European Energy Law and Policy

Charles Seale-Hayne Library
University of Plymouth
(01752) 588 588
LibraryandITenquiries@plymouth.ac.uk

European Energy Law and Policy

AN INTRODUCTION

Heiko Krüger
Attorney-At-Law

Edward Elgar
PUBLISHING

Cheltenham, UK • Northampton, MA, USA

Published by
Edward Elgar Publishing Limited
The Lypiatts
15 Lansdown Road
Cheltenham
Glos GL50 2JA
UK

Edward Elgar Publishing, Inc.
William Pratt House
9 Dewey Court
Northampton
Massachusetts 01060
USA

A catalogue record for this book
is available from the British Library

Library of Congress Control Number: 2016942157

MIX
Paper from
responsible sources
FSC® C013056

ISBN 978 1 78643 033 5 (cased)
ISBN 978 1 78643 035 9 (paperback)
ISBN 978 1 78643 034 2 (eBook)

Typeset by Servis Filmsetting Ltd, Stockport, Cheshire
Printed and bound in Great Britain by TJ International Ltd, Padstow

Contents in brief

Full contents

Abbreviations

3rd Energy Package	3rd legislative package on EU electricity and gas markets comprising Directive 2009/72/EC (Electricity Directive), Directive 2009/73/EC (Gas Directive), Regulation (EC) No 714/2009 (Electricity Regulation), Regulation (EC) No 715/2009 (Gas Regulation), Regulation (EC) No 713/2009 (ACER Regulation)
ACER	Agency for the Cooperation of Energy Regulators
ACER Regulation	Regulation (EC) No 713/2009 of the European Parliament and of the Council of 13 July 2009 establishing an Agency for the Cooperation of Energy Regulators [2009] OJ L 211/1
Altmark criteria	criteria established by the European Court of Justice according to which a compensation granted for discharging public service obligations does not qualify as state aid in the sense of EU state aid rules (see Case C-280/00 *Altmark* [2003] ECR I-7747)
CCP	common commercial policy
CCS	carbon capture and storage
CCT	clean coal technologies
CEER	Council of European Energy Regulators
CEF	Connecting Europe Facility
CJEU	Court of Justice of the European Union
Commission	European Commission (an institution of the European Union)
Council	Council of the European Union (an institution of the European Union)
DG	directorate-general (a department of the European Commission)

DSO	distribution system operator
EC	European Community
ECIs	European critical infrastructures
ECJ	European Court of Justice or Court of Justice (now part of the CJEU)
ECR	European Court Reports
ECSC	European Coal and Steel Community
ECT	Energy Charter Treaty (binding multilateral agreement establishing a legal framework for international cooperation between net exporters of energy, net importers and transit countries)
EEAG	Communication from the Commission, Guidelines on State aid for environmental protection and energy 2014–2020 [2014] OJ C 200/1
EEC	European Economic Community
EED	see Energy Efficiency Directive
EEE–F	European Energy Efficiency Fund
EEPR	European Energy Programme for Recovery
EFSI	European Fund for Strategic Investments
Electricity Directive	Directive 2009/72/EC concerning common rules for the internal market in electricity and repealing Directive 2003/54/EC [2009] OJ L 211/55
Electricity Regulation	Regulation (EC) No 714/2009 of the European Parliament and of the Council of 13 July 2009 on conditions for access to the network for cross-border exchanges in electricity and repealing Regulation (EC) No 1228/2003 [2009] OJ L 211/15
Energy Community	aims at establishing open and transparent energy markets within the contracting states by harmonising the applicable regulatory frameworks; founded by the European Union and a number of south-east European states
Energy Efficiency Directive	Directive 2012/27/EU of the European Parliament and of the Council of 25 October 2012 on energy efficiency,

	amending Directives 2009/125/EC and 2010/30/EU and repealing Directives 2004/8/EC and 2006/32/EC [2012] OJ L 315/1
Energy Taxation Directive	Directive Council Directive 2003/96/EC of 27 October 2003 restructuring the Community framework for the taxation of energy products and electricity [2003] OJ L 283/51
ENP	European Neighbourhood Policy
ENTSO-E	European Network of Transmission System Operators for Electricity
ENTSO-G	European Network of Transmission System Operators for Gas
EPBD	Directive on the Energy Performance of Buildings 2010/31/EU [2010] OJ L 153/13
ERGEG	European Regulators' Group for Electricity and Gas
ErPs	energy-related products
ESA	Euratom Supply Agency
et seq	and the following page(s) or paragraph(s)
EU ETS	EU Greenhouse Gas Emission Allowance Trading Scheme
Euratom	European Atomic Energy Community
Euratom Treaty	Treaty establishing the European Atomic Energy Community
European Council	an institution of the European Union
European energy law	understood here as the legal rules of the EU and Euratom outlining, defining and implementing European energy policy
European energy policy	understood here as the action of the European Union and Euratom that deals with the allocation of rights and duties concerning the exploitation of energy resources
FiT	feed-in tariffs model (type of support schemes for renewable energy)
four freedoms	provisions of the TFEU ensuring that goods, persons, services, capital and payments may move freely within the internal market

Gas Directive	Directive 2009/73/EC concerning common rules for the internal market in natural gas and repealing Directive 2003/55/EC [2009] OJ L 211/94
Gas Regulation	Regulation (EC) No 715/2009 of the European Parliament and of the Council of 13 July 2009 on conditions for access to the natural gas transmission networks and repealing Regulation (EC) No 1775/2005 [2009] OJ L 211/36
GBER	General Block Exemption Regulation, Commission Regulation (EU) No 651/2014 of 17 June 2014 declaring certain categories of aid compatible with the internal market in application of Articles 107 and 108 of the Treaty [2014] OJ L 187/1
GHG	greenhouse gases
GPP	green public procurement
ITC	Inter-Transmission System Operator Compensation
LNG	liquefied natural gas
Merger Regulation	Council Regulation (EC) No 139/2004 of 20 January 2004 on the control of concentrations between undertakings [2004] OJ L 24/1
NRAs	national regulatory authorities
OJ	Official Journal of the European Union
OPEC	Organisation of the Petroleum Exporting Countries
PCA	partnership and cooperation agreement
PPA	power purchase agreements
primary law	comprises the highest-ranking sources of European law, i.e. the TEU, the TFEU and the Euratom Treaty in particular
REMIT	Regulation (EU) No 1227/2011 of the European Parliament and of the Council of 25 October 2011 on wholesale energy market integrity and transparency [2011] OJ L 326/1
Renewable Energy Directive	Directive 2009/28/EC of the European Parliament and of the Council of 23 April

	2009 on the promotion of the use of energy from renewable sources and amending and subsequently repealing Directives 2001/77/EC and 2003/30/EC [2009] OJ L 140/16
RES	renewable energy sources comprising all non-fossil sources that are naturally replenished, in particular sunlight, wind, biomass, hydropower and geothermal energy
SEA	Single European Act
secondary law	acts adopted by EU/Euratom institutions comprising mainly the instruments listed in article 288 of the TFEU, namely regulations, directives, decisions, recommendations and opinions
SGEI	service of general economic interest
SME	small and medium-sized enterprises
TEC	Treaty establishing the European Community
TEN-E	trans-European energy networks
TEU	Treaty on European Union
TFEU	Treaty on the Functioning of the European Union
TSO	transmission system operator
vertically integrated undertaking (electricity sector)	means an electricity undertaking or a group of electricity undertakings where the same person or the same persons are entitled, directly or indirectly, to exercise control, and where the undertaking or group of undertakings perform at least one of the functions of transmission or distribution, and at least one of the functions of generation or supply of electricity (cf article 2(21) Directive 2009/72/EC)
vertically integrated undertaking (gas sector)	means a natural gas undertaking or a group of natural gas undertakings where the same person or the same persons are entitled, directly or indirectly, to exercise control, and where the undertaking or group of undertakings perform at least

one of the functions of transmission, distribution, LNG or storage, and at least one of the functions of production or supply of natural gas (cf article 2(20) Directive 2009/72/EC)

Wholesale Market Regulation — see REMIT

WTO — World Trade Organization

Table of key decisions of EU courts[1]

Main subjects: renewable energy sources, refusal to award green certificates for electricity production installations located outside the member state in question, Renewable Energy Directive (Directive 2009/28/EC), free movement of goods, article 34 TFEU

Main subjects: state monopolies, operation of services of general economic interest, regional distributor imposing on local distributors an exclusive purchasing clause excluding all imports, articles 37, 101, 102 and 106 TFEU

Main subjects: compensation for discharging public service obligations, concept of state aid, article 107 TFEU

Main subjects: renewable energy sources, state aid, concept of 'intervention by the state or through state resources', article 107 TFEU

Main subjects: refusal of access to a facility

Main subjects: state monopolies

---

[1] The main subjects listed here are partly taken from the exact wording of the judgement in the respective case.

Table of key legislation

Introduction

Energy plays a fundamental role in our daily lives. The way we live, the way in which our economy and society work, is inextricably linked with the permanent availability and use of energy. The operation of electrical appliances, the running of industrial machines, the heating of our homes, the powering of our means of transport, the way we produce food, none of this can be imagined without energy. Given its crucial importance, worldwide energy demand has grown exponentially in the last 100 years. Nevertheless we are still some way from reaching the peak of global consumption. World energy needs are in fact projected to at least double by 2050 mainly due to the circumstance that non-OECD countries will raise their standard of living to that of Western nations. This trend is proving critical as the world is still majorly dependent on fossil fuels. Throughout the next few decades fossil energy sources will probably continue to cover around 80% of world energy use.

Considering that these traditional energy sources are limited, nations will face huge challenges when safeguarding their energy needs in future. Without fundamentally rethinking the way we arrange our energy supply, the world community envisages fiercer competition over resources and even more adverse effects on the environment and climate. Against this backdrop, concerted action is needed to steer developments in a way that ensures energy supply for all nations in an amicable and sustainable manner. However, moving forward together remains difficult in view of the strategic nature of national energy supply and the fact that countries disagree on many fundamental issues related to it.

This textbook will give an overview of the common ground the 28 members of the European Union and Euratom have established over the years. Despite significantly deviating national interests and perceptions, these countries have managed to create a partially common energy policy and a corpus of common and harmonised legal rules. Even if it does not cover every European country, this common roof shall be understood here as 'European energy law and policy'. Today's goal of this concept is to make the energy supply of involved nations fit for the future. However, the evolution of this policy is still underway and it remains to be seen whether member states carry on straight ahead down this road to meet all upcoming challenges.

Clarification of what exactly European energy law and European energy policy encompass poses some difficulty.[1] Indeed the Treaty on the Functioning of the European Union (TFEU) includes in article 194 an explicit provision on competences in the field of energy policy. However, this article does not stake out the entire remit of the European Union in relation to energy. Additional competences for the adoption of energy-related measures follow from other titles, for instance those on the environment and trans-European networks. For this reason, the said terms will be understood in a broader sense here. European energy policy will thereby refer to the action of the European Union and Euratom which, broadly speaking, deals with the allocation of rights and duties concerning the exploitation of energy resources.[2] European energy law forms part of this policy and embraces the legal rules of the European Union and Euratom outlining, defining and implementing that policy. Under this approach, both terms include traditional regulation of the power industry and any other regulative approach of an economic, social, environmental or technical nature with a bearing on the utilisation of energy resources. Hence, European energy policy and European energy law as understood here constitute areas which overlap with other fields of policy and law, such as environmental policy. Many authors use the term '*EU* energy law and policy' instead of '*European* energy law and policy' with a view to linguistically assign the regulative activity in question more clearly to the European Union. Here preference shall nevertheless be given to the latter term as this volume covers Euratom activities alongside those of the European Union. The term also seems appropriate as the European Union in fact constitutes the pivot of harmonising activities within Europe, which through the so-called Energy Community and the European Economic Area (EEA) also effects legislation in non-EU member states.

In recent years a range of comprehensive books on EU energy law and policy and detailed monographs focusing on specific aspects of that area have been published.[3] By contrast, the present textbook follows an introductory

---

1 See also M Roggenkamp, C Redgwell, I del Guayo and A Rønne, *Energy Law in Europe* (2nd edn, Oxford University Press 2007) 8 et seq; J Grunwald, *Das Energierecht der Europäischen Gemeinschaften* (de Gruyter 2003) 5 et seq.

2 Following Bradbrook's definition of energy law, see A Bradbrook, 'Energy law as an academic discipline' (1996) 14 JERL 193, 194. See also S W Schill, 'The interface between national and international energy law', in K Talus (ed.), *Research Handbook on International Energy Law* (Edward Elgar Publishing 2014) 44; M Roggenkamp, C Redgwell, I del Guayo and A Rønne, *Energy Law in Europe* (2nd edn, Oxford University Press 2007) 8.

3 See, by way of example, the book series on EU energy law published by Claeys & Casteels Publishing, namely e.g. C Jones (ed.), *EU Energy Law: Volume I, The Internal Energy Market: The Third Liberalisation Package* (3rd edn, 2010); C Jones (ed.), *EU Energy Law: Volume II, EU Competition Law and Energy Markets* (3rd edn, 2011); P Hodson, C Jones and H van Stehen (eds), *EU Energy Law: Volume III, Book 1, Renewable Energy*

approach which will serve students, experts and otherwise interested people as a guide to the numerous facets of the energy policy and law established by the European Union and Euratom. The focus is thereby laid on the legal dimension, meaning European energy law with its treaty rules, legislative acts and judicial decisions, in particular. Besides, the textbook provides an insight into the political dimension. More precisely, a summary is given of the institutional framework of policy-making, procedures of decision-making and the strategic superstructure overarching relevant legislation. The question as to how certain political decisions have come about remains, however, unaddressed, even though specific issues related to that question, such as the disparity of national interests and their reconciliation or the influence of stakeholders, generally have a particular bearing on the legislative outcome in the field of energy.

In detail, Chapter 1 outlines the constitutional framework within which EU and Euratom institutions drive forward their energy agenda. The framework arises out of the EU and Euratom treaties, which were literally speaking not stipulated as an actual constitution, but, nevertheless, function in fact as such. First, Chapter 1 gives an overview of the institutions involved in political and legislative decision-making in relation to energy. Then light is cast on the political life-cycle through which a regulative measure has to pass from the planning stage to reflection on its impact. Law is identified as the chief instrument within this process, and the one that ultimately determines the envisaged measure. Subsequently, Chapter 1 delineates the sources of European energy law, main legal principles, relevant legislative powers and pertinent legislative procedures. Euratom is treated in a separate section.

Chapter 2 concentrates on the fundamental rules giving shape to the internal energy market. Respective rules are principally laid down in the TFEU or result from the case law of the Court of Justice. Treaty provisions, notably the so-called fundamental freedoms and the treaty rules on competition, serve particularly as a yardstick for law-making and as a safety net in the absence of legislative acts. The fact that these rules form the contractually settled core of European energy law does not, however, mean that they stand entirely

---

Law and Policy in the European Union (2010); J Curtin (ed.), *EU Energy Law: Volume VII, Energy Efficiency in the European Union* (2014); J Vinois, (ed.), *EU Energy Law: Volume VIII, The Energy Infrastructure Policy of the European Union* (2014). Cf also book series 'EU Energy Law and Policy Issues' published by Intersentia. Furthermore see, for instance, the following individual books: M Roggenkamp, C Redgwell, I del Guayo and A Rønne, *Energy Law in Europe* (2nd edn, Oxford University Press 2007); A de Hauteclocque, *Market Building Through Antitrust: Long-Term Contract Regulation in EU Electricity Markets* (Edward Elgar Publishing 2013); B Delvaux, *EU Law and the Development of a Sustainable, Competitive and Secure Energy Policy: Opportunities and Shortcomings* (Intersentia 2013); A Johnston and G Block, *EU Energy Law* (Oxford University Press 2013); K Talus, *EU Energy Law and Policy – A Critical Account* (Oxford University Press 2013).

outside the sphere of political influence. Considerable discretion remains partly with the European legislator and the European Commission as regards the implementation of treaty law. In this light, the Commission has especially developed the competition rules to become a primary tool for restructuring the energy sector,[4] which is taken into account in Chapter 2.

Whereas Chapters 1 and 2 focus on parameters fixed in the EU and Euratom treaties, Chapter 3 is concerned with the planning framework underlying current and future legislation pertaining to energy. Thus, Chapter 3 primarily addresses the union's energy-related agenda. This agenda covers a short, medium and long-term horizon and embraces a complex system of targets, several overall strategies and a range of specific planning tools. The so-called 20-20-20 headline targets for the year 2020 and the corresponding 'Energy 2020 strategy' occupy centre stage. In the autumn of 2014 heads of state and government had already put the plans for the successive period until 2030 in concrete terms. Taking this planning step into consideration was crucial not least because it completes the present planning picture, but also as it curbs the EU's original ambitions in terms of climate protection and thus possibly marks a reorientation of energy policy in the medium term.

Chapters 4 and 5 present an outline of legislation in relation to energy that were in large part adopted or revised in the light of the union's energy agenda as set out in Chapter 3. Chapter 4 outlines sector-specific acts and the main instruments provided for within them. Sector-specific acts refer to measures that concern particular subdivisions of the energy sector, meaning the electricity sector, in general, and sectors featuring specific energy resources, namely gas, oil, coal, renewable energy and nuclear fuels. A main point of focus thereby lies in the liberalisation of the electricity and gas markets and pertinent unbundling regimes and provisions on third-party access to grids. Chapter 4 goes on to summarise a range of further relevant sector-specific rules pertaining, for instance, to the security of the electricity, gas and oil supply, and national support schemes in the renewable energy sector.

Chapter 5 deals with cross-sector legislation and therefore with measures that have a bearing on several energy subsectors or even go beyond the energy sector. Measures covered relate specifically to the functioning of

---

4 See also K Talus, 'Wind of change: Long-term gas contracts and changing energy paradigms in the European Union' in C Kuzemko, A Belyi, A Goldthau and M F Keating (eds), *Dynamics of Energy Governance in Europe and Russia* (Palgrave Macmillan 2012) 237 et seq; K Talus, *EU Energy Law and Policy – A Critical Account* (Oxford University Press 2013) 5.

the internal energy market, the increase in energy efficiency, the protection of the environment and of consumers, the strengthening of energy security, including the extension of infrastructures, and the promotion of energy-related projects by means of EU support programmes.

Finally, Chapter 6 deals with the external dimension of European energy policy and law. The European Union's external action primarily aims at safeguarding imports of energy resources from third countries and is, therefore, an essential tool for offsetting member states' scarcity of resources. Aside from outlining the relevant institutional and programmatic settings, Chapter 6 sketches the EU's main instruments of external energy policy. These instruments are deployed at international and regional level and exhibit a multilateral, bilateral, unilateral or introversive nature. Particular importance is attached to energy relations with Russia, given that this country remains the European Union's largest supplier of fossil fuels. However, relations with other actual or potential suppliers and transit countries, especially in the Eastern neighbourhood, will also be highlighted considering their strategic relevance.

It should be pointed out that in the interest of promoting necessary reforms, the European legislator and the European Commission pursue a gradual regulative approach in terms of many energy-related issues. This means that regulative measures are gradually enhanced through several generations of legislation. Furthermore, energy legislation and to some extent also competition law enforcement in the energy sector by the Commission are generally subject to change due to shifting political interests and the altering perceptions of given challenges.[5] This is why European energy law remains in a constant state of flux and must be continuously monitored. For this reason, this and also other textbooks may in many respects only serve as a starting point for a more up-to-date analysis based notably on relevant journals,[6] yearbooks,[7] loose leaf works,[8] official EU websites,[9] case law reports of the

---

5 See in this context also K Talus, *EU Energy Law and Policy – A Critical Account* (Oxford University Press 2013) 5.

6 Cf, for instance, European Energy and Environmental Law Review; European Energy Journal; Oil, Gas & Energy Law (OGEL); Journal of World Energy Law & Business; Renewable Energy Law and Policy Review (RELP).

7 Cf yearbooks 'EU Energy Law and Policy' published by Claeys & Casteels Publishing.

8 Cf R H Tudway (ed.), *Energy Law and Regulation in the European Union* (Sweet & Maxwell).

9 Main websites: http://europa.eu/ (official website of the European Union); http://www.consilium.europa.eu/en/european-council/ (European Council); http://www.europarl.europa.eu (European Parliament); http://www.consilium.europa.eu/en/council-eu/ (Council of the European Union); http://ec.europa.eu/ (European Commission); eur-lex.europa.eu (database on EU law) (all accessed 29 April 2016).

Court of Justice[10] and the latest competition cases decided by the European Commission.[11]

I would like to use this opportunity to acknowledge Mr Alan Wylie for his great job in carefully proofreading all of the chapters. Furthermore, I would like to express my gratitude to Ms Laura Mann and Mr Luke Adams from Edward Elgar Publishing who rendered the publication of this textbook possible.

---

10 See the following website of the Court of Justice: http://curia.europa.eu/jcms/jcms/j_6/ (accessed 29 April 2016).
11 See the following website of the Commission: http://ec.europa.eu/competition/elojade/isef/index.cfm (accessed 29 April 2016).

1

Structure and functioning of the European Union and Euratom

European energy policy has become very complex in recent years and today it features a multitude of layers. As an introduction to this field, the present textbook seeks to systematically break down this complexity. However, illustrations in Chapters 2 to 6 are given on the basis of the reader's general familiarity with the functioning of the European Union and also with the nature of EU law. Given the fact that the mechanics of the European Union differ widely from those of nation states, it seems worthwhile for readers who have not yet been in touch with the European Union to familiarise themselves with this particular organisation first. The present chapter is intended to enable these readers to take their first steps into this distinctive world. After a brief review of its history, the chapter gives an outline of the institutional structures and the functioning of the European Union and of its sister organisation Euratom. This overview includes a short presentation of the general forms of EU action as well as of the legal sources and the legal principles of EU law. Moreover, there is an outline of pertinent legislative powers and the law-making procedures the EU legislator has to observe when adopting measures in the field of energy. Of course, more advanced readers should proceed directly to Chapter 2 or take Chapter 1 as an opportunity to swiftly brush up on their knowledge.

1.1 History of the European Union

A useful starting point is to go back in history and understand how the European Union and the field of European energy policy in particular have evolved and how far integration has come to date. The process of European integration can be traced back to the experiences of the two world wars of the 20th century. Integration was considered a key factor for securing peace between neighbours who had repeatedly been at war in the past. A first step to reconciliation and convergence was taken in 1951 with the establishment of the European Coal and Steel Community (ECSC) between Belgium, France, (West) Germany, Italy, Luxembourg and the Netherlands. The aim of this early predecessor of the European Union was to establish common control over the key resources of those days, particularly concerning coal as the major source of energy. Thus, energy issues were considered among the main drivers of early European integration.

Then in 1957, the next major step followed with the signing of the so-called Treaties of Rome. Consisting of two separate treaties, the EEC Treaty and the Euratom Treaty, this contractual package laid down the foundations for the European Economic Community (EEC) and the European Atomic Energy Community (Euratom or EAEC). In conjunction with the ECSC, consequently three European Communities existed in those days, each concentrating on different political domains. The EEC soon played the leading role. It was created to establish a common market for goods, services and labour among member states. Energy policy was not explicitly mentioned in the EEC Treaty. Nevertheless, over the years the EEC has served as a basis for adopting energy legislation outside the scope of the ECSC and Euratom.

With a view to enhancing European integration, the Treaties of Rome have been amended several times. One of the chief alterations was achieved in 1965 with the so-called Merger Treaty. This treaty unified the institutions of the three existing European Communities and therefore represented a big step towards the institutional structure of the European Union as we know it today. The next major amendment to the treaties was brought about in 1986 with the adoption of the Single European Act (SEA). The SEA led, inter alia, to an extension of EEC competences, strengthened the role of the European Parliament and provided for the creation of a single market by 1993.

The European Union was founded with the Treaty of Maastricht (Treaty on the European Union or TEU) signed in 1992. During the initial years, the European Union functioned as an umbrella only, spanning the three supra-national European Communities and the newly introduced inter-governmental remits of a Common Foreign and Security Policy (CFSP) as well as cooperation in the fields of Justice and Home Affairs (JHA). Apart from that, the Treaty of Maastricht amended once more the Treaties of Rome, particularly changing the name of the European Economic Community (EEC) into the European Community (EC) and initialising the creation of a single currency, the Euro.

In 1995 the European Union already encompassed 12 member states and the Schengen Agreement made it possible for citizens to cross many state boundaries within Europe without border checks. At this point in time Europe had visibly grown together. In subsequent years, integration was further deepened and the European Union was prepared for further enlargement by the Treaty of Amsterdam (1997) and the Treaty of Nice (2001). Ultimately, in 2004 and 2007 the former Cold War division of Europe into an Eastern and a Western part was finally overcome by the accession of 12 new, mostly Eastern-European, member states.

In theory, the next logical step should have been the adoption of a European constitution verbally manifesting the wish to continue building a common European home while further dismissing the traditional concept of national sovereignty. However, at the end of the decade the process of integration was floundering. Politicians were not able to take Europe's citizens down the road towards an ever closer union. Ultimately, the adoption of a European constitution failed due to rejection of it by both a French and a Dutch referendum.

Nevertheless, it was clear that the then union of 27 member states urgently required reforms in order to preserve its capacity to act. For that reason, the respective heads of states and governments adopted the Lisbon Treaty in 2007. Even though the Lisbon Treaty was less ambitious than the draft constitution, it brought about significant changes to the founding treaties as regards EU structures, decision-making and particular policies. In particular, the Lisbon Treaty breathed life into the European Union, vesting it with legal personality and merging in it all supra-national and inter-governmental components established by the founding treaties so far, except Euratom. Furthermore, the role of the European Parliament was strengthened, the Charter of Fundamental Rights became part of European primary law and the former EEC Treaty was renamed as the Treaty on the Functioning of the European Union (TFEU).

Due to national reservations, the European Union and its predecessor organisations have never been provided with an all-encompassing competency in the field of energy. Nonetheless, common energy policy has played an increasingly important role over the decades, especially as regards the European Community.[1] In 1992 energy was formally made an area of its activities, even though the EC Treaty still lacked explicit rules on energy competences at that time. Instead, relevant legislation was based on several other competences, such as those on the approximation of laws and trans-European networks, resulting in a patchwork of energy regulation. For that reason, in 2006 the European Council called for a more coherent approach

---

1 See also D Buchan, 'Energy Policy – Sharp Challenges and Rising Ambitions' in H Wallace, M A Pollack and A R Young (eds), *Policy-making in the European Union* (6th edn, Oxford University Press 2010) 357.

leading to a true European energy policy.[2] Fresh impetus followed in the same year by the Commission's Green Paper on Energy which staked out key issues of a respective common energy policy.[3]

In 2007 the Lisbon Treaty also gave energy policy a broader legal foundation by introducing article 194 into the TFEU. This provision lays down the objectives and corresponding competences of EU energy policy, even though the list of competences is not exhaustive.[4] Accordingly, the common energy policy is supposed to guarantee the functioning of the energy market and ensure security of supply. Furthermore, it is to serve the promotion of renewable energy, energy efficiency and network interconnections. Even though article 194 of the TFEU did not actually broaden the energy competences that could already be inferred from other treaty provisions, it underlined ambitions to strengthen joint action in the field.

In practice, these initiatives have led to increased EU activity in the area of energy policy in recent years. Based on transferred competences, EU institutions have adopted a number of proposals, strategies and concrete legislative measures affecting any energy sub-sector (from the electricity market to that of renewable energy) and covering medium and long-term horizons (for example, '2020 Energy Strategy', '2030 Climate and Energy Policy Framework' and 'Energy Roadmap 2050'). Respective strategies and instruments will be examined in more detail below in Chapters 2 to 6. Compared to the time before 2006, energy legislation has significantly increased and the corpus of rules applicable in that time has undergone substantial changes. Reinforced actions have led to more coherent and harmonised instruments across Europe. However, this finding does not detract from the fact that energy policy remains an area of high strategic relevance to member states. National reticence in the energy field is still impeding the straightforward development of effective common rules in many areas.

1.2   Institutional structure of the European Union

From Chapters 2 to 6 we will see that a range of institutions and bodies wield influence to a greater or lesser degree over EU energy policy. For a better understanding of how the common energy policy is established and implemented throughout the 28 EU member states, we should at this point get

---

2 See European Council 23/24 March 2006, *Presidency Conclusions*, no 44.

3 European Commission, *Green Paper on a European strategy for sustainable, competitive and secure energy* (COM (2006) 105 final).

4 See section 1.4.1 below.

an overview of the institutional structure and of the powers and portfolios assigned to the various institutions.

The European Union appears as a complex entity with a unique institutional structure that results from its special nature. The European Union may be characterised as an economic and political partnership between sovereign states. However, it is neither a federation, nor is it merely a framework of cooperation. It is rather an organisation that combines areas where cross-national institutions exercise legislative powers (supranational elements) with areas where member states cooperate, coordinate and decide unanimously (intergovernmental elements).

Policy-making in supranational areas involves the European Union's four primary institutions: the European Council, the Council of the European Union (Council), the European Parliament and the European Commission. By contrast, in terms of intergovernmental areas (Common Foreign and Security Policy) the European Council and the Council of the European Union in principle alone determine respective policies and actions. However, there are a number of other entities participating in particular processes, assisting primary institutions or monitoring their action. These entities include in particular the Court of Justice, the Court of Auditors, the European Economic and Social Committee, the Committee of the Regions, and various specialised agencies. Let us shed some more light on the institutions and bodies having a bigger say in energy-related matters, which, of course, include the EU's primary institutions (see Figure 1.1).

1.2.1 European Council

The European Council gathers the heads of state or government of member states, the president of the European Council and that of the European Commission. The European Council negotiates and adopts the general political directions and priorities of the European Union including the ones applicable to energy policy. Hence the European Council also indirectly influences concrete energy legislation, even though it does not issue any legislative act itself. Its influence on specific legislative work in the field of climate and energy policy may even grow in the future. As part of the climate and energy deal clinched in October 2014, the heads of state and government declared that the European Council reserves the right to set directions even in regard to rather specific issues.[5]

---

5 See European Council 23/24 October 2014, *Conclusions*.

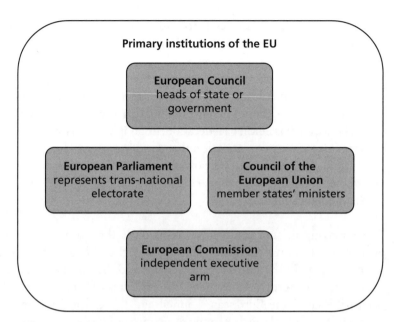

Figure 1.1 The EU's four primary institutions

The European Council is convened at least twice every six months. In general, it decides by consensus. Energy policy is one of many issues the European Council deals with, whereas the importance of energy issues varies from meeting to meeting. One of its most momentous decisions impacting on energy policy was that on the so-called 20-20-20 targets, which represent the European Union's major climate and energy goals in the years to come (see Chapter 3 below).[6]

1.2.2 European Parliament

The European Parliament represents the trans-national electorate of the European Union. It was created to grant the European Union's citizens a say in European affairs and, by doing so, to ensure democratic support for an ever closer European integration. The European Parliament's remit comprises legislative and budgetary functions, which it jointly exercises with the Council of the European Union. Moreover, the European Parliament elects the president of the European Commission, approves the latter's cabinet (as a whole) and exercises political control. Plenary proceedings principally take place in Strasbourg, but also in Brussels.

---

6 See European Council 8/9 March 2007, *Presidency Conclusions, no 32 and annex I.*

Members of the European Parliament (MEPs) are elected every five years by direct universal suffrage. MEPs form standing parliamentary committees which prepare plenary sessions by reviewing legislative proposals and drawing up reports for the plenary. Each proposal is delegated to a particular committee (committee responsible) which also collects the opinions of other relevant committees where required. Within a parliamentary committee a single MEP, called a rapporteur, is nominated and assumes responsibility for drafting a report on a particular legislative proposal. Once a committee responsible has approved the legislative report, which especially entails a draft legislative resolution, the issue is tabled in the plenary.

As regards work on legislative proposals relevant to the field of energy, a number of different parliamentary committees are involved, especially:

- ITRE (Industry, Research and Energy)
- ENVI (Environment, Public Health and Food Safety)
- IMCO (Internal Market and Consumer Protection)
- ECON (Economic and Monetary Affairs).

1.2.3 Council of the European Union

The European Union has two main legislative bodies, the European Parliament and the Council of the European Union. The Council of the European Union (also Council or Council of Ministers) represents the national governments and gathers member states' representatives at ministerial level. Aside from its activity as one of the co-legislators, the Council fulfils several other functions. Accordingly it decides on the EU budget together with the European Parliament, it coordinates member states' policies where provided for in the treaties, it defines the Common Foreign and Security Policy, and it passes resolutions on the conclusion of international agreements.

At every meeting the Council brings together those national ministers who are responsible for the issues tabled. At present, there are ten Council configurations covering all fields of EU policies, from the internal market to the Common Foreign and Security Policy. As regards the area of energy, different configurations may add relevant issues to their agenda due to the fact that energy affects various fields of policy. This particularly applies to the following Council configurations:

- Transport, Telecommunications and Energy Council (TTE)
- Competitiveness Council
- Environment Council

- Economic and Financial Affairs
- Foreign Affairs Council.

Pertinent voting procedures in the Council vary and depend on the agenda item in question. The Treaties provide for three procedures of voting: unanimity, qualified majority voting and simple majority voting. Qualified majority voting (QMV) is determined to be the general voting procedure (article 16(3) TEU).[7] It also applies to most energy-related issues. Energy-related measures of fiscal nature form an exception, for instance, and have to be decided on unanimously (article 194(3) TFEU).

Sessions of the Council are prepared by the Permanent Representatives Committee (COREPER). This assisting body consists of representatives of the member states, strictly speaking their ambassadors to the European Union (COREPER II) and deputy representatives (COREPER I). COREPER may resort to a number of sub-committees and working groups that are composed of national delegates assisting its work.

The presidency of the Council is held by the government of individual member states on a rotating basis. The presidency sets the political agenda of the Council, heads its secessions and organises its work. Thus, member states presiding over the Council may gain significant influence on particular political and legislative items. A member state's presidency ends after six months. Nevertheless, to ensure continuity three consecutive presidencies elaborate common political programmes. The presidency is assisted by a standing secretariat, which helps to organise and coordinate the Council's work on a set agenda.

1.2.4 European Commission

The European Commission (Commission) represents the European Union's executive arm. Even though it is staffed with member states' nationals, it is supposed to function independently of member states. The Commission's main tasks consist in ensuring the implementation of EU treaty law and EU legislation, in executing the European Union's budget and in running various funding programmes. In the field of energy, it supervises in particular the

---

7 The thresholds for a qualified majority and weighting criteria are defined in art 16(4) TEU and art 238(2) and (3) TFEU. The 'double majority' system provided for in these provisions took effect on 1 November 2014. Up to that time the former Nice Treaty Council voting arrangements as laid down in art 3 Protocol on transitional provisions applied. Moreover, between 1 November 2014 and 31 March 2017 a member of the Council may still request that an act has to be adopted in accordance with the former Nice Treaty Council voting arrangements.

national implementation of EU energy legislation, it applies EU competition law, and it manages or oversees the management of several funding programmes, which aim, for instance, at extending energy infrastructures and fostering the use of renewable energy.

Aside from these responsibilities regarding the implementation of EU policies, the Commission furthermore fulfils a crucial function in the process of law-making, even though it does not officially count among the European Union's legislative bodies. In general, legislative acts may be treated and adopted by the European legislature only on the basis of a proposal drafted by the Commission. This means the Commission has the right of initiative, which shall enable it to fulfil its duties as so-called guardian of the treaties. Proper implementation of EU treaty law ultimately requires an adequate degree of legislation. As a consequence, the Commission holds a key position in terms of the European Union's political orientation and legislative planning, which also explains why it is a main addressee for interest groups seeking to influence EU policies and those in the field of energy, in particular.

The Commission consists at present of 28 members (called Commissioners), one national of each member state. It is newly composed after every election to the European Parliament, meaning every five years. The President of the Commission is officially proposed by the European Council and elected by the European Parliament. As regards remaining members of the Commission, the Council adopts a list of candidates, who are suggested by member states. After the European Parliament has given its consent to the cabinet as a whole, the European Council may finally appoint the new Commission.

Each of the Commissioners covers a defined policy area and furthers proposals falling in his or her respective remit. With a view to ensure cooperation among Commissioners, the current president, Jean-Claude Juncker, has set up so-called project teams for particular cross-cutting topics. One of these selected subject areas entitled 'A Resilient Energy Union with a Forward-Looking Climate Change Policy' concerns questions of energy regulation in particular. Project teams are headed by one of the Commission's Vice-presidents and assemble all the Commissioners responsible for the policy areas covered by a given cross-cutting field.

In general the Commission as a whole takes decisions on individual proposals (principle of collective responsibility). In the majority of cases it adopts initiatives by written procedure. Oral decision-making is reserved for issues of major importance only. All Commissioners have their own cabinet assisting them in planning and handling their portfolio. Commissioners are furthermore supported by a range of special departments (so-called Directorates-General or DGs) and services which do most of the preparatory and administrative work.

Given the cross-cutting nature of energy policy, its elaboration and implementation requires the involvement of various Directorates-General, which at present include for example:

- DG Energy (ENER)
- DG Climate Action (CLIMA)
- DG Competition (COMP)
- DG Internal Market, Industry, Entrepreneurship and SMEs (GROW)
- DG Environment (ENV)
- DG Research and Innovation (RTD).

In actual fact it happens quite often that legislative proposals affect the domain of different Directorates-General. In such cases, the DG responsible for drafting the proposal obtains the opinions of all other DGs with legitimate interests. Cooperation between GDs is thereby ensured by the Secretariat-General, which safeguards the consistency of the Commission's work and facilitates its internal and external communication.

1.2.5 Court of Justice of the European Union

Alongside the European Union's four primary institutions, the Court of Justice of the European Union (CJEU) plays a key role in policy areas, such as energy policy, in which both the strict implementation of EU treaty law, namely of EU competition law, and the adoption, transposition and enforcement of complex EU legislation are of crucial importance. The CJEU's general task is to ensure the uniform interpretation and proper application of EU treaty law and legislation by EU institutions and especially by member states.

The CJEU constitutes the whole judicial branch of the European Union and comprises three different courts: the Court of Justice, the General Court and the Civil Service Tribunal. The Court of Justice consists of 27 judges and may sit in different chambers: the full court, a grand chamber (15 judges) and small chambers (five or three judges). Judges are assisted by advocates general who, if required, submit their opinion on individual cases. The Court of Justice has in particular jurisdiction in the following instances:

- **Infringement procedure**: In case a member state fails to fulfil its obligations under EU treaty law, the Commission or any other member state may call on the Court to determine the violation and specify necessary actions. If the member state in question does not comply with measures defined by the Court, it may impose a penalty on that state. However, in order to engage the Court in the case of an infringement of the treaties, the Commission must first conduct a preliminary procedure and give the member state concerned the chance to submit its opinion or to terminate the violation.

- **Actions for annulment**: Member states, EU institutions and even natural or legal persons may call on the court to review legislative acts or measures adopted by EU institutions with legal effect in relation to third parties. Actions may, for instance, be instituted if the lack of an institution's competence or the infringement of treaty law is assumed. If the Court considers the action well founded, it declares the act concerned null and void. The Court of Justice and the General Court share competences to handle such cases. The latter is particularly responsible for claims brought by private individuals and companies.
- **Actions for failure to act**: Moreover, the jurisdiction of the Court of Justice, and also that of the General Court, cover the case in which an EU institution fails to meet a given obligation to act. If a respective action brought about by a member state, EU institution or natural or legal person is admissible and well founded, the Court establishes the failure to act so that the institution concerned is required to adopt necessary measures.
- **Preliminary rulings**: National courts are in charge of implementing EU law throughout their jurisdiction. In case a national court considers EU law to be unclear or invalid, it may, or, if there is no higher judicial authority, it must request the Court of Justice for a ruling on that issue.
- **Appeals**: Furthermore, the Court of Justice exercises jurisdiction over appeals brought against decisions of the General Court in the case of actions for annulment or actions for failure to act, for instance.

The General Court is supposed to reduce the workload of the Court of Justice. It is also composed of 27 judges sitting mostly in chambers of three or five judges. Jurisdiction of the General Court covers, for example, actions for annulment or actions for failure to act brought by natural or legal persons. It is, for instance, also responsible for hearing appeals against decisions of the Civil Service Tribunal.

The Civil Service Tribunal decides at first instance on disputes between the European Union and its servants, which includes disputes on wages, disciplinary measures and sickness, for example. It is composed of seven judges, generally sitting in chambers of three judges.

1.2.6 Other institutions, agencies and bodies relevant to energy policy

In addition to the aforementioned institutions, a range of further institutions, agencies, bodies, committees, platforms and initiatives are involved in the drafting, determination, implementation and reflection of EU policies. The European Union's financial institutions, meaning the European Central Bank (ECB), the European Investment Bank (EIB) and the European Investment Fund (EIF), feature prominently in this respect. In terms of energy policy, the European Investment Bank (EIB) plays a special role considering that it manages several financial instruments meant to foster developments in the area of energy, such as the expansion of energy networks, the extended use of renewable energy sources, the dissemination of energy efficiency solutions and that of other low-carbon technologies.

In addition to financial bodies, a number of agencies entrusted with specific tasks provide support in achieving European Union goals. The Agency for the Cooperation of Energy Regulators (ACER), for instance, is entrusted with promoting the liberalisation and integration of the European Union's electricity and gas markets. ACER's primary tasks consist in assisting national regulatory authorities (NRAs) at EU level and in helping coordinate their work. ACER contributes to the development of common network and market rules, it monitors market developments and delivers opinions on energy infrastructure issues with a European-wide dimension.[8] Other European Union agencies provide data for policy-making (the European Environment Agency (EEA)) or manage EU promotion programmes (for example, the Executive Agency for Small and Medium-sized Enterprises (EASME) and the Research Executive Agency (REA)).

As regards the energy sector, various other platforms and organisations have been established that are intended to ensure cooperation among stakeholders, assist the EU Commission or assume other specific tasks (for further information see also Chapter 4 below). In terms of the electricity and gas sub-sectors, these bodies include, for instance, the European Network of Transmission System Operators for Electricity (ENTSO-E), the European Network of Transmission System Operators for Gas (ENTSO-G), the Electricity Cross-Border Committee, the Gas Committee, the Smart Grids Task Force, the Electricity Regulatory Forum (Florence Forum), the Gas Regulatory Forum (Madrid Forum), the Citizens' Energy Forum (London),

---

8 See Regulation (EC) No 713/2009 of the European Parliament and of the Council of 13 July 2009 establishing an Agency for the Cooperation of Energy Regulators, [2009] OJ L 211/1.

and the Fossil Fuels Forum (Berlin). As regards the nuclear sub-sector, the European Nuclear Safety Regulator Group (ENSREG), the European Nuclear Energy Forum (ENEF), and Fusion for Energy (F4E) are worthy of mention.

1.3 Forms of European Union action

1.3.1 General remarks

There are a range of different forms of action available for EU institutions when exercising their responsibilities. Such actions concern the whole policy life-cycle from planning through determining and implementing concrete measures to reflecting on their impact (see Figure 1.2). However, it must be borne in mind that governance in EU areas of competence does not involve EU institutions alone. Actions at EU level and those at member states' level are intertwined, particularly at the planning and implementing stages. This also applies to the field of energy policy.

a) *Planning*

During the planning phase, institutions perform a complex preparatory process leading to general policies and concrete measures. The preparatory stage comprises the recognition and analysis of given or expected needs, the determination of pertinent goals, the development of regulative measures

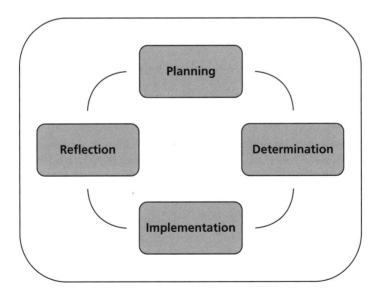

Figure 1.2 Policy life-cycle

and the assessment of their probable impact. The process is mainly completed by the European Commission and its assisting entities, which provides the Commission with wide influence on EU policies. However, in terms of agenda setting, targeting and the determination of general political directions, the Commission has to align itself with the provisions given in the founding treaties and in the conclusions of the European Council. Moreover, the Commission may also be asked by the European Parliament, the Council and EU citizens (at least one million) to prepare draft legislation on a specific issue. Despite these formal stipulations, however, the drafting of legal acts is also quite often pushed by member states or stakeholders.

The Commission works on the basis of annual work programmes reflecting overarching objectives and long-term strategies. As regards energy legislation, strategic frameworks are described in Chapter 3 below and include in particular the '2020 Energy Strategy', the '2030 Climate and Energy Policy Framework' and the 'Energy Roadmap 2050'. Annual work programmes map out both planning instruments and concrete legislative proposals. Planning instruments include, for instance, strategies, communications, green papers (to launch public consultations) and white papers (to set out initiatives that are at an advanced level of drafting). Legislative proposals may be tabled individually or tied up in legislative packages. Before proposing a concrete legislative act, the Commission, in principle, conducts an impact assessment to analyse the economic, social and environmental effects of the initiative. In addition, an exchange of views in the form of consultations and expression of opinions takes place with stakeholders, national governments and parliaments with sometimes considerable impact on the draft.

b)   Determination

Once a proposal has passed the planning phase, it is submitted to the competent decision-maker. Depending on the initiative in question, this may be in particular the European legislature (adoption of legislative acts), the European Council and the Council (both adopt actions in the area of the Common Foreign and Security Policy (CFSP)) and the Commission (determines delegated acts). The European legislature basically means the European Parliament and the Council acting in conjunction.[9] Proposals are put into practice by being converted into law. When it comes to energy policy it is legislative acts, such as regulations and directives that constitute the crucial legal means at the disposal of the European Union. Key aspects of

---

9 By way of exemption, the Commission may also adopt legislative acts according to arts 45(3)(d) and 106(3) TFEU.

EU law and of the various forms of legal acts will be outlined in the following section.

c) *Implementation*

After a policy initiative has been converted into an applicable act by the decision-maker responsible, it requires proper implementation. Implementation is understood here in a broader sense and encompasses all legislative, judicial and executive measures necessary to bring a given act into effect within the circle of member states, companies or individuals addressed by it.

Respective responsibilities for implementation of EU acts are shared among member states and the European Union. Article 4(3) of the TEU establishes the general rule that member states have to ensure the fulfilment of the obligations resulting from EU acts within their national territory by any appropriate measure, which may be, depending on the respective legal and factual requirements, of a legislative, judicial or executive nature. This principle is further specified, for instance, in article 291(1) TFEU as regards the implementation of binding EU acts and in article 288(3) TFEU in relation to the transposition of EU directives. Accordingly, member states bear the primary responsibility for the implementation of EU acts.

However, founding treaties also provide for the involvement of various EU organs in the implementation of EU acts. The Commission is the EU institution with the broadest implementing powers.[10] First, it has the responsibility to ensure the application of European law throughout the European Union. It assumes the role of the guardian of the treaties and as such it especially observes the proper implementation of EU acts in member states. For that reason, the Commission may collect all necessary information and carry out required checks (article 337 TFEU). If it finds that a member state does not comply with an EU measure, it initiates an infringement procedure (article 258 TFEU). In case a member state does not terminate its violation as required by the Commission, the latter may submit the case to the Court of Justice of the European Union for a definitive decision on the case. Besides, the Commission is granted special controlling competences as regards the observance of the European Union's competition and state aid rules (articles 105 and 108 TFEU).

---

10 See also A Staab, *The European Union Explained: Institutions, Actors, Global Impact* (Indiana University Press 2008) 45 et seq.

Second, in addition to its guardian role, the Commission may also be empowered to directly adopt implementing measures itself. This occurs when the legislature considers uniform conditions for implementation necessary (article 291(2) TFEU). However, in such cases the adoption of an implementing act by the Commission remains subject to the control of member states through the so-called comitology procedure (article 291(3) TFEU).

Third, as the Commission is also the European Union's administrative body, it has the duty to implement EU acts regarding the internal functioning of the European Union. Furthermore, it exercises executive responsibilities where the treaties so provide. Accordingly, the Commission is particularly responsible for executing the EU budget, for managing EU programmes and, together with national authorities, for enforcing EU competition rules.

d) Reflection

The policy life-cycle closes with reflection on the effects of adopted and implemented measures. In theory, reflection requires monitoring and analysis of both positive and negative effects, including goal attainment and side effects. As regards EU policies, the Commission is in general in charge of carrying out respective evaluations. Results of reflection may urge EU institutions to rethink, amend and supplement already adopted measures or to improve their implementation. Consequently, evaluations of already existing legal frameworks have significant influence on the planning of new initiatives.

1.3.2 Key aspects of EU law

The adoption and implementation of legal rules represents the pivot of the policy life-cycle and of governance in general. This is true for energy policy, but also for any other policy area. The European Union is equipped with its own legal system which comprises various forms of legal rules and which exhibits some main principles we should be aware of when dealing with EU energy law. Before we turn our attention to these principles, it is useful to take a closer look at the sources of EU law and the various forms of legal rules first.

EU law or European law, as understood here as the law of the EU and Euratom, consists of four main components: primary law, secondary law, supplementary law and international agreements (see also Figure 1.3 below). Details on the classification of certain sources of law remain somewhat controversial, but this is of minor importance for this introduction.[11]

a)   *Primary law*

Primary law comprises the highest-ranking sources of European law laying down the primary values and supreme rules of the functioning of the European Union and Euratom. It includes the treaties founding, amending and extending the European Union, Euratom and all their internal structures. The current state of integration accrues from the consolidated versions of the following three treaties representing the core of present primary law:

- the Treaty on European Union (TEU);
- the Treaty on the Functioning of the European Union (TFEU); and
- the Treaty establishing the European Atomic Energy Community (Euratom Treaty).

All three treaties set out the core principles, institutional structures, powers and general functioning of the European Union and Euratom. They particularly define EU and Euratom competences in individual fields and corresponding procedures of decision-making and law-making respectively. They furthermore determine the fundamental rights and freedoms of citizens, residents and companies.[12]

The three treaties also create the legal framework for European energy policy. The TFEU contains on the one hand a set of directly applicable provisions safeguarding the general functioning of the European energy market (for example, the European Union's four freedoms). On the other hand it lays down competences for the adoption of energy legislation. In contrast, the TEU establishes rules for external EU action, which may adversely affect energy issues. The Euratom Treaty ultimately covers questions of nuclear energy policy. The European Atomic Energy Community (Euratom) established by the Euratom Treaty must be formally distinguished from the European Union, even though Euratom and the European Union are run

---

11 See, for instance, the slightly deviating classification in N Foster, *EU Law – Directions* (Oxford University Press 2008) 73 et seq.

12 Fundamental rights are laid down in the Charter of Fundamental Rights of the European Union of 7 December 2000 which is declared as applicable by article 6 TEU. In respect of the limited application of the Charter to Poland and to the United Kingdom, see the Protocol on the application of the Charter of Fundamental Rights of the European Union to Poland and to the United Kingdom, appended to the Lisbon Treaty.

by the same set of institutions. Details regarding the Euratom Treaty will therefore be the subject of a separate consideration below.

b) Secondary law

The TFEU vests European institutions with law-making powers. Within their sphere of competences, empowered institutions may adopt legal acts, which form the European Union's secondary law. The corpus of secondary law comprises mainly the instruments listed in article 288 TFEU, namely regulations, directives, decisions, recommendations and opinions. The first three types of legal acts are also considered as legislative acts or EU legislation.[13]

- **Regulations**: Regulations have general application. They are binding in their entirety and directly applicable in all member states.
- **Directives**: Directives are flexible legal instruments directed to member states. Directives set out targets and more or less concrete provisions, which have to be transposed into national law by member states. Member states have leeway with regard to how to achieve defined results. Directives are principally not directly applicable to individuals and companies. However, by way of exception, natural and legal persons may refer to individual provisions of a directive in case it was not properly implemented or not transposed in due time and the provision in question is clear, precise and unconditional (vertical direct effect).[14] This exemption does not apply for claims between individuals (no horizontal direct effect).[15] Considering their more flexible nature, directives are less restrictive for member states as compared to regulations. Given that, they figure particularly prominently in politically sensitive areas such as energy policy. Although the European legislator has not refrained completely from adopting regulations pertaining to the energy sector, directives appear as the dominant instruments of EU energy policy.
- **Decisions**: Decisions are binding acts, which are especially used to regulate individual cases. When applied like this, a decision is binding on those individual member states, natural or legal persons addressed by it. Besides, treaties provide for the deployment of decisions in other situations as well. Decisions form, for instance, the primary instruments in the field of the Common Foreign and Security Policy (CFSP).

---

13 Cf art 289 TFEU. See also http://ec.europa.eu/legislation/ (accessed 29 April 2016).
14 Cf, for instance, Court of Justice Cases 41/74 *Van Duyn v Home Office* [1974] ECR 01337 and 152/84 *Marshall v Southampton Health Authority* [1986] ECR 00723.
15 Cf Court of Justice Case 152/84 *Marshall v Southampton Health Authority* [1986] ECR 00723.

- **Recommendations and Opinions**: Recommendations and opinions have no binding force. They may nevertheless take effect through their persuasive power or in case they provide interpretation on legal acts, or in case the adoption of a legal act requires the recommendation of a certain institution.

c) Supplementary law

Supplementary sources of law comprise the case law of the European Court of Justice, general principles of law and rules of public international law. Supplementary sources primarily serve to bridge gaps left in primary and secondary law or to interpret these sources of law. General principles of law include, for instance, the principles the European Court of Justice has identified as being common to the member states' legal systems, in particular fundamental rights. Even international law has served as 'a source of inspiration' for the Court of Justice when substantiating general principles of law.[16]

d) International agreements

The European Union is considered as a subject of international law. It may conclude international agreements with third states and international organisations, which are binding upon the European Union, its institutions, and member states (article 216 TFEU). International agreements belong to the corpus of EU law and even take priority over secondary law.

e) Legal principles

EU law is determined by a number of legal principles filtered by the Court of Justice of the European Union out of the legal sources detailed above, including in particular the following cornerstone principles:

i) Hierarchy of sources of EU law

EU law is characterised by an order of priority (see Figure 1.3). Primary law is the highest rank of EU law, and all provisions of primary law have generally equal priority. General principles of law have the same legal ranking as primary law. International treaties concluded by EU institutions rank below primary law, but before secondary law. Acts of secondary law are

---

16 See http://europa.eu/legislation_summaries/institutional_affairs/decisionmaking_process/l14533_en. htm, accessed 5 January 2016.

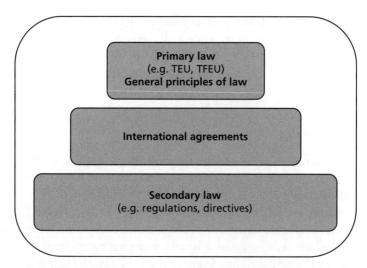

Figure 1.3 Hierarchy of main sources of EU law (simplified representation)

subordinate to primary law, general principles of law and international treaties. This means in particular that secondary law may never derogate from primary law. Rather, secondary law may put primary law in concrete terms and it must be interpreted in terms of primary law.

ii)   *Supremacy*

The doctrine of supremacy is relevant in relation to the national law of EU member states. According to the European Court of Justice, the doctrine says that EU law is always superior to national law.[17] In case of conflict, EU law takes precedence over national law. This means that national law derogating from EU law must not be applied in such a case, even though it remains valid and may be applied in cases without any connection to EU law.

The doctrine of supremacy is generally accepted in all EU member states. Nevertheless, not every highest court at national level has aligned itself with the very strict approach of the European Court of Justice, which subordinates even the constitutional law of member states to EU secondary law. The German Federal Constitutional Court for instance held that, in principle, it will no longer review secondary law on the basis of the German constitution. Nevertheless it made clear on several occasions that it reserves the right to do so under certain circumstances, notably in case the level of protection of

17 See Case 6/64 *Falminio Costa v ENEL* [1964] ECR 585, 593.

fundamental rights under EU law lags behind the indispensable level of protection offered under the German constitution.[18]

iii)   *Direct effect*

Given that EU law addresses in large part member states, the question arises whether under certain conditions specific provisions of EU law nevertheless bear direct effect, meaning that individuals or companies may invoke them before national or European courts. In a series of cases the Court of Justice has answered this question in respect of every major source of EU law. Accordingly a provision of primary law shall be directly applicable if it contains a sufficiently clear, precisely stated and unconditional obligation, the implementation of which does not require any additional measure.[19] This is in particular true for most of the fundamental freedoms, which are the object of consideration below in Chapter 2.

In addition to primary law, EU legislation may also bear direct effect. By their very nature, regulations always exhibit direct effect.[20] Pursuant to article 288 TFEU, regulations are directly applicable, meaning that they may have effect in favour of or to the disadvantage of individuals without requiring any further national act of implementation. As already mentioned above, directives have direct effect in a vertical dimension in cases where they are not properly implemented or not implemented in due time and the provisions in question are clear, precise and unconditional.[21] A decision is generally binding on anyone to whom it is addressed. However, an individual may also invoke a provision of a decision imposed on member states if it can be ascertained that this provision is 'capable of producing direct effects in the legal relationships between the addressee of the act and third parties.'[22]

iv)   *Effectiveness of EU law ('effet utile')*

Pursuant to article 4(3) TEU, member states must take all appropriate measures to ensure the fulfilment of the obligations arising out of the treaties or resulting from EU acts. This obligation includes in particular the duty of member states' courts to interpret and apply national law in the light

---

18 Bundesverfassungsgericht cases 2 BvR 197/83, "Solange II", BVerfGE 73, 339; 2 BvL 1/97, "Bananenmarkt-Entscheidung", BVerfGE 102, 147.

19 Case 26/62 *Van Gend en Loos v Nederlandse Administratie der Belastingen* [1963] ECR 1.

20 Court of Justice Case 43/71 Politi s.a.s. v Ministry for Finance of the Italian Republic [1971] ECR 01039.

21 Cf, for instance, Court of Justice Cases 41/74 *Van Duyn v Home Office* [1974] ECR 01337 and 152/84 *Marshall v Southampton Health Authority* [1986] ECR 00723. See above section 1.3.2b) Secondary law.

22 See Court of Justice case 9/70 *Franz Grad v Finanzamt* [1970] ECR 825.

of the wording and the purpose of EU directives in order to give effect to these EU acts and to avoid conflicts.[23] This means that national law must be interpreted in light of a directive irrespective of whether national law was adopted before or after the directive or whether it was explicitly meant to implement the directive. Therefore EU directives have importance even after implementation in national law.

1.4 Law-making in the field of energy policy

The preceding sections have conveyed a basic idea of the European Union's internal structure, its general functioning and the meaning of EU law for the determination and implementation of the common energy policy. Legislation constitutes the chief instrument of action in the field of energy policy, which is hardly surprising for an area generally coming under the European Union's supranational domain. But how exactly do legislative acts of the European Union come about?

In general, the adoption of a certain legislative act requires both the European Union's competence to act and the execution of the applicable procedure by the European legislature. Let us scrutinise both aspects in the following two sub-sections.

1.4.1 Legislative powers

a) *General remarks*

The remit of the European Union accrues from the competences member states have transferred to it (principle of attributed powers or principle of conferral).[24] Accordingly, the European Union's legislative powers are confined to the very areas where such competences were conferred. Any competence not transferred to the European Union remains with the member states. In contrast to member states, the European Union is furthermore not in a position to open up new fields of activity.

However, explicit European Union competences as designated for individual fields are extended by the doctrine of implied powers and by articles 3(2) and 352 TFEU. Under the doctrine of implied powers the treaties confer upon

---

23 See Court of Justice Cases 14/83 *Colson and Kamann* [1984] ECR 1891; C-106/89 *Marleasing* [1990] ECR I-04135.

24 Cf article 5 TEU; see also A von Bogdandy and J Bast (eds), *Principles of European Constitutional Law* (2nd edn, Hart Publishing and C.H. Beck 2010) 280.

the European Union all powers being indispensable in order to carry out the tasks assigned to it, regardless of whether respective powers were explicitly stated in the treaties or not.[25] Article 3(2) TFEU concedes in particular to the European Union the competence to conclude international agreements, even if not explicitly provided for in the treaties, in cases where such competence is necessary to exercise internal powers. Ultimately, according to Article 352 TFEU (the so-called 'flexibility clause') the European Union may adopt a measure if it proves necessary, within the framework of a defined policy field, to attain a certain EU objective, even though the treaties do not specifically set out the competence for such action.

Pursuant to Article 2 TFEU, legislative competences can generally be put into three main groups: exclusive competences (Article 3 TFEU), shared competences (Article 4 TFEU) and supporting competences (Article 6 TFEU). In areas of exclusive competences the European Union is solely responsible for legislation.[26] Member states' framework for action is limited here to the implementation of European Union acts and to the fields where the European Union itself empowers them to act. The fields of exclusive competences include, for instance, the customs union and the common commercial policy. The latter also covers, in part, the European Union's external energy action.

The vast majority of EU policies come under the category of shared competences.[27] In these areas, the European Union acts only if and so far as a given objective cannot be sufficiently achieved by the member states, but can rather, by reason of the scale or effect of the proposed action, be better attained at European Union level (principle of subsidiarity).[28] If these conditions are not met or if the European Union does not exercise a given competence, the member states remain responsible for policy-making.

In the fields of supporting competences (for example, research, education, tourism) member states remain fully responsible for legislation.[29] Here the European Union may only support, coordinate or supplement the action of member states.

---

25 See Joined Cases 281, 283, 284, 285 and 287/85 *Germany and others v Commission* [1987] ECR 3203. See also A von Bogdandy and J Bast (eds), *Principles of European Constitutional Law* (2nd edn, Hart Publishing and C.H. Beck 2010) 282.

26 However, there are some exceptions to the rule, which are for instance provided for in arts 346 and 347 TFEU.

27 See art 4 TFEU.

28 See art 5(1) and (3) TEU and the Protocol on the application of the principles of subsidiarity and proportionality.

29 Art 2(5) and art 6 TFEU.

Finally, the European Union has to observe the principle of proportionality when using its competences. According to this principle, the content and form of a European Union measure shall not exceed what is necessary to achieve the relevant objective of the treaties.[30] For instance, if a certain objective can be effectively attained by means of a regulation or a directive, the European Union must use a directive since this instrument leaves the member states the choice of the implementing measure, which is less restrictive than a regulation.

b) *Energy-related legislative powers*

Energy policy was considered an EC/EU domain of minor importance for many years. Even though energy policy had played a role at European level since the European Community's very beginnings, member states struggled for a long time to delegate crucial energy responsibilities to the Community and avoided introducing an explicit, comprehensive and coherent portfolio of energy competences. This is why a number of considerable deficiencies in the legal framework for energy could be discerned over many years,[31] some of which even remain to this day. Nevertheless, the European Community and the European Union respectively, have continuously expanded their energy-related legislation on the basis of different competences in the last decades, indicating the considerably increased importance of common European action in the energy sector.[32]

However, energy law and policy continue to be characterised by a carefully balanced division of powers between the European Union and its member states: First, most areas of EU energy policy and its related policies such as environmental policy come under the shared competences.[33] This means that action at European Union level is admissible only under the principle of subsidiarity. Second, article 194(2) TFEU determines that the European Union's energy competence is not all-encompassing. Correspondingly, EU action shall not affect member states' right to determine the conditions for exploiting their energy resources, their choice between different energy sources and the general structure of their energy supply. For that reason,

---

30 Cf art 5(1) and (4) TEU and the Protocol on the application of the principles of subsidiarity and proportionality. See also N Foster, *Foster on EU Law* (4th edn, Oxford University Press 2013) 386 et seq.

31 See European Commission, *White Paper 'An Energy Policy for the European Union'* (COM (1995) 682 final); M Roggenkamp, C Redgwell, I del Guayo and A Rønne, *Energy Law in Europe* (2nd edn, Oxford University Press 2007) 229.

32 See also D Buchan, 'Energy Policy – Sharp Challenges and Rising Ambitions' in H Wallace, M A Pollack and A R Young (eds), *Policy-making in the European Union* (6th edn, Oxford University Press 2010) 357.

33 Cf art 4 TFEU.

the usage of nuclear power, for instance, is still left to every member state's discretion. Under specific conditions, measures of environmental policy may take precedence over the last-mentioned two national reservations, but only if the Council and therefore basically the member states unanimously decide so.[34] Third, measures of energy policy which are primarily of a fiscal nature also require unanimous Council decisions and therefore the consent of every member state's representative.[35] Fourth, member states retain the right to take measures necessary to ensure their energy supply in the event of serious internal disturbances, a serious international tension or war.[36] However, in such a case member states shall try to collectively prevent disturbances of the internal market caused by such measures.

Thus, member states' ambit continues to comprise crucial energy competences. The free choice of energy sources remains surely a pivotal element. It allows member states to determine the individual national energy mix beyond the mandatory national targets for renewable energy.[37] Within this scope of discretion, Germany has initiated the so-called 'Energiewende' (energy transition) in particular, under which renewable energies are being substantially developed while the use of nuclear power is phased out. As energy grids are already connected throughout Europe, the process presents neighbouring states with huge challenges, especially in terms of grid overload. However, this exemplifies just the general fact that the national choice of the energy mix is actually far from being a concern of individual countries alone. Of course, also the adherence of individual states to the conversion of fossil fuels or of nuclear fuels as the predominant means of producing electricity affects a range of other countries in view of resulting environmental impacts and safety hazards. In this light, common approaches have to be found and amplified at EU level, which would in effect further curtail the room for national leeway. However, this route already seems to be predetermined considering that the European Union has already decided to establish a functioning internal energy market and to step up common climate protection efforts, which exclude isolated national decision-making.

---

34 Cf art 194(2) subparagraph 2 TFEU in conjunction with art 192(2)(c) TFEU. See J Schwarze (ed.), *EU-Kommentar* (3rd edn, Nomos 2012) art 194 notes 28 et seq.

35 See art 194(3) TFEU.

36 See art 347 TFEU and Declaration no 35 appended to the Final Act adopted by the Conference of the Representatives of the Governments of the Member States in Brussels on 23 July 2007.

37 Respective targets are laid down in Directive 2009/28/EC of the European Parliament and of the Council of 23 April 2009 on the promotion of the use of energy from renewable sources and amending and subsequently repealing Directives 2001/77/EC and 2003/30/EC [2009] OJ L 140/16.

i)   *Core competences in the field of energy policy*

With the 2007 Lisbon Treaty, member states established an explicit and comprehensive competence of the European Union in the field of energy policy. Respective stipulations were laid down in article 194 TFEU which defines the overall objectives of EU energy policy, energy-related competences, the aforementioned reservations for national action and applicable legislative procedures.

Pursuant to article 194, energy policy has to be developed with regard to the completion of the internal market, the need for environmental protection and improvement and the solidarity between member states. Considering these general prerequisites, EU energy policy aims to:

(a)   ensure the functioning of the energy market;
(b)   ensure security of energy supply in the European Union;
(c)   promote energy efficiency and energy saving and the development of new and renewable forms of energy; and
(d)   promote the interconnection of energy networks.

Subparagraph (a) determines the general aim of the European Union to create a competitive internal energy market. Despite considerable efforts in recent years, difficulties still remain in this respect due to the divergent state of market liberalisation in member states, the disparity in national regulation and the modest progress of cross-border electricity trading.[38] Legislative acts pertaining to the creation of the internal energy market (for example, the 3rd energy package) used to be based on article 95 TEC (now article 114 TFEU concerning the approximation of laws). From the entry into force of the Lisbon Treaty onwards, article 194 TFEU has to be considered as *lex specialis* in relation to article 114 TFEU.

Subparagraph (b) addresses one of the most critical issues of energy policy: security of energy supply. In this respect the European Union will be presented with particular challenges in the decades to come, considering the growing demand for energy and the threatening dependence from single suppliers. In order to forestall and overcome potential problems subparagraph (b) allows for the adoption of necessary legislation, for instance, in view of setting up minimum stocks of crude oil, petroleum products and natural gas, or establishing measures to properly cope with supply

---

38 See S Breier in C Lenz and K Borchardt, *EU-Verträge* (5th edn, Bundesanzeiger Verlag 2010) article 194 note 8.

disruptions. According to article 194 TFEU, ensuring the security of every member state's energy supply has to be understood as a common task. It requires solidarity among member states and is therefore a source of help in times of supply shortages.[39]

Pursuant to subparagraph (c), the European Union undertakes to foster energy efficiency, energy saving, renewables and new forms of energy. This target serves both security of energy supply and the environmental sustainability of energy production and consumption. It is hence closely intertwined with the EU policies on security of supply and on climate protection. Based on subparagraph (c), the European Union may adopt prescriptive measures or funding programmes promoting required technical innovation. By contrast, instruments to support the generation of renewable energy or its feeding into the grid are still subject to EU environment policy and the corresponding article 192 TFEU.[40]

Finally, pursuant to subparagraph (d) the European Union is charged with promoting the interconnection of networks, which constitutes a logical step given objectives (a) to (c). A well-functioning, secure and sustainable energy sector presupposes stronger links between national energy systems and also between remote net segments or newly-arising power generation facilities and core networks. Subparagraph (d) goes beyond article 170(1) TFEU according to which the European Union shall only contribute to the development of trans-European networks.[41] Under article 194, the European Union may also fully finance single projects. Furthermore, this article extends the European Union's competences in the area of planning even though it has to carefully consider the principle of subsidiarity here.[42]

ii)   *Additional competences*

Ultimately, the introduction of article 194 TFEU through the Lisbon Treaty did not materially increase the European Union's competences in the field of energy policy.[43] Based on several other treaty provisions, EC/EU institutions

---

39 S Hirsbrunner in J Schwarze (ed.), *EU-Kommentar* (3rd edn, Nomos 2012) article 194 note 10.

40 C Calliess in C Calliess and M Ruffert, *EUV/AEUV* (4th edn, C.H. Beck 2011) article 194 note 15; S Hirsbrunner in J Schwarze (ed.), *EU-Kommentar* (3rd edn, Nomos 2012) article 194 note 17.

41 See also article 171(1) subparagraph I TFEU.

42 C Calliess in C Calliess and M Ruffert, *EUV/AEUV* (4th edn, C.H. Beck 2011) article 194 note 16 et seq; S Breier in C Lenz and K Borchardt, *EU-Verträge* (5th edn, Bundesanzeiger Verlag 2010) article 194 note 12.

43 See also S Breier in C Lenz and K Borchardt, *EU-Verträge* (5th edn, Bundesanzeiger Verlag 2010) article 194 note 3; A M Schneider, *EU-Kompetenzen einer Europäischen Energiepolitik* (Nomos 2010) 310.

had already gradually stepped up their energy-related activities in the course of the preceding years.[44] The provisions on competences used before the coming into effect of the Lisbon Treaty were principally carried over from the former EC Treaty to the TFEU and may theoretically even today serve as a legal basis for the adoption of legislative acts.[45] These provisions include, for instance, article 114 TFEU (approximation of laws/internal market), articles 170 et seq. TFEU (trans-European networks) and articles 191 et seq. TFEU (environment).

However, now any issues covered by article 194 must principally be based on this provision, given its nature as *lex specialis*.[46] This namely holds true for the approximation of laws intended to ensure the functioning of the energy market (cf article 194 para 1a), measures on minimum gas and oil storage (cf article 194 para 1b), promotion of energy efficiency (cf article 194 para. 1c) and fostering the interconnection of energy networks (cf article 194 para 1d).[47]

Nevertheless, article 194 does not constitute an exhaustive legal basis for energy-related policies, as follows from its paragraph 2. In case article 194 does not appear as *lex specialis*, other provisions may apply, such as article 122 covering situations of severe supply difficulties[48] or article 192 as regards the economic promotion of renewable energies (by contrast, the promotion of the technological development comes under article 194).[49] However, in practice, the choice of the appropriate legal basis may cause some difficulty. This applies especially to the area where the policies on energy, environment and climate overlap.[50] The European Court of Justice has established particular rules which have to be considered in such cases.[51] Accordingly, the choice of the legal basis must rest on objective factors (in particular the aim and the content of the measure). If a measure pursues a twofold purpose or it has a twofold component, the act must be based on the legal basis the main or predominant purpose or component requires.[52]

---

44 See also A Johnston and G Block, *EU Energy Law* (Oxford University Press 2013) 4.

45 See the wording of article 194(2) subparagraph 1 TFEU "Without prejudice to the application of other provisions of the Treaties".

46 W Kahl and S Bings in R Streinz (ed.), *EUV/AEUV* (2nd edn, C.H. Beck 2012) article 194 note 39.

47 C Calliess in C Calliess and M Ruffert, *EUV/AEUV* (4th edn, C.H. Beck 2011) article 194 notes 9 et seq.

48 See also A Johnston and G Block, *EU Energy Law* (Oxford University Press 2013) 240; A M Schneider, *EU-Kompetenzen einer Europäischen Energiepolitik* (Nomos 2010) 312.

49 C Calliess in C Calliess and M Ruffert, *EUV/AEUV* (4th edn, C.H. Beck 2011) article 194 note 15.

50 W Kahl and S Bings in R Streinz (ed.), *EUV/AEUV* (2nd edn, C.H. Beck 2012) article 194 note 39.

51 See, inter alia, ECJ Cases C-336/00 *Huber* [2002] ECR I-7699, para 31; C-281/01 *Commission v Council* [2002] ECR I-12049, para 38; C-338/01 *Commission v Council* [2004] ECR I-04829, para 55 et seq.

52 ECJ, C-338/01 *Commission v Council* [2004] ECR I-04829, para 55.

In case one of the four objectives included in article 194 TFEU is primarily pursued, the measure must be founded on article 194 TFEU as the pertaining *lex specialis*. However, legal acts frequently serve more than one *primary* purpose. If this is the case, the measure has generally to be founded on the different applicable legal bases.[53]

iii)   *General scope of competences*

In general, energy responsibilities of the European Union, as defined in the TFEU, cover all energy sub-sectors, from the coal, electricity and gas sectors to the oil and renewable energy sectors. The nuclear sector, however, constitutes an exception. As regards nuclear energy policy, the Euratom Treaty provides for special provisions and it is controversial whether the TFEU may with regard to article 106a(3) of the Euratom Treaty serve as a subsidiary legal basis.[54]

1.4.2   Legislative procedures

European Union institutions resort to different procedures when exercising their legislative powers. The so-called ordinary legislative procedure, formerly known as the codecision procedure, constitutes the most frequently used procedure. Beyond that the TFEU provides for several special legislative procedures applicable to issues of particular sensitivity to member states. Special legislative procedures include, for instance, the consent procedure (formerly known as the assent procedure) and the consultation procedure.

The applicable legislative procedure follows from the treaty provisions which cover an issue in question. In terms of energy policy and related areas, such as environmental policy and trans-European networks policy, the ordinary legislative procedure is generally determined as the relevant procedure. Nonetheless, some sensitive energy-related issues are also subject to special legislative procedures. This applies, for instance, to measures of a primarily fiscal nature (article 194(3) TFEU) and measures of environmental policy significantly affecting a member state's choice between different energy sources (article 192(2)(c) TFEU).

---

53 Ibid para 56 et seq.

54 Cf D Hackländer, *Die allgemeine Energiekompetenz im Primärrecht der Europäischen Union* (Peter Lang Verlag 2010) 107; Bundeskanzler, *Anfragenbeantwortung* (GZ: BKA-353.110/0060-I/4/2012, 13 April 2012) [answer to a parliamentary request from Austrian Federal Chancellor dated 13 April 2012] http://www.parlament.gv.at/PAKT/VHG/XXIV/AB/AB_10448/fnameorig_249761.html (accessed 29 April 2016).

a)   *Ordinary legislative procedure*

The ordinary legislative procedure (formerly known as the codecision procedure) has developed as the primary legislative procedure in the course of various treaty amendments. This evolution goes hand in hand with the strengthening of the European Parliament's power. The ordinary legislative procedure ultimately involves the Council and the Parliament on an equal footing. This means that the Parliament may also reject a draft act or propose its own amendments. The ordinary legislative procedure is set out in article 294 TFEU and may be summarised as follows.

(a) **Legislative initiative**: In general, the Commission sets the legislative process in motion. It has the 'right of initiative' and, correspondingly, it is its task to prepare and officially submit a legislative proposal to the legislature, namely the Parliament and Council. Considering the special significance of a proposal for the final act, the Commission occupies a central position and is the object of intense lobbying. The drafting process, which is often triggered by requests of the Parliament and Council, consists of several stages of evaluation, consultation and preparation (see above section 1.3.1). After completion, the Commission forwards a proposal to the Parliament and Council, but also to the national parliaments and, where the treaties so determine, to the Committee of the Regions (CoR) and the European Economic and Social Committee (EESC). National parliaments, CoR and EESC may give their opinion on a draft act. The influence of member states' parliamentarians on a proposal along this path is, however, limited given that national parliaments are formally only called upon to send a reasoned opinion on whether the draft act complies with the principle of subsidiarity.

(b) **First reading**: On a first reading the European Parliament adopts its position on the proposal. The position is prepared by the relevant parliamentary committee (committee responsible) or, to be more precise, by one of its members (rapporteur). After being adopted by the committee responsible, the draft position (called 'report') is forwarded to the plenary for debate. The plenary assembly revises the text and adopts the Parliament's position by a simple majority (majority of the members taking part in the vote). Afterwards the position is sent to the Council.

If the Council accepts the position of the Parliament, the act is adopted. If not, the Council prepares a revised draft and sends it back to the Parliament with a statement of reasons. The Council generally acts by a qualified majority (as defined in the treaties).

(c) **Second reading**: When receiving a deviating position from the Council, the Parliament may approve, reject or amend the proposed draft. In case of approval with a simple majority, the act is adopted in the wording of the Council's version. The same is true in cases where the Parliament does not take any decision. If the Parliament rejects the position of the Council by absolute majority (majority of the Parliament's component members), the act is deemed to have failed.

In cases where the Parliament decides to amend the Council's draft by absolute majority, the proposed new text is forwarded to the Council and the Commission, which then gives an opinion. If the Council then approves the amendments proposed by the Parliament by a qualified majority, the act is adopted. In cases where the Commission has rejected the Parliament's proposal, the Council must decide unanimously on the amendments.

If the Council does not accept the Parliament's amendments, a meeting of the Conciliation Committee is convened. The Conciliation Committee is composed of delegations of the European Parliament and the Council and elaborates a joint text of both institutions. If the Conciliation Committee does not reach agreement on a joint position, the act is deemed to have failed. Otherwise, a third reading takes place.

(d) **Third reading**: In the third reading the European Parliament, acting by a simple majority, and the Council, acting by a qualified majority, decide on the joint text. If both approve the draft, the act is deemed to have been adopted. If not, the act has ultimately failed.

b) *Special legislative procedures*

The special legislative procedures include in particular the consent procedure (assent procedure) and the consultation procedure. Under the consent procedure the Council adopts legislative acts after obtaining the consent of the Parliament. The European Parliament can either accept or reject the proposal (right of veto). The TFEU does not provide for the Parliament being able to table amendments. The Commission is again responsible for preparing the proposal and initiating the legislative process. The consent procedure is, for instance, applicable in the case of article 352 TFEU (flexibility clause).

The consultation procedure is used for legislation in particularly sensitive areas. This especially applies to energy measures of a fiscal nature (article 194(3) TFEU) and environmental measures significantly affecting a member state's choice between different energy sources (article 192(2)(c) TFEU). Under the consultation procedure, the Council acts on a proposal of the Commission after simply consulting Parliament and, where provided for, after consulting the Economic and Social Committee and the

Committee of the Regions (see for example, article 192(2)(c) TFEU). The Council is, however, neither bound by the Parliament's stance nor by the viewpoints of both committees. The Council thus adopts legislation alone acting either unanimously or by a qualified majority subject to the applicable treaty provision.

1.5 Euratom

As set forth in the introduction, within this textbook the concept of European energy policy comprises energy related strategies as well as the activities of two organisations, namely the European Union and Euratom. This section is dedicated to the latter organisation. However, the presentation is confined to merely sketching the contours of Euratom considering the fact that its functioning is similar to that of the European Union.

The European Atomic Energy Community (Euratom or EAEC) is a supranational organisation dedicated to nuclear energy policy. Euratom and the European Union have the same member states and share the same institutions responsible for defining and implementing energy policies. Thus, from a political perspective at least, there are good arguments for pooling both organisations' energy competences under one and the same major policy field, namely that of a European energy policy. However, from a legal point of view Euratom must be distinguished from the European Union. Whereas the European Union is based on the Treaty on European Union (TEU) and the Treaty on the Functioning of the European Union (TFEU), Euratom is established on the Euratom Treaty (EAEC Treaty).

Euratom was founded in 1957 by the Rome Treaties in order to foster cooperation in the nuclear field. Even today, it aims at pooling and coordinating member states' strengths and resources in the nuclear sector. Euratom pursues a number of objectives including:

- the creation of a nuclear common market
- the promotion of research
- the dissemination of information
- the establishment of uniform safety standards
- securing the establishment of necessary infrastructure
- ensuring the security of atomic energy supply
- supervising that nuclear materials are not diverted to purposes other than those for which they are intended
- the promotion of peaceful uses of nuclear energy.

However, the Euratom Treaty does not affect the member states' general right to opt in favour of or oppose nuclear energy as a component in their energy supply.

1.5.1 Structure and general functioning of Euratom

Euratom is designed as a supranational organisation. Its decisions are taken by transnational European institutions and require application throughout the member states. As mentioned before, Euratom and the European Union share the same set of institutions, namely comprising the European Council, the Council, the European Parliament, the European Commission (Commission), the Court of Justice of the European Union, the European Central Bank and the Court of Auditors.

It is also the European Council gathering the heads of state or government, the president of the European Council and the president of the Commission that defines the general political directions and priorities.[55] The Council (also Council of the European Union or Council of Ministers) represents the main decision-making body giving shape to nuclear energy policy. The Council configuration entrusted with deciding on Euratom issues is the Transport, Telecommunications and Energy Council (TTE), which constitutes an assembly of responsible representatives of each member state at ministerial level. The European Parliament plays a minor role in the nuclear sector. In general, the Council must only consult the Parliament before adopting a certain measure. The Industry, Research and Energy Committee (ITRE) constitutes the specialised committee of the Parliament responsible for Euratom matters.

The Commission occupies a key position in the field of nuclear policy. It drafts and proposes Euratom actions, performs coordinating and executive functions, and supervises the Euratom Supply Agency. Tasks are principally distributed among two Directorates-General, DG Energy (responsible for nuclear energy, transport, international relations, nuclear safeguards, waste management) and DG Research (responsible for research in nuclear energy). The Commission's in-house science service, the Joint Research Centre (JRC), provides necessary scientific and technical assistance in designing, implementing and monitoring instruments of nuclear policy. The JRC was originally founded as the Joint Nuclear Research Centre dedicated to nuclear research only, but the focus of the centre has been extended to other

---

55 Article 15 TEU.

important policy fields over the years. In addition to the JRC, a Scientific and Technical Committee Euratom (STC) was installed as an advisory body attached to the Commission specialising in nuclear matters.[56] It particularly advises the Commission in the elaboration of nuclear research and training programmes.[57]

Apart from these institutions, some other agencies and bodies support the goals of Euratom. The following ones count among these bodies: the Euratom Supply Agency (ESA), the 'European Joint Undertaking for ITER and the Development of Fusion Energy' (Fusion for Energy), the European Nuclear Energy Forum (ENEF), the European Nuclear Safety Regulator Group (ENSREG), and the Sustainable Nuclear Energy Technology Platform (SNETP).

Euratom Supply Agency (ESA): The Euratom Supply Agency is a body established by the Euratom Treaty to ensure a regular and equitable supply of ores and nuclear fuels for Community users.[58] Its particular tasks are to provide for fair distribution by ensuring equal access to sources and to secure long-term supply and avoid dependence on single suppliers. In order to fulfil its tasks, ESA has a right of option on ores, source materials and special fissile materials produced in the territories of member states.[59] Furthermore, it is equipped with an exclusive right to conclude contracts relating to the supply of ores, source materials and special fissile materials originating from inside or outside of the Euratom area. Located in Luxembourg, ESA operates under the supervision of the Commission, which has the authority to issue directives, veto decisions of the agency and appoint its Director General.

Fusion for Energy (F4E): The 'European Joint Undertaking for ITER and the Development of Fusion Energy' (Fusion for Energy or F4E) constitutes Euratom's contribution to the International Thermonuclear Experimental Reactor partnership (ITER). ITER is the world's largest research and engineering project to demonstrate that fusion is a feasible energy source in future. F4E, based in Barcelona, Spain, was established under the Euratom Treaty and will be in operation for 35 years from 2007 onwards. Besides ITER, F4E supports the construction of demonstration fusion power plants (DEMO). Furthermore, F4E is responsible for implementing the 'Broader

---

56 See article 134 Euratom Treaty.
57 See article 7(1) Euratom Treaty.
58 Cf articles 2(d) and 52(2)(b) Euratom Treaty.
59 Cf article 52(2)(b) Euratom Treaty.

Approach', which is an advanced partnership between Euratom and Japan to complement ITER and promote the realisation of fusion energy.[60]

European Nuclear Energy Forum (ENEF): The European Nuclear Energy Forum (ENEF or the Bratislava/Prague forum) is meant to serve as a discussion platform of stakeholders in the nuclear field. The forum brings together member states, Euratom institutions, industry, and consumers, and may address any topic of nuclear energy policy.

European Nuclear Safety Regulator Group (ENSREG): The European Nuclear Safety Regulator Group (ENSREG) is an independent expert body to promote the improvement of nuclear safety and radioactive waste management. ENSREG was originally founded as the European High Level Group (HLG) on Nuclear Safety and Waste Management. ENSREG gathers officials from national regulatory or nuclear safety authorities and from the European Commission.[61]

Sustainable Nuclear Energy Technology Platform (SNETP): The Sustainable Nuclear Energy Technology Platform (SNETP) is a stakeholder forum to foster research and development in the nuclear sector with particular focus on nuclear fission technologies. It brings together stakeholders from industry, technical safety organisations, NGOs and academia. SNETP members also take the lead in the Sustainable Nuclear Initiative established by the SET-Plan.

1.5.2 Forms of Euratom action

In principle, Euratom may resort to the same types of instruments as the European Union does, when drafting, defining, implementing and evaluating its policies.[62] Legal forms of action serve as chief instruments here, too. Just like EU law, Euratom law particularly comprises sources of primary and secondary law. The revised Euratom Treaty constitutes the main source of Euratom's primary law. The treaty sets out Euratom's tasks, major objectives, competences, structure and functioning. It also directly imposes obligations on member states, for instance in terms of the creation and maintenance of the nuclear common market. Euratom's secondary law also

---

60 See http://www.f4e.europa.eu/understandingfusion/broaderapproach.aspx (accessed 29 April 2016).

61 See http://www.ensreg.eu/members-glance (accessed 29 April 2016).

62 See above section 1.3.

consists mainly of regulations, directives, decisions, recommendations and opinions.[63]

1.5.3   Euratom decision-making and legislation

Euratom action is limited to the very areas where competences have been transferred to it (principle of conferral). Euratom competences correspond to the Euratom objectives, for example, the promotion of research, the establishment of uniform safety standards, the security of atomic energy supply, or the creation of the nuclear common market. This book is not the place for a detailed description of these competences. The following key points are only to provide a brief insight into the sphere of Euratom action. For further details on secondary law adopted on the basis of theses competences, see Chapter 4.6 below.

- **Nuclear research**: For instance, to promote research in the field of nuclear energy, Euratom may determine research and training programmes, which are implemented by Euratom regulations and decisions (Council regulations and decisions) and operated by the Commission (see article 7 Euratom Treaty). The current Euratom Research and Training Programme runs from 2014 until 2018.[64]
- **Uniform safety standards**: Articles 30 to 32 provide for the establishment of basic standards within the Community for the protection of the health of workers and the general public against the dangers arising from ionising radiations. Euratom has already made use of this competence by adopting Council Directive 96/29/Euratom. Member states have to ensure compliance with the basic standards contained in the directive, by adopting appropriate national provisions.
- **Security of atomic energy supply**: Article 52 of the Euratom Treaty provides the basis for a common atomic energy supply policy. This policy is supposed to be guided by the principle of equal access to sources of supply and is to prohibit privileged positions for certain users. Moreover, based on article 52, the ESA has been established in order to safeguard a regular and equitable supply of nuclear fuels. Details on competences and functioning of ESA are laid down in articles 53 et seq.
- **Nuclear common market**: The functioning of the nuclear common market is safeguarded by articles 92–100 and article 195 of the

---

63 See art 106a(1) Euratom Treaty in conjunction with art 288 TFEU; see above section 1.3.

64 Council Regulation (Euratom) No 1314/2013 of 16 December 2013 on the Research and Training Programme of the European Atomic Energy Community (2014–2018) complementing the Horizon 2020 Framework Programme for Research and Innovation.

Euratom Treaty. These provisions particularly provide for the abolition of all customs duties, charges having equivalent effect and quantitative restrictions on imports and exports in respect of defined nuclear materials (article 93). Furthermore, subject to certain restrictions, non-discrimination is guaranteed for skilled employees coming from another member state as well as for individuals and companies participating in the construction of nuclear installations (articles 96 and 97). In terms of certain issues, Euratom may also adopt legal acts to specify details. This is, for instance, the case in respect of safeguarding the mobility of workers in the nuclear sector (article 96(2)) and with regard to facilitating the conclusion of insurance contracts covering nuclear risks (article 98(2)).

Relevant decision-making procedures arise from the treaty provisions applicable to individual issues. As regards legislative acts, it is in general up to the Council to decide (unanimously or by a qualified majority) on the basis of a proposal of the Commission. In this context, other institutions, such as the European Parliament, the Economic and Social Committee and the Scientific and Technical Committee, are involved for consulting purposes only.

 REVIEW QUESTIONS

1. What are the European Union's primary institutions that also have significant influence over the European energy policy? Which institutions are the two EU co-legislators? *See section 1.2.*
2. What are the general areas of responsibility of the European Commission in the field of energy? *See section 1.2.4.*
3. Why does the European Commission occupy a key position as regards EU energy legislation? *See section 1.2.4.*
4. Once a legislative act has been adopted by the EU legislator, how is it ensured that member states properly implement the act? *See section 1.3.1c).*
5. Which three treaties represent the core of present primary law and why do they form the framework of European energy policy? *See section 1.3.2a).*
6. Which forms of legal acts are considered as legislative acts and how are they distinguished from each other? *See section 1.3.2b).*
7. What does it mean when a specific provision of EU law has direct effect? *See section 1.3.2e).*
8. Most areas of European energy policy come under the category of shared competences, what does this mean? *See section 1.4.1a).*
9. From which provision accrue the core competences for policy-making in the field of energy? *See section 1.4.1b).*
10. Which legislative procedure is generally applicable in terms of the adoption of legislation in the area of energy policy? *See section 1.4.2.*

FURTHER READING

Elizabeth Bomberg, John Peterson and Richard Corbett, *The European Union: How Does It Work?* (3rd edn, Oxford University Press 2012)

Nigel Foster, *Foster on EU Law* (4th edn, Oxford University Press 2013)

Paul Craig and Grainne de Burca, *EU Law: Text, Cases, and Materials* (5th edn, Oxford University Press 2011)

John Peterson and Michael Shackleton (eds), *The Institutions of the European Union (The New European Union Series)* (3rd edn, Oxford University Press 2012)

Helen Wallace, Mark A Pollack and Alasdair R Young (eds), *Policy-making in the European Union* (6th edn, Oxford University Press 2010)

2

Treaty rules promoting the internal energy market

The EU treaties lay the legal foundation for the European Union and its actions in the various policy areas. The Treaty on the Functioning of the European Union (TFEU) represents the pivotal document when it comes to energy policy or any other field of economic policy. The TFEU does not only determine the European Union's legislative powers in the area of energy policy, as shown above in Chapter 1. It also contains crucial provisions that are used by EU institutions to foster the creation and functioning of the internal energy market. Given that, this textbook concentrates first on these fundamental rules before the focus is laid on energy-related legislation in the subsequent chapters.

The relevant provisions of the TFEU which are scrutinised in the following sections include:

- the fundamental freedoms (free movement of goods, persons, services and capital),
- the rules on cartels and dominant positions on the market,
- the rules on state aid, and
- the rules on taxation.

This corpus of rules is of vital importance to the proper functioning of the internal energy market. It prevents member states and undertakings from hindering trade and distorting competition. The provisions are directly binding upon member states and, in part, they produce direct effect, meaning that individuals and companies may rely on them before national or European courts.

In principle, the rules of the TFEU cover all energy sectors. The Euratom Treaty sets forth some special rules for the nuclear sector only.[1] This means

---

1 Cf in particular articles 93, 96 and 195 of the Euratom Treaty. As regards the relationship between the TFEU and the Euratom Treaty in the field of competition law, see section 2.2 below and, for instance, R Ptasekaite,

that the TFEU rules are also applicable to the coal sector which used to be subject to the European Coal and Steel Community Treaty (ECSC Treaty). The ECSC Treaty expired in 2002.

2.1 Fundamental freedoms: free movement of goods, persons, services, capital and payment

Establishing and guaranteeing an internal market remains a crucial mission of the European Union. In order to accomplish this objective the Union relies considerably on the so-called 'four freedoms of movement'. The four freedoms are designed to ensure that goods, persons, services, capital and payments may move freely within the internal market. The freedoms constitute basic conditions for the functioning of the single market. They are benchmarks for EU legislation[2] and they serve as a legal safety net. Thus, recourse to the four freedoms comes into consideration where the European Union has not exercised its legislative powers and exhaustively harmonised a certain issue. In cases where a particular question is covered by an exhaustive act of harmonisation, it has to be answered in light of this act and not on the basis of primary law, including the freedoms of movement.[3] In other words, if the compatibility of a certain member state's measure is called into question, it has to be checked solely in the light of the harmonising measure and included exemptions, in as far as they exist.

Member states are obligated to comply with the four freedoms when exercising their powers. This pertains to any national institution and authority, be it legislature, government or judiciary, and be it on federal, regional or local level.[4] National law contradicting the four freedoms may not be applied. On several occasions the European Court of Justice has confirmed that the freedoms of movement are also applicable in the energy sector, apart from a few narrowly defined exceptions.

The four freedoms have been incorporated into the Treaty on the Functioning of the European Union, as depicted in Figure 2.1.

'Competition law and nuclear regulation: A European perspective' in B Delvaux, M Hunt and K Talus (eds), *EU Energy Law and Policy Issues* (vol 4, Intersentia 2014) 93 et seq.

2 M Ruffert, in C Calliess and M Ruffert, *EUV/AEUV* (4th edn, C.H. Beck 2011) art 288 AEUV note 9; W Kahl, in C Calliess and M Ruffert, *EUV/AEUV* (4th edn, C.H. Beck 2011) art 114 AEUV note 29.

3 Cases C-309/02 *Radlberger v Land Baden-Württemberg* [2004] ECR I-11763, para 53; C-37/92 *Vanacker v Lesage* [1993] ECR I-4947, para 9; C-324/99 *DaimlerChrysler* [2001] ECR I-9897, para 32; C-573/12 *Ålands Vindkraft AB v Energimyndigheten*, para 57.

4 See art 4(3) EU Treaty; case C-71/02 *Karner v Troostwijk* [2004] ECR I-3025, para 34.

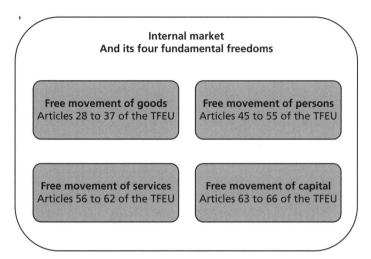

Figure 2.1 The four freedoms

2.1.1   Free movement of goods

a)   *General remarks*

Ensuring the internal market for goods remains one of the European Union's top priorities. In order to address this issue properly, the European Union resorts to both the adoption of specially tailored legislation and the enforcement of various treaty rules, wherein the principle of the free movement of goods plays a pivotal role. This principle accrues from several provisions of the TFEU and generally bans any kind of barriers to the trade of goods. Strictly speaking, the free movement of goods prohibits firstly the imposition of custom duties on imports and exports between member states, and of charges having an equivalent effect (articles 28 and 30 TFEU). Furthermore, it comprises the prohibition of quantitative restrictions on imports and exports and all measures having equivalent effect (articles 34 and 35 TFEU). Special rules are provided for state monopolies of a commercial character (article 37 TFEU), which may become especially relevant to the energy sector. Correspondingly, member states have to adjust state monopolies in such a way as to exclude any discrimination regarding the conditions under which goods are procured and marketed. Besides, as regards taxation, member states must also observe article 110 TFEU, which prohibits the imposition of taxes on products of other member states in excess of the taxes applicable to similar domestic products.

The central rule of the free movement of goods is laid down in article 34 TFEU banning quantitative restrictions on imports and all measures having equivalent effect if no proportionate justification is at hand. In a series of well-known cases the European Court of Justice has interpreted this provision in detail.[5] 'Measures having equivalent effect' are of particular relevance in practice. The Court of Justice assumes such measures in the case of national trading rules which are capable of hindering, directly or indirectly, actually or potentially, intra-Community trade (*Dassonville case*).[6] Pursuant to the Court's understanding the prohibition covers in this context not only measures bearing a discriminatory effect, but also those generally showing a restrictive effect.[7] Nevertheless, this interpretation does not apply to every rule which possibly impinges on the trading of goods. At the very least, selling arrangements (opening hours for shops, staff training requirements, and so on), which apply to all relevant traders and affect domestic and imported products in the same manner, are principally excluded from the prohibition (cf joined cases of *Keck and Mithouard*).[8] Consequently, product-related measures remain banned if not justified.

Justification may particularly be given on the basis of the Cassis de Dijon doctrine or article 36 TFEU. In the *Cassis de Dijon case* the Court of Justice held that a national measure must be accepted so far as it is necessary in order to satisfy mandatory requirements relating for instance to the fairness of commercial transactions or to the protection of public health or that of consumers.[9] Later on the Court acknowledged environmental protection as another mandatory requirement that has a special bearing on the assessment of restrictive national measures in the field of renewable energy.[10] The *Cassis de Dijon doctrine* has sparked some debates among scholars considering that its normative derivation remains unclear. The first debate revolves around its systematic allocation. The question is whether the doctrine is subordinate to article 34 and, thus, constitutes another limitation of the scope of this article

---

5 As regards the interpretation of article 35 concerning the export of products, see the more restrictive case law following from Cases 15/79 *Groenveld BV v Produktschap* [1979] ECR 03409 and C-108/01 *Consorzio del Prosciutto di Parma, Salumificio S. Rita* [2003] ECR I-05121. For the respective debate among scholars, see T Kingreen in C Calliess and M Ruffert, *EUV/AEUV* (4th edn, C.H. Beck 2011) arts 34–36 AEUV notes 127 et seq; D Chalmers, G Davies and G Monti, *European Union Law* (3rd edn, Cambridge University Press 2014) 794 et seq.

6 Case 8/74 *Procureur du Roi v Benoît and Gustave Dassonville* [1974] ECR 837.

7 Cases 8/74, *Procureur du Roi v Benoît and Gustave Dassonville*, para 5; 120/78 *Rewe-Zentral AG v Bundesmonopolverwaltung für Branntwein* [1979] ECR 649, para 8 (Cassis de Dijon case).

8 Joined Cases C-267/91 and C-268/91 *Bernard Keck and Daniel Mithouard* [1993] ECR I-6097. See for a more detailed discussion in the context of the Keck case and the post-Keck case law: N Foster, *EU Law – Directions* (Oxford University Press 2008) 272 et seq; T Kingreen in C Calliess and M Ruffert, *EUV/AEUV* arts 34–36 AEUV notes 186 et seq.

9 Case 120/78 *Rewe-Zentral AG v Bundesmonopolverwaltung für Branntwein* [1979] ECR 649.

10 See, for instance, Cases C-524/07 *Commission v Austria* [2008] I-00187, para 57; C-573/12 *Ålands Vindkraft AB v Energimyndigheten*, para 77.

beside the *Keck/ Mithouard* formula, or whether it represents a separate category of grounds of justification alongside article 36. Meanwhile the Court of Justice seems to take the latter point of view,[11] as the following sections take into account. A second debate concerns the question as to whether directly and/or indirectly discriminating national measures may also be justified under the *Cassis de Dijon doctrine*.[12] Legal scholars are divided in this respect. Many opine that *Cassis* does not cover direct discriminations.[13] However, the Court's law practice is inconsistent in this respect or remains at least odd.[14] In one of the latest cases with relevance to the energy sector (the *Ålands Vindkraft* case) the Court seemingly held that the doctrine may serve as a basis for the justification of discriminating measures.[15] However, ultimately its stance remained unclear as it did not clearly refer to the discriminating nature of the measure in question and it, in parallel, referred to article 36 as a basis of justification.[16] Considering this, the Court actually stoked up further speculations instead of clearing up the issue.[17]

Beside the *Cassis de Dijon doctrine*, article 36 TFEU has to be taken into account as a conceivable basis of justification for national measures actually or potentially hindering intra-union trade. Accordingly a national restriction may be justified on grounds of public morality, public policy, public security, the protection of health and life of humans, animals or plants; and other reasons provided that the measure in question does not constitute a means of arbitrary discrimination or a disguised restriction. As will be shown subsequently, article 36 can take on particular importance in the energy field, especially in the context of security of supply and the promotion of renewable energy.

Last but not least, when assessing the compatibility of a national measure with article 34, it must be held to particular scrutiny as to whether it complies with the principle of proportionality. Otherwise the measure may not be exempted

---

11 See, for instance, C-524/07, *Commission v Austria*, para 57; C-573/12, *Ålands Vindkraft AB v Energimyndigheten*, paras 76 et seq.

12 See T Kingreen in C Calliess and M Ruffert, arts 34–36 AEUV note 210.

13 Cf D Chalmers, G Davies and G Monti, *European Union Law*, 779; N Foster, *EU Law – Directions* (Oxford University Press 2008) 277; T Kingreen in C Callies and M Ruffert, arts 34–36 AEUV note 83.

14 See T Kingreen in C Callies and M Ruffert, arts 34–36 AEUV note 82; A Johnston and G Block, *EU Energy Law* (Oxford University Press 2013) 344.

15 C-573/12 *Ålands Vindkraft AB v Energimyndigheten*, paras 76 et seq.

16 In this context see also Joined Cases C-204/12 to C-208/12 *Essent Belgium*, para 122 showing even more uncertainty in respect of the discriminative nature of the measure at issue ('may potentially be subjected to differential treatment').

17 See also É Durand and M Keay, 'National support for renewable electricity and the single market in Europe: the Ålands Vindfraft case' (August 2014) Oxford Energy Comment, https://www.oxfordenergy.org/wpcms/wp-content/uploads/2014/08/National-support-for-renewable-electricity-and-the-single-market-in-Europe-the-%C3%85lands-Vindkraft-case.pdf accessed 29 April 2016.

from article 34 despite a given justification under the *Cassis de Dijon doctrine* or under article 36. Proportionality means that the measure at issue must be suitable (objective attainable by measure), necessary (no measures available that are less restrictive of intra-union trade) and proportionate in a strict sense (weighing of the respective member state's objective and the harm done to intra-union trade) for attaining the objective pursued, provided that the objective is legitimate.[18] The question as to whether a national measure can pass the proportionality test is often the decisive factor for the outcome of the review under EU law and depends very much on the details of the individual case.

b) Energy-related cases

Article 34 concerning the import of products also features prominently in the energy sector. In a number of cases the Court of Justice has pointed out that the interpretation of the free movement of goods principle, as outlined above, also applies to the energy sector.

i) No harmonising legislation

To start with, the Court has stressed that also in relation to measures concerning the energy sector, recourse to article 34 comes into consideration only if no exhaustively harmonising EU legislation is in place.[19] As subsequently shown in Chapter 4, national regulation in the various energy subsectors has been subject to more or less intense harmonisation through secondary law. In the electricity and gas sectors in particular, harmonisation has made major progress in recent years. Considering the elaborate stipulations provided for in the so-called Electricity and Gas Directives (Directives 2009/72/EC and 2009/73/EC) but also in other legislative acts, it must be generally scrutinised in a given case relating to the electricity or gas market as to whether there is any remaining scope for taking recourse to provisions of the TFEU.

A prime example of a controversial discussion in this respect concerns the check of the legal admissibility of national support schemes exclusively promoting the production of domestic green electricity.[20] The Court of Justice dealt with the issue in the *Ålands Vindkraft case* which, among other things, raised the question as to how article 34 and the Renewable Energy Directive

---

18 In detail: T Kingreen in C Calliess and M Ruffert, arts 34–36 AEUV notes 88 et seq; Case C-189/95 *Franzén* [1997] ECR I-5909, para 75.

19 Case C-573/12 *Ålands Vindkraft AB v Energimyndigheten*, paras 56 et seq.

20 Cf N Grabmayr, M Kahles and F Pause, 'Warenverkehrsfreiheit in der Europäischen Union und nationale Förderung erneuerbarer Energien' Würzburger Berichte zum Umweltenergierecht Nr. 4, dated 18 June 2014, p 8.

(Directive 2009/28/EC) interrelate. The Court ultimately found that the current harmonisation brought about by this directive does not show the extent that could preclude recourse to article 34 as regards the territorial restriction in question.[21]

ii)   *Scope of article 34 TFEU*

Second, given its fugacity, the question may well be raised as to whether energy can be generally considered as a legally protected good under article 34. In principle, the provision refers to the understanding of 'goods' in the sense of article 28(2) and article 29 TFEU, which cover products originating in member states as well as those products coming from third countries which are in free circulation in member states. As regards the concept of 'goods' itself the Court of Justice held that these are products which can be valued in money and which are capable, as such, of forming the subject of commercial transactions.[22] This is also true for the various energy sources or forms of energy, respectively, such as oil,[23] gas,[24] electricity,[25] heat,[26] waste[27] and coal, with the result that these have to be considered as falling within the scope of article 34. Furthermore, production and processing machines for energy sources must also be understood accordingly as goods in the sense of these provisions.

By contrast, natural and enriched uranium, other nuclear materials, and even the machinery used to generate nuclear energy come under the more specific rules of the Euratom Treaty. The abolition of customs duties, charges having equivalent effect and all quantitative restrictions on imports and exports in the nuclear sector is regulated by the Euratom Treaty.[28]

iii)   *National measures falling under article 34 TFEU*

Third, the Court of Justice, of course, proceeds from the assumption that its case law defining the forms of market restrictions being subject to the

---

21 Case C-573/12 *Ålands Vindkraft AB v Energimyndigheten*, paras 56 et seq.
22 Case 7/68 *Commission v Italy* [1968] ECR 423.
23 See J Schwarze, 'European energy policy in Community law' in E Mestmäcker (ed.), *Natural Gas in the Internal Market, A Review of Energy Policy* (Nomos 1993) 157 et seq.
24 Case C-159/94 *Commission v France* [1997] ECR I-5815.
25 Cases C-393/92 *Almelo v NV Energiebedrijf Ijsselmij* [1994] ECR I-1477, para 28; C-158/94 *Commission v Italian Republic* [1997] ECR I-5789, para 17; C-379/98 *PreussenElektra AG v Schleswag AG* [2001] ECR I-02099, para 72.
26 According to Commission Decision 2006/598/EC [2006] OJ L 244/8, para 37.
27 Case C-2/90 *Commission v Belgium* [1992] ECR I-4431, para 28.
28 See section 1.5.3 above.

prohibition of article 34 also applies to the energy sector. This means that the review of a national measure affecting the trade of energy has to be conducted on the basis of the above-mentioned principles following from *Dassonville*, *Keck/Mithouard* and subsequent case law. Considering the many years of judicature in the field of energy, it is impossible to compile an exhaustive list of measures the Court regarded as prohibited under these principles. Thus, the following measures just provide a glimpse of member states' actions the Court found to be covered by article 34: national rules which require importers to purchase a certain proportion of a given product (for example, petroleum products, electricity produced from renewable energy sources) from a national supplier;[29] a system of marketing quotas which determines the quantities of petroleum products that distribution companies may purchase from suppliers of their choice;[30] a national support scheme giving advantages for domestic producers of renewable energy over those established in another member state.[31]

iv) *Exceptions*

Fourth, a national measure violating article 34 may appear as justified by virtue of the *Cassis de Dijon doctrine* or article 36 provided, in particular, that the measure is proportionate and that harmonising secondary law does not generally preclude recourse to the particular ground of justification in question.[32] Considering the exceptional economic relevance of a secure energy supply, national measures serving that interest may potentially invoke public security and public policy in the sense of article 36 as grounds of justification.[33] Besides the protection of health and life of humans, animals and plants (article 36) and environmental protection (*Cassis de Dijon doctrine*) may also possibly serve as a basis of an exception from the principle of free movement of goods in the energy sector.

Public security and public policy: As regards public security and public policy in the sense of article 36 in particular, the Court of Justice established that these grounds may be drawn on only 'if there is a genuine and sufficiently

---

29 Cases 72/83 *Campus Oil Limited v Irish Minister for Industry and Energy* [1984] ECR 2727, summary para 4; C-379/98 *PreussenElektra AG v Schleswag AG* [2001] ECR I-02099, para 72.
30 Case C-347/88 *Commission v Hellenic Republic* [1990] ECR I-4747, paras 51 et seq.
31 C-573/12 *Ålands Vindkraft AB v Energimyndigheten*, paras 65 et seq.
32 As regards the exclusion of a recourse to grounds of justification, see Case 251/78 *Denkavit Futtermittel GmbH v Minister für Ernähung, Landwirtschaft und Forsten des Landes Nordrhein-Westfalen* [1973] ECR 3369, para 14.
33 See also M Roggenkamp, C Redgwell, I del Guayo and A Rønne, *Energy Law in Europe* (2nd edn, Oxford University Press 2007) 239.

serious threat to a fundamental interest of society'.[34] The *security of supply doctrine* as developed by the Court in the context of energy supply has to be seen against this background. In the corresponding momentous *Campus Oil case* the Court stated that the aim of ensuring a minimum supply of petroleum products at all times is capable of constituting a serious public security concern in accordance with article 36.[35] The Court held that petroleum products are of exceptional importance as an energy source and that an interruption of supplies results in dangers to a country's very existence.[36] Based on this reasoning the Court accepted Irish rules which required importers to cover a certain proportion of their needs by purchasing from an Irish refinery at prices fixed by the Irish state ministry in order to keep the refinery's capacity at constant availability. However, the Court made clear that in order to comply with the principle of proportionality the prices must be especially based on the operational costs of the refinery; and the quantities of petroleum products covered by the scheme must not exceed the minimum supply requirements without which the public security of Ireland would be affected.[37]

By contrast, in its decision *Commission v Greece*, the Court held that Greek rules which, on the one hand, required companies engaged in the distribution of petroleum products to have their annual supply programs approved by national authorities and, on the other hand, established a system of marketing quotas, were not compliant with the principle of free movement of goods.[38] In this case, Greece failed to provide substantial evidence that the rules were *essential* in order to ensure a minimum supply of petroleum products for the country at all times under the terms of the *Campus Oil case*. In another judgment involving Greece, the Court decided that a Greek law which obligated distribution companies to purchase petroleum products from Greek refineries to which they had transferred their statutory obligation of holding emergency stocks, was in contradiction to the free movement of goods principle.[39] The Court once more underscored the findings of the *Campus Oil case* holding that the Greek rules were to be considered as discriminating against petroleum products from refineries situated in other member states. In the case at hand a justification under the security of supply

---

34 Cases C-54/99 *Église de Scientologie* [2000] ECR I-1335, para 17; C-36/02 *Omega v Bonn* [2004] ECR I-9609, para 30; C-503/99 *Commission v Belgium* [2002] ECR I-4809, para 47.

35 Case 72/83 *Campus Oil Limited v Irish Minister for Industry and Energy* [1984] ECR 2727.

36 Case 72/83, *Campus Oil Limited v Irish Minister for Industry and Energy*, para 34.

37 For further details see Case 72/83, *Campus Oil Limited v Irish Minister for Industry and Energy*; A Johnston and G Block, *EU Energy Law*, 242 et seq.

38 Case C-347/88 *Commission v Hellenic Republic* [1990] ECR I-4747, para 60.

39 Case C-398/98 *Commission v Hellenic Republic* [2001] ECR I-7915.

doctrine failed as, first, the reasons Greek relied on were purely of an economic nature and therefore not sufficient to substantiate a public security concern and, second, the objective of public security could have been met in any case by less restrictive measures.

However, considering today's partially comprehensive legislation seeking to secure energy supply, it needs to be determined in a given case whether there is any scope for article 36 and the according security of supply doctrine and, thus, the national measure at hand must be assessed on the basis of secondary law only.[40] This may particularly apply to measures relating to the electricity, gas and oil sectors. As regards the electricity and gas sectors we have to bear in mind the Electricity and Gas Directives,[41] the Electricity Security of Supply Directive[42] and the Gas Security of Supply Regulation[43] establishing a common policy of security of supply. As regards the oil sector, the European Union's legislation on minimum oil stocks needs to be taken into particular consideration.[44]

Other grounds of justification: Aside from public security and public policy, other grounds of justification may also come into consideration in terms of national restrictions in the field of energy. As mentioned above, these grounds include in particular environmental protection (*Cassis de Dijon doctrine*)[45] and the protection of health and life of humans, animals or plants (article 36). *PreussenElektra* represents one of the groundbreaking and mostly discussed cases of the Court of Justice in this context and especially raised the question as to whether directly discriminative measures may be justified on the basis of the *Cassis de Dijon doctrine*. In *PreussenElektra* the judges found that a German law placing an obligation on power companies to purchase a certain percentage of their supplies from renewable energy sources which are located in Germany, is capable of hindering intra-Community trade.[46] However, the Court subsequently stated that the law is nevertheless compatible with the free movement of goods principle. It particularly established that the German law contributes to the reduction in

---

40 As regards the exclusion of a recourse to grounds of justification in general, see Case 251/78 *Denkavit Futtermittel GmbH v Minister für Ernährung, Landwirtschaft und Forsten des Landes Nordrhein-Westfalen*, [1973] ECR 3369, para 14.
41 Directive 2009/72/EC (Electricity Directive) and Directive 2009/73/EC (Gas Directive).
42 Directive 2005/89/EC.
43 Regulation (EU) 994/2010.
44 Cf Directive 2009/119/EC. See also A Johnston and G Block, *EU Energy Law*, 243 in this context.
45 See, for instance, Cases C-524/07 *Commission v Austria* [2008] I-00187, para 57; C-573/12 *Ålands Vindkraft AB v Energimyndigheten*, para 77.
46 Case C-379/98 *PreussenElektra AG v Schleswag AG* [2001] ECR I-02099, para 70 et seq. For a detailed discussion on the case see A Johnston and G Block, *EU Energy Law*, 242 et seq.

greenhouse gases and therefore serves the protection of the environment, something that should seemingly indicate its justification under the *Cassis de Dijon doctrine*. Besides, the Court added a range of further considerations. It especially noted that the German Act was furthermore aimed at protecting the health and life of humans, animals and plants (in the sense of the current article 36 TFEU) and that environmental protection requirements have to be considered when implementing European policies (within the meaning of the current article 6 TFEU). The ruling engendered criticism as the mere listing of arguments did not provide any clarity on the systematic approach the Court took. Therefore it remained unclear whether environmental protection or other grounds not contained in what is now article 36 are capable of justifying directly discriminative national measures.[47]

To this day, nothing much has changed in view of the Court's ambiguity in this particular regard. In the more recent cases from 2014, the *Ålands Vindkraft case*[48] and the *Essent Belgium case*,[49] the Court held a similar multi-faceted justification hinting at the *Cassis de Dijon doctrine* and article 36 TFEU being applicable at the same time.[50] In the first of the two cases the Finnish energy company Ålands Vindkraft operated a windfarm on the Finnish Åland islands which feature a grid connection to Sweden. Irrespective of this particularity, the Swedish Energy Agency refused to authorise the award of renewable certificates to Ålands Vindkraft, placing it at a competitive disadvantage in relation to domestic producers of renewable energy. Although the Court found that this practice generally constituted a prohibited barrier to trade pursuant to article 34 TFEU, it held the Swedish scheme to be justified and proportionate and therefore compatible with EU law.

As regards the justification of the territorial limitation of the support scheme, the Court basically followed the rather hazy reasoning of the *PreussenElektra case*. Among other considerations it particularly cited the circumstance that the underlying legislation in question sought to promote the use of renewable energy sources and therefore served the protection of the environment in the sense of the *Cassis de Dijon doctrine* and the protection of health and life of humans, animals and plants within the meaning of article 36 TFEU. However, again the Court did not clarify that the national trade barrier at hand constituted a directly discriminative restriction and it

---

47 A Johnston and G Block, *EU Energy Law*, 344.

48 C-573/12 *Ålands Vindkraft AB v Energimyndigheten*.

49 Joined Cases C-204/12 to C-208/12 *Essent Belgium*.

50 Case C-573/12 *Ålands Vindkraft AB v Energimyndigheten*, paras 76 et seq; Joined Cases C-204/12 to C-208/12 *Essent Belgium*, paras 89 et seq.

held both grounds, separately from one another, as a basis of its justification. In doing so, it continued to eschew an answer to the crucial question as to whether reasons coming under the *Cassis de Dijon doctrine* are capable of justifying directly discriminative measures.[51]

v)   *Proportionality test*

Ultimately, the Court's ruling in the *Ålands Vindkraft case* was remarkable in other ways, namely in view of the proportionality test. The case raised the crucial question as to whether the ultimate goal of the Swedish scheme to protect the environment might just as well be pursued by the promotion of green electricity produced in Finland. If this had been the case, the support scheme could not have been considered as necessary and, thus, not as proportionate either. However, the Court rejected this chain of thought. The ultimate reason for this was the fact that in the absence of EU law to harmonise support policies, it remains up to every member state to establish a national support scheme that matches its starting points and allows it to attain its individually binding renewable target. In this context the Court particularly pointed out that a member state must remain in a position to control the effect and costs of its support scheme, which obviously might be difficult without territorial restrictions. Against this background it remains clear that when assessing national support schemes in future, the evolution of harmonising law in this area must continue to be closely observed even in regard to the proportionality test.

Besides the *Ålands Vindkraft case*, the parallel *Essent Belgium case* was also interesting in view of the principle of proportionality.[52] In this case a Flemish support scheme provided for the issuance of certificates for green electricity produced in the Flemish Region of Belgium while in parallel setting forth the obligation of suppliers of electricity to surrender annually to the competent authority a certain number of those green certificates. Instead of submitting such certificates the energy supplier Essent Belgium NV, however, presented guarantees of origin demonstrating the production of green electricity in other countries and was ultimately fined for not fulfilling its quota obligation. In terms of the proportionality test, the Court fundamentally confirmed its reasoning given in the *Ålands Vindkraft case*. With a view to ensure proportionality, it particularly underscored that, so as to enable suppliers to obtain green certificates, member states must provide for mechanisms on the basis

---

51 See also E Durand and M Keay, 'National support for renewable electricity and the single market in Europe: the Ålands Vindfraft case'.
52 Joined Cases C-204/12 to C-208/12 *Essent Belgium*.

of which a genuine market for certificates can be created and furthermore that also the fines imposed for not meeting quota obligations must not be excessive. In the end, the Court deemed the Flemish scheme proportional.

vi)   *State monopolies*

As mentioned above, article 37 TFEU provides for specific rules on state monopolies of a commercial character, which are especially relevant to the energy sector. Compared with article 34 TFEU, the scope of article 37 is narrower. It exclusively affects measures originating from state trading monopolies. The concept of state trading monopolies comprises any entity through which a member state, in law or in fact, either directly or indirectly supervises, determines or appreciably influences imports or exports between member states (article 37(1) TFEU). This also includes monopolies delegated by the state to others. Article 37 does not require member states to dissolve their monopolies, it rather determines that existing or new monopolies shall be operated without any discrimination between nationals of member states in view of the conditions under which goods are procured and marketed. Considering the systematic position of article 37, measures originating from state trading monopolies can be justified neither by article 36 nor by the *Cassis de Dijon doctrine*.[53] However, a justification might come into play pursuant to article 106(2) TFEU in terms of undertakings entrusted with the operation of services of general economic interest or having the character of a revenue-producing monopoly.[54]

The Court of Justice has dealt with national energy monopolies in a series of cases: In the case *Commission v Italy*, the Court established, for instance, that exclusive electricity import and export rights, which were transferred to a state-owned entity (in this case: ENEL), constitute discrimination against exporters and importers based in other member states.[55] Such exclusive rights are therefore prohibited under article 37. In the case at hand, the Court however did not assume a violation of EU law as it considered a justification pursuant to article 92(2) of the EC Treaty, the now article 106(2) TFEU, conceivable.[56] According to this provision a grant of exclusive rights may remain in place if it is necessary to enable the monopoly to perform the particular tasks assigned to it, given that the development of trade is not affected

---

53 Cases C-157/94 *Commission v the Netherlands* [1997] ECR I-5699, para 24; C-159/94 *Commission v France* [1997] ECR I-5815, para 41; Kingreen in Calliess and Ruffert, art 37 AEUV note 12.

54 Cases C-157/94 *Commission v the Netherlands*, para 25; C-159/94 *Commission v France*, para 42; Kingreen in Callies and Ruffert, art 37 AEUV note 12.

55 Case C-158/94 *Commission v Italian Republic* [1997] ECR I-5789, para 23.

56 Case C-158/94 *Commission v Italian Republic*, para 38 et seq.

to such an extent as would be contrary to the interests of the Union.[57] The Court of Justice confirmed these findings in the cases *Commission v the Netherlands* (regarding the Dutch SEP)[58] and *Commission v France* (regarding the French energy companies EDF and GDF),[59] wherein it extended its considerations to the gas sector.

However, these cases are added here just to demonstrate the structure of treaty law. At least in terms of the electricity and gas sectors, in many cases *direct* recourse to article 106(2) as a potential basis of justification should have fallen short for a considerable time as was already indicated by the Court in the *VEMW case*.[60] With the introduction of the Electricity and Gas Directives,[61] the European legislator has established a harmonised language on the prohibition of discrimination between electricity undertakings and between system users and has set forth a special scheme of conceivable exemptions. These exemptions, however, also provide for recourse to article 106(2), but only under certain harmonised conditions.[62] Ultimately, the granting of exclusive import or export rights in the electricity and gas sectors, as specific category of cases quoted here, should be generally banned given the clear harmonising obligation arising out of the Electricity and Gas Directives to guarantee equality of access to the net.[63]

2.1.2 Free movement of persons

The free movement of persons constitutes another mainstay of the common European market. The principle entails two constituent parts: the freedom of movement for workers and the freedom of establishment.

The *freedom of movement for workers* and corresponding determinations are laid down in articles 45 to 48 TFEU. Pivotal provisions arise from article 45. Thus, the freedom of movement of workers comprises particularly the rights to accept offers of employment actually made, to move freely within the territory of member states for this purpose and to stay in a member state

---

57 See art 106(2) and Case C-158/94 *Commission v Italian Republic*, paras 43 and 60.
58 Case C-157/94 *Commission v the Netherlands* [1997] ECR I-5699.
59 Case C-159/94 *Commission v France* [1997] ECR I-5815.
60 Case C-17/03 *Vereniging voor Energie, Milieu en Water* [2005] ECR I-04983, para 89. See also A Johnston and G Block, *EU Energy Law*, 246.
61 Directive 2009/72/EC concerning common rules for the internal market in electricity and repealing Directive 2003/54/EC [2009] OJ L 211/55 (Electricity Directive); Directive 2009/73/EC concerning common rules for the internal market in natural gas and repealing Directive 2003/55/EC [2009] OJ L 211/94 (Gas Directive).
62 See art 3(2) of both directives.
63 See arts 32 and 3(2) of the Electricity Directive and arts 32 and 3(2) of the Gas Directive.

for the purpose of employment.[64] Furthermore, article 45 obligates member states to eliminate any discrimination based on nationality between workers of the member states as regards conditions of work and employment, such as employment per se or remuneration. However, the Court of Justice found that member states are generally[65] also prohibited from imposing any indiscriminate restrictions on workers precluding or deterring them from leaving their country of origin in order to exercise their right to freedom of movement.[66] All these provisions do not, however, apply to employment in the public service (article 45(4)). National measures covered by article 45 may be justified on grounds of public policy, public security or public health. In terms of non-discriminative measures, overriding reasons relating to the general interest may also serve as a basis for an exception.

The freedom of movement for workers is also applicable to the energy sector, concerning in practice especially the common employment of foreign specialists in the area. Article 45 spans even employees being on the payroll of state-owned energy companies since the exception of article 45(4) (employment in the public service) does not generally encompass employment by a private natural or legal person.[67] Regarding the justification of discriminatory or generally restrictive national measures, security of supply concerns may come into play as a ground of public security. However, practical pertinence of such concerns in terms of the freedom of movement for workers is limited compared to their impact on the free movement of goods.

The *freedom of establishment* is embodied in articles 49 to 55 of the TFEU. It entails the right to take up and pursue activities as self-employed persons and to set up and manage undertakings in another member state under the conditions applicable to nationals of that state. The freedom of establishment pertains to natural persons being nationals of member states and companies having their registered office or principal place of business within the European Union. Article 49 generally bans national restriction on the freedom of establishment or on the setting-up of agencies, branches or subsidiaries. It furthermore prohibits any discrimination on grounds of nationality. Article 51 excludes activities from the ambit of the freedom of establishment which involve a direct and specific connection with the exercise of a member

---

64 Cf art 45(3).

65 The limiting approach adopted by the Court of Justice in the Joined Cases *Keck and Mithouard* is applicable by analogy. See Case C-415/93 *Bosman* [1995] ECR I-04921, paras 102 et seq.

66 Case C-415/93 *Bosman*, para 96.

67 Court of Justice, Case C-283/99 *Commission v Italian Republic* [2001] ECR I-04363, para 25.

state's official authority.[68] Furthermore, as article 52 determines, national action treating foreign nationals differently may be justified on grounds of public policy, public security or public health. Non-discriminating measures may also be excluded from the scope of article 49 if justified by overriding reasons relating to the general interest.[69]

The freedom of establishment may also be of considerable relevance in the energy sector. Energy-related activities frequently presuppose the granting of governmental concessions constituting a key instrument for member states to regulate access to the market. This in particular bears the potential of treating foreign players differently and contrary to article 49. Such discrimination has been assumed by the European Commission, for instance, in cases where a member state awarding concessions in the power sector gives preference to operators which already hold a concession. Other operators, including foreign companies, are therefore virtually excluded from bidding for such concessions. Besides the granting of concessions, the allocation of so-called 'Golden Shares' represents another governmental tool to exert influence within the energy branch, and accordingly this merits scrutiny under article 49 (see also below under section 2.1.4).

Given the crucial role the energy sector plays in any member state, grounds of justification, especially public security concerns, pose a focal point for discussion when applying article 49 in the branch. In respect thereof, in the *Commission v Belgium* case the Court of Justice transferred its security of supply doctrine to the freedom of establishment.[70] Accordingly, a national measure may be justified if it is assigned to ensure a minimum supply of petroleum products at all times and is in accordance with, beyond that, the principle of proportionality.

2.1.3 Free movement of services

The free movement of services, also called the freedom to provide services, accrues from article 56 TFEU. Further details are laid down in articles 57 to 62.[71] Under the free movement of services, citizens and companies of EU member states possess the freedom to offer and to provide services in another EU member state. On the one hand the freedom requires member states to eliminate all discrimination on grounds of nationality against service

---

68 Court of Justice, Cases C-53/08 *European Commission v Republic of Austria* [2011] ECR I-04309, para 45; 2/74 *Reyners* [1974] ECR 631, paras 44 and 45.
69 Court of Justice, Case C-400/08 *Commission v Spain* [2011] ECR I-01915, para 73.
70 Case C-503/99 *Commission v Belgium* [2002] ECR I-4809, paras 44, 46 and 59.
71 See also Chalmers, Davies and Monti, *European Union Law*, 798 et seq.

providers. On the other hand member states must abolish any restriction, even if such is non-discriminatory, which is capable of prohibiting, impeding or rendering less advantageous the activities of a services provider established in another member state.[72]

Services falling within the remit of article 56 are normally provided for remuneration and can be characterised by their temporary nature (in contrast to the permanent nature of an establishment) and the provider's self-employed status (in contrast to an employment relationship). The concept of service particularly embraces activities of an industrial or commercial character, activities of craftsmen, and those of the professions (see article 57). Moreover, article 56 covers only those services by which either the service provider, or the service recipient, or the service itself moves across the border.

The scope of article 56 also covers energy-related services which meet the requirements. The distinction between the application of article 56 and that of the provisions on the free movement of goods appears to be a pivotal point because activities governed by other freedoms are excluded from the material reach of article 56. If the delivery of products is combined with a service, the application of article 56 TFEU (freedom to provide services) instead of articles 34 and 35 TFEU (free movement of goods) depends principally on whether the delivery of goods is entirely secondary in relation to the service.[73] The supply of electricity or gas, for instance, generally comes under the free movement of goods, and not under the freedom to provide services, with the result that the application of article 56 is excluded.[74] The delivery of these goods seems to be prior to the provision of services, at least it is not clearly subordinate to it.

A national measure contravening the freedom to provide services may be justified with reference to articles 62 and 52. Thus, special treatment for foreign nationals, and also general restrictive measures, may be justified on grounds of public policy, public security or public health. Besides, as regards non-discriminatory restrictions[75] and obviously also hidden discrimination[76] unwritten grounds of justification also come into consideration, namely overriding reasons relating to the general interest (for example, the protection of workers, consumer protection).

---

72 Cases C-272/94 *Guiot* [1996] ECR I-1905, para 10; C-3/95 *Reisebüro Broede* [1996] ECR I-6511, para 25.
73 Cases C-275/92 *Schindler* [1994] ECR I-1039, para 22; C-36/02 *Omega* [2004] ECR I-9609, para 26.
74 W Kluth in C Calliess and M Ruffert, *EUV/AEUV* (4th edn, C.H. Beck 2011) arts 56, 57 AEUV note 18.
75 Case C-288/89 *Stichting Collectieve Antennevoorziening Gouda* [1991] ECR I-4007, paras 13, 14, 27.
76 For the corresponding discussion see Kluth in Calliess and Ruffert, arts 56, 57 AEUV notes 75 et seq.

2.1.4 Free movement of capital and payment

Articles 63 to 66 TFEU provide for two more essential elements of the common European market: the free movement of capital and that of payment. Both principles complete the freedoms of movement and allow the European Single Market to function properly. Under article 63 all restrictions on the movement of capital or on payments between member states and between member states and third countries are prohibited. The concept of 'capital movement' covers every cross-border transfer of monetary and real capital out of a member state, which is primarily proceeded for investment purposes.[77] For instance, this includes direct investments, investments in real estate and operations on securities dealt on the capital market (bonds, shares and other securities of a participating nature). By contrast, the term 'payment' refers to proceeds especially from the sale of products and the provision of services, but it also covers wages of employees.

Articles 64 and 65 set forth exceptions from the stipulations of article 63. Whereas article 64 refers to particular national restrictions on the free movement of capital between member states and third countries, article 65 affects restrictions on the free movement of capital and payments between member states. Article 65 permits member states to take all measures which are requisite to prevent infringements of national law and regulations, especially in the field of taxation and the prudential supervision of financial institutions, or measures which are justified on grounds of public policy or public security. Moreover, member states may also invoke overriding requirements of the general interest in order to justify restrictions, provided that these are proportionate and applicable to all persons and undertakings.[78]

Given the paramount importance of energy supply, member states attempt to retain influence within the bigger energy companies which used to be under state control in former times. The so-called 'Golden Shares' constitute the most prominent instrument for maintaining governmental influence, and as such they are particularly subject to critical judgment. 'Golden Shares' are connected with privileges often held by authorities to control the acquisition of shares or to oppose certain management decisions.

In a series of cases, the European Court of Justice held that Golden Shares fall within the scope of both the free movement of capital and the freedom

---

77 J Bröhmer in C Calliess and M Ruffert, *EUV/AEUV* (4th edn, C.H. Beck 2011) art 63 AEUV note 8.
78 Case C-503/99 *Commission v Belgium* [2002] ECR I-4809, para 45.

of establishment.[79] They are liable to impede or render less attractive the acquisition of shares by undertakings established in other member states in a manner that affects both freedoms.[80] Compatibility with EU law may be reached only if the provision of Golden Shares is covered by an exception as mentioned above. In this regard, the Court particularly confirmed its findings from the Campus Oil case (the security of supply doctrine) and held these transferable to the free movement of capital and to the freedom of establishment, respectively. Accordingly, national measures, such as the establishment of Golden Shares, do not infringe the free movement of capital if they are designed to ensure a minimum supply of petroleum products at all times, even in the event of a crisis, in as much as proportionality is observed.[81] In some cases the Court particularly held that the system of Golden Shares at issue was ultimately not proportionate as it went beyond what is necessary to ensure a minimum supply. Consequently, these systems contravened the free movement of capital. This was especially true for the case *Commission v France* regarding French rights in the oil company Société Nationale Elf-Aquitaine;[82] and the case *Commission v Spain* regarding the Spanish energy companies Repsol and Endesa.[83] The case *Commission v Belgium* constitutes an exception since the Belgium rules vesting Golden Shares in companies engaged in the transportation and supply of gas were considered to be strictly limited and therefore less intensive; and the commission did not identify any other measure that is less restrictive.[84] Ultimately, the introduction of the latest internal energy market and security of supply legislation brings up the question of the extent to which justification may still be sought today under the outlined approach of the Court.[85]

2.2 Treaty law on competition

Fair competition constitutes one of the building blocks of the European market economy. A well-functioning internal European market presupposes abolishing restraints of competition and safeguarding fair play among undertakings and member states. It is therefore not surprising that the Treaty on

---

79 For details see also A Johnston and G Block, *EU Energy Law*, 243 et seq.

80 Cases C-367/98 *Commission v Portugal* [2002] ECR I-4731; C-483/99 *Commission v France* [2002] ECR I-4781; C-503/99 *Commission v Belgium* [2002] ECR I-4809; C-463/00 *Commission v Spain* [2003] ECR I-4581; C-98/01 *Commission v Great Britain* [2003] ECR I-4641; C-174/04 *Commission v Italy* [2005] I-04933. See also the more recent case C-326/07 *Commission v Italy* [2009] ECR I-2291.

81 Cases C-503/99 *Commission v Belgium* [2002] ECR I-4809, para 46; C-174/04 *Commission v Italy* [2005] I-04933 para 40.

82 Case C-483/99 *Commission v France* [2002] ECR I-4781, para 53.

83 Case C-463/00 *Commission v Spain* [2003] ECR I-4581, para 80.

84 See Case C-503/99 *Commission v Belgium* [2002] ECR I-4809, paras 48–55.

85 See also A Johnston and G Block, *EU Energy Law*, 244.

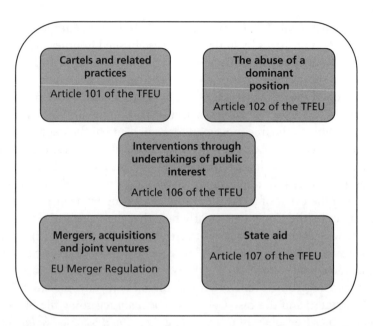

Figure 2.2 EU competition law: covered competition practices and governmental measures

the Functioning of the European Union itself attends to the matter and lays down a range of basic rules designed to guarantee free competition.

EU competition rules address both aspects, namely distortions of competition caused by undertakings and those induced by member states (see also Figure 2.2). Anti-competitive actions pursued by companies, such as the establishment of cartels and the abuse of dominant positions within the market, come under articles 101 to 106 TFEU (see sections 2.2.1 to 2.2.3 below). Governmental measures distorting competition, namely intervention through undertakings of public interest and state aid, are governed by articles 106 and 107 to 109 TFEU (see sections 2.2.3 and 2.2.5). Apart from treaty rules, competition is also subject to EU legislation. Specific emphasis must be laid on the 'Merger Regulation' which relates to mergers, acquisitions and joint ventures involving undertakings with a certain turnover (see section 2.2.4).[86] There are other conceivable forms as to how member states impair competition, such as the restriction of imports and exports or the collection of unequal taxes. Such measures, however, do not formally count among the competition rules but are nevertheless addressed by the TFEU (see sections 2.1 and 2.3).

---

86 Council Regulation (EC) No 139/2004 of 20 January 2004 on the control of concentrations between undertakings [2004] OJ L 24/1.

EU competition law applies in principle to the whole energy branch.[87] This holds true for the electricity and gas sectors in particular, but also for the coal branch and generally for the nuclear industry. Although the electricity and gas markets face extensive harmonising legislation, the European legislator still proceeds from the assumption that the establishment and maintenance of the internal market requires both EU competition law and sector-specific legislation.[88] These two instruments are supposed to be complementary and augment each other. Besides EU competition law also applies to the coal sector. The coal branch used to be covered by the special provisions of the ECSC Treaty, but this expired in 2002. As regards competition in the nuclear industry, according to the apparently prevailing view of scholars, the rules of the TFEU on antitrust (articles 101 and 102) and the rules on mergers apply as well, except where the Euratom Treaty provides for specific rules.[89] The situation is less clear in respect of the applicability of the TFEU rules on state aid. However, there seems to be a trend to hold that these provisions also apply in the nuclear sector, except in areas regulated by the Euratom Treaty.[90] An exception is, for instance, assumed for research and investments.[91]

Both the European Commission and the Court of Justice have examined and decided on numerous cases where competition in the energy sector had been restrained, shedding considerable light on the applicability of treaty law in this area. Indeed it seems that there has been no other area in recent years in which the Commission and Court have dealt with a comparably high number of cases.[92] That said, the following sections only aim at demonstrating how competition rules are principally applied in the area. For a more comprehensive insight into the decision-making practices and a more detailed illustration of individual cases it is necessary to resort to literature

---

87 See L Ritter and D Braun, *European Competition Law: A Practitioner's Guide* (3rd edn, Kluwer Law International 2004) 914; J Grunwald, *Das Energierecht der Europäischen Gemeinschaften* (de Gruyter 2003) 183; W Weiß in C Calliess and M Ruffert, *EUV/AEUV* (4th edn, C.H. Beck 2011) art 101 AEUV notes 3 et seq; W Cremer in C Calliess and M Ruffert, *EUV/AEUV* (4th edn, C.H. Beck 2011) art 107 AEUV note 7.

88 Cf recital 37 of Directive 2009/72 and recital 33 of Directive 2009/73. See also M Simm, 'The interface between Energy, Environment and Competition Rules of the European Union' (Institutional Report to the FIDE Congress 2012) pp 8 et seq http://www.fide2012.eu/General+and+EU+Reports/id/217/ accessed 29 April 2016.

89 For more details see R Ptasekaite, 'Competition law and nuclear regulation: A European perspective' in B Delvaux, M Hunt and K Talus (eds), *EU Energy Law and Policy Issues* (vol 4, Intersentia 2014) 102 et seq; A Johnston and G Block, *EU Energy Law*, 384 et seq.

90 Cf R Ptasekaite, 'Competition law and nuclear regulation: A European perspective', 106 et seq.; A Johnston and G Block, *EU Energy Law*, 384 et seq.

91 R Ptasekaite, 'Competition law and nuclear regulation: A European perspective', 106 et seq.

92 C Jones (ed.), *EU Energy Law: Volume II, EU Competition Law and Energy Markets* (3rd edn, Claeys & Casteels Publishing 2011) 1.

specialising on competition matters in the energy branch[93] and to revert to the relevant decision databases.[94]

2.2.1 Article 101: cartels and related practices

a) *General remarks*

i) *Scope*

Article 101 of the TFEU establishes a far-reaching prohibition of cartels and related practices. It bans all agreements between undertakings, decisions by associations of undertakings and concerted practices with the potential to affect trade between member states if they have as their object or effect the prevention, restriction or distortion of competition within the internal market. Article 101 enumerates conducts which are particularly critically gauged. These include for instance agreements, decisions or practices, which directly or indirectly fix purchasing or selling prices; limit or control production, markets, technical development, or investment; share markets or sources of supply. In principle, no difference is made between horizontal and vertical agreements. Accordingly, article 101 concerns in general both kinds of agreements, those between competitors and also those between companies belonging to different levels of a supply chain.

However, to be subject to the prohibition a relevant conduct must affect trade and competition at least to an appreciable extent.[95] Whether or not this is the case depends on the circumstances of any given case, such as on the nature and the quantity of the product in question as well as the respective market and the standing of the parties in that market.[96] This principally requires scrutiny in every individual case whilst taking into account the case law and the official notices and guidelines of the European Commission. The latter statements include, for instance, the Commission notice on agreements of minor

---

93 See, for instance, Jones (ed.), *EU Energy Law: Volume II, EU Competition Law and Energy Markets*; P Cameron, *Competition in Energy Markets: Law and Regulation in the European Union* (2nd edn, Oxford University Press 2007); U Scholz and S Purps, 'The application of EU competition law in the energy sector' (2013) 4(1) Journal of European Competition Law & Practice 63–82; A de Hauteclocque, *Market Building Through Antitrust: Long-Term Contract Regulation in EU Electricity Markets* (Edward Elgar Publishing 2013).

94 Details regarding decisions adopted by the Commission and the Court of Justice are provided on the Commission's website: http://ec.europa.eu/competition/index_en.html, accessed 29 April 2016. For rulings of the Court see also http://curia.europa.eu/jcms/jcms/j_6/, accessed 29 April 2016.

95 See for instance Court of Justice, Case 22/71 *Béguelin Import Co. v S.A.G.L. Import Export* [1971] ECR 949, paras 16 to 18.

96 See for instance Court of Justice, Case 22/71 *Béguelin Import Co. v S.A.G.L. Import Export*, paras 16 to 18.

importance (de minimis),[97] the guidelines on the effect on trade concept,[98] the notice on the definition of the relevant market,[99] the guidelines on vertical restraints[100] and the guidelines on horizontal cooperation agreements.[101] These various publications ultimately give guidance on the assessment of individual practices and may thus also help companies in the energy sector, which are under special surveillance, to weigh up critical agreements in advance.

ii) *Exemptions*

Not every cartel is undesirable. Some cartels appear to be thoroughly economically reasonable. Against this backdrop, article 101(3) provides for exemptions from the prohibition regarding agreements, decisions or practices, which contribute to improving the production or distribution of goods or to promoting technical or economic progress, if consumers may have a fair share in the resulting benefit. However, such actions may not grant an undertaking the possibility to substantially eliminate competition in the affected area. According to Regulation EC 1/2003, the company or the association of companies in question bear the onus of proving that the prerequisites of article 101(3) are present. However, the Commission has introduced various block exemptions, under which it assumes certain categories of agreements, decisions or concerted practices as being permissible. This is especially true for certain vertical agreements and concerted practices,[102] and certain research and development agreements[103] and specialisation agreements (such as joint production agreements)[104] as regards cooperation at horizontal level. Apart from that the Commission has published its criteria for assessment under article 101(3), giving even further orientation for companies acting within the energy branch.[105]

---

97 Commission Notice on agreements of minor importance which do not appreciably restrict competition under Article 81(1) of the Treaty establishing the European Community (de minimis) [2001] OJ C 368/14.

98 Commission Notice – Guidelines on the effect on trade concept contained in Articles 81 and 82 of the Treaty [2004] OJ C 101/81.

99 Commission notice on the definition of relevant market for the purposes of Community competition law [1997] OJ C 372/5.

100 Commission Notice, Guidelines on Vertical Restraints (SEC(2010) 411 final).

101 Guidelines on the applicability of Article 101 of the Treaty on the Functioning of the European Union to horizontal co-operation agreements [2011] OJ C 11/01.

102 Commission Regulation (EU) No 330/2010 of 20 April 2010 on the application of Article 101(3) of the Treaty on the Functioning of the European Union to categories of vertical agreements and concerted practices.

103 Commission Regulation (EU) No 1217/2010 of 14 December 2010 on the application of Article 101(3) of the Treaty on the Functioning of the European Union to certain categories of research and development agreements.

104 Commission Regulation (EU) No 1218/2010 of 14 December 2010 on the application of Article 101(3) of the Treaty on the Functioning of the European Union to certain categories of specialisation agreements.

105 Communication from the Commission, *Guidelines on the application of Article 81(3) of the Treaty* [2004] OJ C 101/97.

Apart from article 101(3), article 106(2) provides another possible exemption for undertakings entrusted with the operation of services of general economic interest or having the character of a revenue-producing monopoly, as will subsequently be outlined in section 2.2.3.

b)   Energy-related cases

Critical collaboration may also occur between undertakings belonging to the energy sector. Concerted conduct that requires scrutiny under article 101 may be found at the horizontal level (for example, joint production, joint construction, joint selling and price fixing) and as well as at the vertical level (for example, exclusive supply agreements and specific long-term supply contracts).[106] When determining whether or not a certain action is covered by article 101, not only the aforementioned Commission publications should be considered, but also the various decisions of the Commission and rulings of the Court which have been adopted in relation to the energy branch over the years.[107] As already noted, considering the high number of cases dealt with in the energy sector, the following remarks are to be understood as an introduction to the area of competition law only and, thus, merely single out individual critical practices and some related cases with a view to illustrating the principal application of competition rules in the energy sector. For a comprehensive insight please refer to literature with a more specialised focus on competition law.[108]

i)   Division of markets

In a range of cases the Commission stressed that arrangements leading to a division of energy-related markets are principally illegal under article 101. One of the more recent cases concerned an agreement among the two power exchanges *EPEX Spot* and *Nord Pool Spot*.[109] The Commission ascertained that these two leading spot power exchanges in Europe had agreed not to compete with one another and to allocate European territories between themselves and therefore clearly infringed article 101. The *Pre-Insulated Pipe Cartel case* serves as another prime example in this

---

106 See also M Roggenkamp, C Redgwell, I del Guayo and A Rønne, *Energy Law in Europe*, 256.

107 Commission cases available at: http://ec.europa.eu/competition/index_en.html, accessed 29 April 2016. See also the annual reports on competition policy issued by the Commission.

108 See, for instance, C Jones (ed.), *EU Energy Law: Volume II, EU Competition Law and Energy Markets*; Cameron, *Competition in Energy Markets: Law and Regulation in the European Union*; A Johnston and G Block, *EU Energy Law*.

109 European Commission, *Antitrust: Commission fines two power exchanges € 5.9 million in cartel settlement* (press release of 5 March 2014, IP/14/215).

context. In this case the Commission examined a series of arrangements revealing the establishment of an illegal cartel in the district heating sector. The Commission found that the Danish, German and Italian undertakings involved, contrary to EU competition law, had divided national markets amongst themselves, agreed prices and allocated individual projects to certain producers.[110] The Commission imposed fines on these undertakings to the amount of around EUR 92 million in total.[111] Finally, the case of *E.ON/GDF* also exemplifies an illegal market-sharing agreement under which undertakings had agreed not to enter a certain market. In this case the German company E.ON and the French enterprise GDF had come to an understanding not to access each other's home markets, prohibiting GDF from supplying German customers and E.ON from supplying French customers.[112]

ii)   *Joint selling/marketing*

In the case of the Norwegian Gas Negotiation Committee (*GFU case*), the Commission declared that a scheme under which a single national entity, which is permanently comprised of the two largest national gas producers, negotiates the terms of all gas supply contracts, on behalf of all gas producers located in the given country, with EU gas buyers, is incompatible with European competition law.[113] The case was settled by the agreement to discontinue the joint sales and marketing activities and to market the gas individually. This approach was confirmed in the case of the cooperation of Danish gas producers – DUC – and the Danish wholesaler DONG (*DUC/DONG case*).[114]

iii)   *Exclusion of access to a market*

In its decision in the case of a cooperation agreement between the Dutch firm SEP and Dutch electricity generators (*IJsselcentrale case*), the Commission underscored that provisions which avoid competition in a certain territory and discourage third parties from gaining access in

---

110 European Commission Case no IV/35.691/E-4 *Pre-Insulated Pipe Cartel* [1999] OJ L 24/1.

111 M Roggenkamp, C Redgwell, I del Guayo and A Rønne, *Energy Law in Europe*, 262.

112 Case COMP/39.401 *E.ON/GDF*.

113 European Commission, *Commission successfully settles GFU case with Norwegian gas producers* (17 July 2002, press release, IP/02/1084); M Roggenkamp, C Redgwell, I del Guayo and A Rønne, *Energy Law in Europe*, 257.

114 European Commission, *Commission and Danish competition authorities jointly open up Danish gas market* (24 April 2003, press release, IP/03/566).

the affected national market, infringe article 101.[115] In the case at hand a provision of the said cooperation agreement prohibited at the horizontal level energy generators from freely exporting and importing and required these generators at the vertical level to impose the same ban on their distributors.

iv)   *Sales restrictions*

As regards vertical agreements, the European Commission confirmed that so-called territorial restriction clauses (also destination clauses) and clauses with similar effect, namely the use of restriction arrangements and profit splitting mechanisms, restrain competition in the gas sector under the terms of article 101.[116] Territorial restriction clauses prevent wholesalers from reselling the gas outside the countries where they are established. In one of the cases at hand, the Commission assessed a transportation and a service contract, concluded by the French company GDF with the Italian energy providers ENI and ENEL prohibiting both Italian companies from selling natural gas in France which GDF had transported.[117] The Commission conceived this as a concrete obstacle to the creation of a genuinely competitive EU gas market, as French consumers are kept from obtaining their supplies from the two Italian providers. This stance was confirmed in other cases such as the *Gazprom/ENI case.*[118]

v)   *Exclusive purchase clauses*

In the *Almelo case*, the Court of Justice held that exclusive purchase clauses between a regional and a local distributor, that is, clauses prohibiting a local distributor from purchasing electricity supplies from suppliers other than the regional distributor, have a restrictive effect on competition and are therefore in principle prohibited.[119] However, the Court also made clear that even such agreements might be excluded from the prohibition of article 101 under article 106(2) TFEU, which is outlined below.

---

115 European Commission Decision 91/50/EEC [1991] OJ L 28/32. See also L Ritter and D Braun, *European Competition Law: A Practitioner's Guide* (3rd edn, Kluwer Law International 2004) 929.

116 See also K Talus, 'Wind of change: Long-term gas contracts and changing energy paradigms in the European Union' in C Kuzemko, A Belyi, A Goldthau and M F Keating (eds), *Dynamics of Energy Governance in Europe and Russia* (Palgrave Macmillan 2012) 237 et seq.

117 European Commission, *Commission confirms that territorial restriction clauses in the gas sector restrict competition* (26 October 2004, press release, IP/04/1310).

118 European Commission, *Commission reaches breakthrough with Gazprom and ENI on territorial restriction clauses* (06 October 2003, press release, IP/03/1345).

119 Case C-393/92 *Almelo v NV Energiebedrijf Ijsselmij* [1994] ECR I-1477, paras 34–50.

vi)   *Long-term supply contracts*

The Commission does not hold long-term supply contracts as incompatible with EU competition law as such, especially where they are necessary to pay off significant investments, for example, in a new gas field.[120] However, the Commission monitors whether an incompatibility arises in individual cases and a long-term arrangement forecloses the market.[121] In this regard, the Commission looks at contract duration in addition to other aspects (for example, certain contractual clauses, such as exclusive clauses, and market characteristics).[122] In the case of the Spanish oil and gas company REPSOL, for instance, the Commission investigated long-term exclusive supply agreements with service stations and indicated that these hamper competition in the Spanish petrol stations market.[123] The case was ultimately closed after REPSOL had committed to free hundreds of service stations from these contracts.

2.2.2   Article 102: the abuse of a dominant position

a)   *General remarks*

i)   *Scope*

Whereas article 101 has its focus on coordinated action among companies, article 102 addresses the abuse of a dominant position through one or several undertakings. A dominant position relates to a position of economic strength which enables an undertaking to prevent effective competition by giving it the power to behave to an appreciable extent independently of its competitors, customers, and consumers.[124] However, holding a dominant position by one or more undertakings *per se* is not illegal. Rather there must be an abuse of such a position that additionally may affect trade between member states. An abuse includes any behaviour of a company in a dominant position that may influence the structure of a market where, as a result of

---

120 See European Commission, *XXXIInd report on competition policy 2002*, point 80; European Commission *Commission clears gas supply contracts between German gas wholesaler WINGAS and EDF-Trading* (12 September 2002, press release, IP/02/1293). See also Ritter and Braun, *European Competition Law: A Practitioner's Guide*, 926; M Roggenkamp, C Redgwell, I del Guayo and A Rønne, *Energy Law in Europe*, 260.

121 See European Commission, *XXXIInd report on competition policy 2002*, point 80; European Commission, *XXVIth report on competition policy 1996*, point 103. See also Ritter and Braun, *European Competition Law: A Practitioner's Guide*, 926; M Roggenkamp, C Redgwell, I del Gayo and A Rønne, *Energy Law in Europe*, 260.

122 See European Commission, *Energy sector competition inquiry – final report – frequently asked questions and graphics* (of 10 January 2007, memo 07/15).

123 European Commission, *Competition: Commission increases competition in Spanish service station market* (12 April 2006, press release, IP/06/495).

124 ECJ Case 27/76 *United Brands* [1978] ECR 702, para 65.

the very presence of the company in question, the degree of competition is already weakened and which, through recourse to unusual methods, has the effect of hindering the maintenance of the degree of competition still existing or the growth of that competition.[125]

According to article 102, an abuse of a dominant position may particularly apply in the following practices: directly or indirectly imposing unfair purchasing or selling prices or other unfair trading conditions; limiting production, markets or technical development to the prejudice of consumers; applying dissimilar conditions to equivalent transactions with other trading parties, thereby placing them at a competitive disadvantage.

Before a dominant position can be ascertained, the relevant market must be identified. The relevant market involves a product dimension and a geographical dimension.[126] The respective product market presupposes that there is a sufficient degree of interchangeability between all the products forming the same market.[127] If products are hardly substitutable, they belong to a different product market. The European Commission particularly considers the markets for electricity, gas and district heating as separate markets as there is very low substitutability.[128]

According to the Commission, the respective geographical market 'comprises the area in which the undertakings concerned are involved in the supply and demand of products or services, in which the conditions of competition are sufficiently homogeneous and which can be distinguished from neighbouring areas because the conditions of competition are appreciably different in those areas'.[129] The geographical market may coincide with a certain national market, but it must not necessarily do so. As the Commission already pointed out in several cases, geographical markets in relation to energy sources may be local, regional, national or pan-European.[130]

---

125 ECJ Case 85/76 *Hoffmann-La Roche* [1979] ECR 461, para 91.
126 For details, see also A Jones and B Sufrin, *EC Competition Law: Text, Cases, and Materials* (3rd edn, OUP 2008) 352 et seq.
127 ECJ Case 85/76 *Hoffmann-La Roche* [1979] ECR 461, para 28. See also L Ritter and D Braun, *European Competition Law: A Practitioner's Guide*, 26; A Jones and B Sufrin, *EC Competition Law: Text, Cases, and Materials*, 353.
128 European Commission, press release IP/94/805 of 02 September 1994. See also M Roggenkamp, C Redgwell, I del Guayo and A Rønne, *Energy Law in Europe*, 264 et seq.
129 Commission notice on the definition of relevant market for the purposes of Community competition law [1997] OJ C 372/5, para 8.
130 For details, see M Roggenkamp, C Redgwell, I del Guayo and A Rønne, *Energy Law in Europe*, 264. See also European Commission, press release IP/99/197 of 29 March 1999 and press release IP/99/387 of 10 June 1999.

ii)　　*Exemptions*

In contrast to article 101, there is no exemption from article 102, at least apart from article 106(2).[131]

b)　　*Energy-related cases*

As is the case with article 101, the Commission has also given guidance on the application of article 102 through several public notices which should be taken into account when assessing individual cases. These publications particularly include the notice on the definition of the relevant market[132] and the guidelines on the effect on trade concept.[133] Furthermore it is also necessary to consider the relevant decision-making practice of both the Commission and the Court, and an insight into this is provided in the following.

i)　　*Predatory pricing (price squeeze/margin squeeze)*

First, in a number of energy-related cases the Commission has particularly covered the crucial issue of pricing. Dominant companies are generally in a position to drive competitors out of the market through a predatory pricing policy. Squeezing margins constitutes one practice coming under this category. A margin squeeze exists, for instance, if a dominant vertically integrated firm possessing an essential electricity or gas network sets a high price for network access while at the same time offering unprofitable prices on the retail market. In this case competitors on the retail market may economically not be able to match the retail prices, especially due to the excessive costs incurred for network access.

Within the context of predatory pricing, the Commission pointed out that a company in a dominant position may be under the obligation to arrange its price so as to allow a reasonably efficient manufacturer a margin sufficient to enable it to survive in the long term (*National Carbonising case*).[134] In a case regarding a dominant Dutch transmission system operator the Commission held that the company's charges for electricity transmissions must always be linked to the actual cost in order to avoid abuse as laid out in article 82 of

---

131　For further details regarding Article 106(2), see section 2.2.3 below.
132　Commission notice on the definition of relevant market for the purposes of Community competition law [1997] OJ C 372/5.
133　Commission Notice – Guidelines on the effect on trade concept contained in Articles 81 and 82 of the Treaty [2004] OJ C 101/81.
134　Commission Decision 76/185/ECSC [1976] OJ L35/6.

the EC Treaty (now article 102 of the TFEU).[135] In another case concerning the German company RWE, the Commission opposed gas transmission tariffs that might have been intentionally set at an artificially high level with a view to squeezing RWE's competitors' margins.[136] Of course, predatory pricing presupposes that prices are not totally fixed by national regulators. This is, however, not the case if the regulator leaves some leeway in pricing, for instance, by setting only maximum prices.[137]

ii)   *Access to infrastructure*

Proper functioning of trade in energy presupposes access to existing networks. The joint use of pipelines, grids and other facilities appears as a pivotal element of an internal energy market.[138] In order to address this issue EU institutions, namely the Commission and the European Court of Justice, have frequently fallen back on article 102 (formerly article 82 of the EC Treaty). Under the so-called *essential facilities doctrine* established by the Court of Justice, the refusal of access to infrastructure or to any other facility essential for transmission or distribution by an undertaking holding a dominant position may be incompatible with article 102.[139] Article 102 applies if the refusal of access to a facility is likely to eliminate all competition in the given market on the part of a company requesting access and there is no actual or potential substitute to the facility, so that access appears to be indispensable for the requesting company to carry on its business.[140] According to the Court of Justice, the denial of access may be justified by objective reasons.[141] Such reasons may include a lack of distribution or transmission capacity; or a lack of solvency of the party seeking access.[142] The *Marathon case* is one of the most noted cases regarding network access which the Commission has dealt with. In this instance, the Commission opposed several European gas companies which had jointly rejected allowing the Norwegian gas producer Marathon access to continental European pipelines.

---

135 See European Commission, *XXIXth report on competition policy 1999*, p 165.
136 European Commission, press release IP/09/410 of 18 March 2003.
137 B Willems and E Ehlers, 'Cross-subsidies in the electricity sector' (2008) 9(3) Competition and Regulation in Network Industries 216.
138 Cf, for instance, R Pisal, *Entflechtungsoptionen nach dem Dritten Energiebinnenmarktpaket* (Nomos 2011) 35 with further references.
139 See ECJ Case C-7/97 *Bronner* [1998] ECR I-07791, paras 37–46; see also A de Hauteclocque, *Market Building through Antitrust: Long-Term Contract Regulation in EU Electricity Markets*, 123 et seq.
140 ECJ Case C-7/97 Bronner, ibid, paras 37–46; L Ritter and D Braun, *European Competition Law: A Practitioner's Guide*, 929; G Monti, *EC Competition Law*, 225; W Weiß in C Calliess and M Ruffert, *EUV/AEUV* art 102 AEUV note 40.
141 ECJ Case C-7/97 *Bronner*, ibid, para 41.
142 See M Roggenkamp, C Redgwell, I del Guayo and A Rønne, *Energy Law in Europe*, 267.

The Commission shelved the case only after the companies involved, including for example, Thyssengas, Gaz de France and Ruhrgas, pledged to grant access to their networks more effectively.[143]

In principle, the essential facilities doctrine applies to all sub-sectors belonging to the energy branch. However, as regards network access in the areas of electricity and gas, both article 102 and the essential facilities doctrine give way to EU legislation governing the issue specifically, namely the Electricity Directive[144] and the Gas Directive.[145][146] Both directives, as well as corresponding national acts of transposition, aim at guaranteeing objective, transparent and non-discriminatory access to transmission and distribution systems.[147] Thus, article 102 and the doctrine function at best as a safety net and take effect only in case the directives fall short.[148]

iii)   *Long-term contracts*

Long-term contracts occur as another crucial means dominant undertakings can use to foreclose competition.[149] Depending on their concrete duration and the volume of supplies fixed therein, long-term contracts may discourage other potential suppliers from market entry. Accordingly the Commission has especially scrutinised long-term contracts in the downstream sector in the past in light of article 102.[150] In one of the better known cases it accused, for instance, the Belgian gas supplier Distrigas of abusing its dominant position by virtue of its strong market position and the long

---

143 See European Commission, press release IP/01/1641 of 23 November 2001 and press release IP/04/573 of 30 April 2004; M F Salas, R Klotz, S Moonen and D Schnichels, 'Access to gas pipelines: lessons learnt from the Marathon case', in European Commission, Competition Policy Newsletter (no 2, summer 2004) 41 et seq; J Ashe-Taylor and V Moussis, 'EU competition law and third party access to gas transmission networks' (2005) Utilities Law Review 105–10.

144 See Directive 2009/72/EC concerning common rules for the internal market in electricity and repealing Directive 2003/54/EC.

145 See Directive 2009/73/EC concerning common rules for the internal market in natural gas and repealing Directive 2003/55/EC.

146 See also in context of the previous Electricity and Gas Directives, Ritter and Braun, *European Competition Law: A Practitioner's Guide*, 929; M Roggenkamp, C Redgwell, I del Guayo and A Rønne, *Energy Law in Europe*, 267.

147 See sections 4.1.1 c) v) and 4.2.1 c) below.

148 M de Rijke, 'Third-Party Access: Implementing EU legislation' (8 November 2004) http://www.internationallawoffice.com/Newsletters/detail.aspx?g=dbc384ba-54af-4770-9083-6a1ed81e8fa1 accessed 29 April 2016 (in context of the previous directives 2003/54/EC and 2003/55/EC).

149 For details see also A de Hauteclocque, *Market Building Through Antitrust: Long-Term Contract Regulation in EU Electricity Markets*; K Talus, 'Wind of change: Long-term gas contracts and changing energy paradigms in the European Union', 237; A Johnston and G Block, *EU Energy Law*, 225 et seq.

150 Cf K Talus, 'Wind of change: Long-term gas contracts and changing energy paradigms in the European Union', 237.

duration of its gas supply contracts of beyond five years with large customers, which furthermore strengthened its dominance and had therefore a potential to frustrate competitors.[151] The Commission closed the case after Distrigas committed to reduce the duration of its contracts and to ensure that an appropriate volume of gas, strictly speaking at least 65%, stipulated in its contracts returns to the market every year in order to allow more competition. A similar approach was pursued by the Commission in a case concerning the French company EDF.[152] The Commission accused EDF of abusing its dominant position through the conclusion of long-term supply contracts with large electricity customers as these were bound to EDF and therefore not accessible to EDF's competitors. In this case the Commission accepted EDF's commitments to reduce the duration of contracts (future contracts with large customers generally not beyond five years) and to guarantee that each year at least 60% of the total contracted volumes return to the market.

In addition, it is worth pointing out that the Commission has also dealt with a range of cases concerning long-term contracts in the upstream sector, which are nonetheless classified under article 101. Here the Commission urged the companies concerned to eliminate critical clauses typically included in long-term contracts, namely territorial restriction clauses (destination clauses) and provisions with similar effect, such as the use of restriction arrangements and profit-splitting mechanisms.[153]

iv)   Cross-subsidisation

Cross-subsidisation represents another practice by which companies possessing a dominant position may decisively hamper competition. Cross-subsidisation means that a profitable part of a company or trust supports a loss-making part by using its profits. It may be used to offer products and services at prices competitors cannot match. Vertically integrated undertakings in the electricity and gas sectors serve as a prime example where cross-subsidisation can take place. Such firms cover several sections of the supply chain by operating transmission and/or distribution networks while they also produce and/or sell the transported electricity or gas. Cross-subsidisation

---

151 Commission Decision of 11 October 2007, Case COMP/B-1/37966 – *Distrigaz; Commission*, press release IP/07/1487 of 11 October 2007. For a discussion of the case see, for instance, A Johnston and G Block, *EU Energy Law*, 225 et seq.

152 Commission Decision of 17 March 2010, Case COMP/39.386 – *Long-term contracts France*; Commission, press release IP/10/290 of 17 March 2010.

153 See section 2.2.1 b) iv) and, for instance, the *Gazprom/ENI case*, IP/03/1345 of 6 October 2003. In addition see section 2.2.1 b) vi).

is present if such a company uses profits generated by the transmission or distribution business to support its production or retail activities.[154]

However, cross-subsidising products or services is not illegal as such unless the preconditions of article 102 TFEU are met. The Commission has found on several occasions that cross-subsidisation may particularly infringe article 102 in the event that an incumbent company supports activities open to competition by allocating their costs to reserved services or monopoly activities.[155] Nevertheless, cross-subsidisation can only fall under article 102 if it is capable of affecting intra-union trade. This may, for instance, be the case if an undertaking uses cross-subsidisation to facilitate predatory pricing and the squeezing of margins, in particular.[156] As article 102 prohibits these practices anyway, as shown above, one may question whether cross-subsidisation constitutes a separate category of practices which are capable of restraining trade. It rather appears as a means of enabling potentially harmful and therefore prohibited conduct, which are nonetheless sufficient grounds to observe cross-subsidisation practices carefully.

As regards the prevention of critical cross-subsidisation by vertically integrated undertakings in the electricity and gas sectors, the Electricity and Gas Directives provide for complementary instruments, namely the provisions on unbundling. These provisions are not only intended to reveal cross-subsidisation by requiring transparent and unbundled accounts. They are also designed to avoid cross-subsidisations through the separation of transmission activities from generation and retail businesses (for details see below, Chapter 4).[157] However, it remains to be seen how effectively these instruments ultimately function in forestalling unfair practices such as predatory pricing.

v)   Division of markets

As mentioned earlier in the context of article 101, arrangements between several companies leading to a territorial division of markets are principally prohibited. However, depending on its market power, a division of markets can also be effected by a single incumbent. It is reasonable that such cases also have to be examined critically under EU competition law, namely under

---

154 B Willems and E Ehlers, 'Cross-subsidies in the electricity sector', 201 et seq.
155 Notice from the Commission on the application of the competition rules to the postal sector [1998] OJ C 39/2, point 3.3; Guidelines on the application of EEC competition rules in the telecommunications sector [1991] OJ C 233/2, para 104.
156 See also B Willems and E Ehlers, 'Cross-subsidies in the electricity sector', 224 et seq.
157 Chapter 4 sections 4.1.1 c) and 4.2.1 c).

article 102. The *Gazprom case*, albeit as yet unresolved at the time of writing this textbook, serves as a prime example in this respect.[158] Gazprom is the dominant gas supplier in a range of Central and Eastern European countries. The Commission has accused Gazprom of pursuing a strategy to partition Central and Eastern European gas markets. It has found that Gazprom, for instance, imposes territorial restrictions, including export bans and destination clauses, in its gas supply contracts with wholesalers and individual industrial customers. This practice may have put Gazprom in a position to charge way too high and therefore unfair gas prices in five EU member states.

2.2.3   Article 106: undertakings of special public interest

a)   *General remarks*

Article 106 of the TFEU complements the treaty rules on competition. Article 106(1) initially clarifies that public undertakings and those enjoying exclusive or special rights granted by member states come under the rules of the treaties, namely those on competition in particular. It furthermore determines that member states may not adopt any measure in relation to such a company which is contrary to the treaties. This means two things: member states shall not violate provisions of the treaties by themselves, for instance by favouring such undertakings in the process of public procurement. Furthermore, they may not prompt or oblige such companies to infringe EU law. It follows from the preceding points that the statutory creation of a dominant position, for instance by conferring exclusive rights, is not in itself contrary to EU law.[159] However, the Court of Justice made clear that a member state is acting in violation of article 106(1) if it creates a situation where an undertaking could not avoid infringing a certain provision of treaty law, such as article 102 TFEU.[160]

The imperative to ensure equal treatment of undertakings of special public interest encounters a significant limitation within the terms of article 106(2). The provision seeks to strike the balance between the Union goal to liberalise European markets and some member states' interest to pursue economic and social policies through certain undertakings.[161] Depending on how political and social attitudes have evolved, member states show quite

---

158 See European Commission, *Antitrust: Commission sends Statement of Objections to Gazprom for alleged abuse of dominance on Central and Eastern European gas supply markets* (22 April 2015, press release, IP/15/4828).

159 ECJ Case C-41/90 *Höfner and Elser* [1991] ECR I-01979, para 29.

160 ECJ Case C-41/90 *Höfner and Elser*.

161 ECJ Case C-265/08 *Federutility* [2010] ECR I-03377, para 28.

divergent intent to interfere in particular markets.[162] However, article 106(2) determines that undertakings entrusted with the operation of services of general interest or having the character of a revenue-producing monopoly are governed by the rules of the treaties only insofar as the application of such rules does not obstruct the performance of the particular tasks assigned to them. Thus, based on article 106(2), the conduct of both member states and undertakings may be exempted from the competition rules mentioned above, but also from other treaty rules, such as the rules on state aid or those on the adjustment of state monopolies contained in article 37 TFEU.[163] The Court of Justice sets high standards for invoking this exception.[164] In particular it examines with special attention questions concerning the principle of proportionality.[165] The Court especially requires that an exemption from article 106(2) must be necessary to ensure the performance of the particular tasks assigned to a company.[166] Besides, it must also be scrutinised closely whether a situation goes beyond the line drawn in article 106(2) sentence 2. According to this particular provision, the development of trade must not be affected to such an extent as would be contrary to the interests of the Union.

b)   *Energy-related cases*

In order to safeguard a basic supply of energy at all times and in all regions, energy companies, particularly energy suppliers, are often constituted as public undertakings or equipped with exclusive or special rights. Thus, article 106 plays a special role with regard to the energy sector which has also been demonstrated by the Court of Justice and the European Commission. Both have dealt with a number of cases concerning, for instance, undertakings with a supply monopoly, companies with exclusive rights to import and export gas or electricity, and firms with privileged access to energy sources.[167]

The application of article 106(1) TFEU primarily means that member states have to observe EU competition law in particular when establishing public

---

162 In terms of national approaches regarding the electricity market, see T von Danwitz, 'Regulation and liberalization of the European electricity market – A German view' (2006) 27 Energy Law Journal 423 et seq.

163 C Jung in C Calliess and M Ruffert, *EUV/AEUV* art 106 AEUV note 34; ECJ Cases C-157/94 *Commission v the Netherlands* [1997] ECR I-5699, para 25; C-159/94 *Commission v France* [1997] ECR I-5815, para 42.

164 E.g. Cases C-159/94 *Commission v France* [1997] ECR I-5815, para 53; C-242/95 *GT-Link* [1997] ECR I-04449, para 50.

165 See, for instance, ECJ, Case C-265/08 *Federutility* [2010] ECR I-03377, para 33.

166 See, for instance, ECJ, Case C-320/91 *Corbeau* [1993] ECR I-2533 para 14; C Jung in C Calliess and M Ruffert, *EUV/AEUV* art 106 AEUV note 50.

167 Cases C-157/94 *Commission v the Netherlands* [1997] ECR I-5699; C-158/94 *Commission v Italian Republic* [1997] ECR I-5789; C-159/94 *Commission v France* [1997] ECR I-5815; European Commission, press releases IP/99/291 of 3 May 1999 and IP/09/1226 of 6 August 2009.

energy undertakings or granting exclusive rights to public or private energy firms. A prime example of a violation of article 106(1) in conjunction with competition law is constituted by the case of an underperforming monopoly. Such a case is present if a member state entrusts an undertaking with the exclusive right to carry on a certain service while the undertaking is apparently incapable of satisfying the existing demand for that service.[168] Such a situation was, for instance, assumed by the Commission in a case involving the French state and Gaz de France.[169] France was accused of violating article 90 of the EC Treaty (later article 86 and now article 106 TFEU) as it prevented non-nationalised distributors from extending their service to certain municipalities. The reason for this was that French law conceded to Gaz de France a monopoly in the supply of gas almost throughout France. However, Gaz de France refused to install distribution networks in the areas concerned with reference to the lack of profitability of required investments.

As regards the exemption provided for in article 106(2) TFEU the first crucial question is whether secondary law, especially the Electricity Directive and the Gas Directive, preclude its application in the energy sector. As secondary law may not overturn primary law, reference to article 106(2) becomes redundant only in cases where harmonising secondary law establishes provisions, which are in terms of their functioning tantamount to article 106(2) and include a corresponding proviso for the operation of services in the public interest.[170]

Liberalisation in the energy sector is still under way and has most significantly progressed in the electricity and gas sub-sectors. As regards the latter two sectors, harmonisation is mainly brought about by the said Electricity and Gas Directives.[171] However, both directives explicitly stipulate in their article 3(2) that recourse to article 86 of the EC Treaty (now article 106 TFEU) remains conceivable, albeit subject to the observance of the corresponding harmonising provisions set out in those directives regarding, for instance, transparency and non-discrimination of public service obligations. Accordingly, under the provisions given in the directives and article 106(2),

---

168 Case C-41/90 *Höfner and Elser* [1991] ECR I-01979.

169 European Commission, press release IP/99/291 of 3 May 1999.

170 Cf Opinion of Advocate General to ECJ Case C-17/03 para 45 (within the context of the previous Electricity Directive 96/92/EC); P van Vormizeele in J Schwarze (ed.), *EU-Kommentar* (3rd edn, Nomos 2012) AEUV art 106 note 56.

171 Directive 2009/72/EC concerning common rules for the internal market in electricity and repealing Directive 2003/54/EC [2009] OJ L 211/55 ('Electricity Directive'); Directive 2009/73/EC concerning common rules for the internal market in natural gas and repealing Directive 2003/55/EC [2009] OJ L 211/94 ('Gas Directive').

member states may impose on electricity and gas undertakings specific public service obligations relating to security, regularity, quality and price of supplies and environmental protection. Consequently, the Electricity and Gas Directives also allow for state intervention related to the imposition of such obligations, such as the granting of financial compensation or exclusive rights to entrusted undertakings.[172] The Court of Justice has ultimately underpinned this assumption in the *Federutility case* concerning state intervention on the price of the supply of natural gas.[173]

Once clarification has been reached in terms of the applicability of article 106(2), the presence of all of its conditions must be examined. Within the scope of the Electricity and Gas Directives the same applies to the conditions set out therein, including by virtue of reference the determinations of article 106(2).[174] As mentioned above, at first the undertaking concerned must accordingly be entrusted with the operation of a service of general economic interest. Both the Court of Justice and the Commission already confirmed back in the 1990s that ensuring the supply of energy, for instance, constitutes such a service.[175] Furthermore, the Electricity and Gas Directives are clearly based on the assumption that companies operating in the electricity or gas sector can be entrusted with the performance of such services, considering the fact that member states may impose on them public service obligations.[176]

Moreover, an exemption from the application of a certain provision of EU primary law, such as articles 101 or 102 TFEU, presupposes that its application obstructs a company from fulfilling the task assigned to it. In this regard, the Court of Justice has underlined when deciding on a case regarding exclusive rights to import electricity that it is not necessary for the survival of

---

172 See also article 3(6) Electricity Directive (Directive 2009/72/EC); B Delvaux, *EU Law and the Development of a Sustainable, Competitive and Secure Energy Policy: Opportunities and Shortcomings* (Intersentia 2013) 159 et seq. For the treatment of compensation under the European Union's state aid rules, see section 2.2.5 b) i) below.

173 The case nevertheless dealt with the second Gas Directive 2003/55/EC which in its article 3(2) sentence 1 provided for determinations that were almost identical to those of the present third Gas Directive 2009/73/EC. See ECJ Case C-265/08 *Federutility* [2010] ECR I-03377; furthermore see Case C-242/10 *Enel Produzione* [2011] ECR I-13665, paras 38 et seq.

174 See article 3(2) sentences 1 and 2 Electricity Directive (Directive 2009/72/EC) and article 3(2) sentences 1 and 2 Gas Directive (Directive 2009/73/EC). See also ECJ, Case C-265/08 *Federutility*, para 24 et seq.

175 Cases C-393/92 *Almelo v NV Energiebedrijf Ijsselmij* [1994] ECR I-1477; C-157/94 *Commission v the Netherlands* [1997] ECR I-5699; C-158/94 *Commission v Italian Republic* [1997] ECR I-5789; C-159/94 *Commission v France* [1997] ECR I-5815; Commission Decision 91/50/EEC of 16 January 1991 [1991] OJ L 28/32 – *IJsselcentrale*. See also A Johnston and G Block, *EU Energy Law*, 241 and 245.

176 Article 3(2) Electricity Directive (Directive 2009/72/EC); article 3(2) Gas Directive (Directive 2009/73/EC).

the entrusted company to be put at risk when complying with EU law.[177] An exemption may already come into consideration if the execution of its special obligations is rendered impossible. However that may be, as regards the specific cases of exclusive import and export rights in the electricity and gas sectors, an exemption should in principal no longer be possible. The reasons for this are the harmonising provisions of the Electricity and Gas Directives, as was already explained in more detail earlier in this chapter.[178]

In general, an obstruction of performance may not be assumed if secondary law sets out a concrete harmonising concept which safeguards the proper discharge of the services in the public interest.[179] In such a case the public service obligations can be fulfilled without infringing EU treaty law. However, even within the electricity and gas sectors, exemptions remain conceivable in individual categories of cases. The Electricity and the Gas Directives do not provide for harmonised concepts for all relevant aspects. Given that, both directives still proceed on the assumption that under their special requirements recourse to article 106 is possible.[180]

The examination of a possible exemption pursuant to article 106(2) ultimately includes an assessment of proportionality. Apart from the conditions mentioned above,[181] the Court of Justice has particularly held in the *Federutility case* that the public service obligation imposed on an undertaking may compromise European Union law, or strictly speaking the Gas Directive in the case at hand, only insofar as is necessary to achieve the objective in the general economic interest pursued. It further argued that the violation of EU law may therefore endure for a limited period of time only.[182]

2.2.4 Merger control

Mergers and acquisitions of companies are practices especially spread among larger undertakings in order to augment innovation capacity and reduce production and distribution costs. A merger or acquisition enables a company to enhance its market force, which may lead to more competition or even to the

---

177 Case C-157/94 *Commission v the Netherlands* [1997] ECR I-5699, para 52 et seq.
178 See section 2.1.1 b) iv) above; see also A Johnston and G Block, *EU Energy Law*, 246.
179 A M Schneider, *EU-Kompetenzen einer Europäischen Energiepolitik* (Nomos 2010) 232 et seq.
180 Cf article 3(2) and (6) Directive 2009/72/EC and article 3(2) Directive 2009/73/EC.
181 See general remarks regarding art 106(2) above.
182 Case C-265/08 *Federutility*, para 33 (within the context of the previous Gas Directive 2003/55/EC); S Wernicke in E Grabitz and M Hilf (eds), *Das Recht der Europäischen Union: EUV/AEUV* (C H Beck 2013) art 106 note 102.

precise opposite. Hence, mergers and acquisitions create sufficient ground for an effective public control.

Merger control within the European Union involves at administrative level the union as a whole and member states. Concentrations with an EU dimension, meaning mergers, acquisitions and full function joint ventures featuring a defined amount of aggregate turnover, come under the ambit of the European Union, strictly speaking of the European Commission.[183] Member states generally retain jurisdiction over concentrations where the thresholds are not reached or where each of the undertakings involved achieves more than two-thirds of its aggregate EU-wide turnover within one member state.[184]

Merger control is determined by secondary law, primarily by the 'Merger Regulation'.[185] If a concentration exhibits a European Union dimension, the Commission must be notified. It appraises whether or not the merger is compatible with the internal market. In the assessment the Commission examines whether the concentration would significantly impede competition whereby it takes especially into consideration the structure of the markets concerned, the actual or potential competition and the market position and economic power of the companies involved.[186] Depending on the result of the evaluation, the Commission approves the concentration, requires certain commitments, or indeed issues a refusal.

The Commission attaches particular importance to merger control using this tool to foster the liberalisation of energy markets. It is especially critical of mergers sought by former national monopolies which might even expand their dominant positions.[187] On the other hand, it sees mergers of energy suppliers from different member states as a means to pave the way for expanded trans-European networks and therefore for an enhanced common energy market.[188]

---

183 For details see articles 1 and 3 of the Merger Regulation (Council Regulation (EC) No 139/2004).

184 See article 1 Merger Regulation (Council Regulation (EC) No 139/2004); European Commission, Case COMP/M.3986 – *Gas Natural/Endesa*.

185 Council Regulation (EC) No 139/2004 of 20 January 2004 on the control of concentrations between undertakings [2004] OJ L 24/1 (Merger Regulation).

186 See article 2 Merger Regulation.

187 See M Monti, 'The single energy market: the relationship between competition policy and regulation', European Commission, press releases database SPEECH/02/101 of 07 March 2002 http://europa.eu/rapid/press-release_SPEECH-02-101_en.htm accessed 29 April 2016.

188 See T von Danwitz, 'Regulation and liberalization of the European electricity market – A German view', 433.

In practice, the Commission has dealt with a range of merger and acquisition cases.[189] In 2004, for example, it prohibited the acquisition of joint control over Gás de Portugal (GDP), by Energias de Portugal (EDP) and the Italian company ENI as it expected the concentration to have an excessive effect on competition.[190] In many other cases the Commission has approved mergers and acquisitions subject to significant conditions and obligations, for example, ownership unbundling, the disinvestment of business, increasing the capacity of an interconnector and granting fair third-party access to transmission networks.[191] These cases include for instance the merger of Gaz de France and Suez,[192] the merger of the German VEBA and VIAG,[193] and the acquisition of subsidiaries of the Hungarian oil and gas incumbent MOL by E.ON.[194]

The European view on mergers and acquisitions does not necessarily coincide with the member states' angle. In particular, the takeover of a so-called national champion sought by foreign companies with government involvement raises considerable concerns and has sparked protectionist counteractions in the past. The merger of Gaz de France and Suez, for instance, was claimed to have in fact been engineered by the French government in order to thwart an envisaged takeover of the French enterprise Suez by the Italian company Enel.[195] Protectionist state intervention has also been exemplified by the ultimately abortive attempt of the German concern E.ON to take over the Spanish firm Endesa. The European Commission had originally cleared the deal, which did not keep the Spanish government from frustrating the plan afterwards. The latter broadened the powers of its national energy regulator CNE, which then imposed stringent conditions on E.ON's bid. Subsequently, the European Commission found that the Spanish intervention violated the European Union's Merger Regulation and articles 43 and 56 TFEU (freedom of establishment and free movement of capital) and required the imposed conditions to be lifted.[196] As Spain failed to do so, the Commission referred the case to the European Court of Justice which ultimately underscored the Commission's decision.[197]

---

189 See, for instance, C Jones and V Landes, 'Part 4 – Merger Control' in Jones (ed.), *EU Energy Law: Volume II, EU Competition Law and Energy Markets*, 433 et seq.

190 European Commission, press release IP/04/1455 of 09 December 2004.

191 For more details, see M Roggenkamp, C Redgwell, I del Guayo and A Rønne, *Energy Law in Europe*, 280 et seq.

192 European Commission, press release IP/06/1558 of 14 November 2006.

193 European Commission, press release IP/00/613 of 13 June 2000.

194 European Commission, press release IP/05/1658 of 21 December 2005.

195 The Independent, 'French ministers blocked Suez deal, claims Enel', 03 March 2006; The New York Times, 'EU studies Enel claim of foul play by French', 2 March 2006.

196 European Commission, press release IP/06/1426 of 18 October 2006.

197 Case C-196/07 *Commission v Spain* [2008] ECR I-00041.

2.2.5   State aid

a)   *General remarks*

Member states may not only encroach upon competition by imposing customs duties, restricting imports and exports, granting exclusive rights and impinging on mergers. They may also resort to state aid as one of the most significant tools of state intervention used to steer market developments in a certain direction. State aid does not necessarily have to represent a critical instrument of national protectionism. It is also used to offset regional imbalances, to foster social developments and to boost technological innovation. For this reason, state aid forms an inherent part of the political repertoire at EU and national level, even though it is subject to strict control.

European state aid control is based on articles 107 to 109 TFEU. Pursuant to article 107(1) any aid granted by a member state or through state resources which distorts or threatens to distort competition by favouring certain undertakings or the production of certain goods is prohibited insofar as it affects trade between member states. State aid in this sense encompasses all measures which 'mitigate the charges which are normally included in the budget of an undertaking and which, without therefore being subsidies in the strict meaning of the word, are similar in character and have the same effect'.[198] For that reason, the European concept of state aid does not only comprise traditional subsidies but also any form of allowance granted without adequate consideration, such as the remission of public charges or the sale of state-owned property at prices below market value.[199]

So as to counterbalance the general ban on state aid, article 107(2) and (3) and some legislative acts define several exemptions from the prohibition. Paragraph 2 determines, for instance, that aid having a social character and aid to make good the damage caused by natural disasters are compatible with the internal market. Under paragraph 3 the Commission enjoys discretion to exempt further benefits, such as aid to promote the economic development of areas of abnormally low living standards or aid to promote projects of common European interest. Furthermore, the Commission may by means of regulation exempt certain categories of aid, what it has especially done in the form of the so-called 'De minimis regulation'.[200] According to this

---

198 ECJ Case C-75/97 *Belgium v Commission* [1999] ECR I-03671, para 23.
199 See also M Roggenkamp, C Redgwell, I del Guayo and A Rønne, *Energy Law in Europe*, 285; W Cremer in C Calliess and M Ruffert, *EUV/AEUV* (4th edn, C.H. Beck 2011) art 107 AEUV note 10.
200 Commission Regulation (EC) No 1998/2006 of 15 December 2006 on the application of Articles 87 and 88 of the Treaty to de minimis aid [2006] OJ L 379/5.

regulation, aid granted up to a ceiling of 200,000 Euro over a period of three fiscal years is not covered by the prohibition.

Member states have to notify the Commission of any plan to grant or alter state aid.[201] After being informed, the Commission examines whether such a plan is compatible with the internal market. In assessing individual proposals the Commission refers to guidelines and frameworks which establish general principles of state aid control. Ultimately, member states may not grant any aid unless the Commission has authorised it.

b) Energy-related cases

State aid also features prominently in the energy sector. Member states have made ample use of it in various forms and in all energy sub-sectors from coal, oil and nuclear industry to the production of renewable energy and district heating.[202] The construction of power plants and energy grids, the extension of alternative energies and the development of new technologies serve as prime examples of activities backed by state support. Thus, the decision-making practice of the Court of Justice and that of the Commission feature a range of individual cases and determinations for categories of cases in relation to the energy industry. The following section offers merely a brief glimpse into this practice. More details are given on the Commission's competition website.[203]

i) Public service obligations

As already mentioned above within the context of article 106, member states may under certain conditions impose public service obligations on energy undertakings, for instance, relating to security of supply and environmental protection. When conferring such tasks they not only have to adhere to applicable secondary law, meaning the Electricity and Gas Directives in particular, but possibly also to the provisions of the TFEU. Thus, it is particularly open to question whether compensation paid for the performance of public services obligations also has to be measured against the state aid rules.

In its famous *Altmark judgment*, the Court of Justice addressed this question and found that where an undertaking receives a compensation for discharg-

---

201 Cf article 108(3) TFEU.
202 See also M Roggenkamp, C Redgwell, I del Guayo and A Rønne, *Energy Law in Europe*, 283 et seq.
203 See   http://ec.europa.eu/competition/sectors/energy/electricity/electricity_en.html   and   http://ec.europa.eu/competition/elojade/isef/index.cfm?clear=1&policy_area_id=3, accessed 29 April 2016.

ing public duties, it does indeed not enjoy a financial advantage and it is thus not put in a more favourable competitive position. Consequently, the Court decided that such compensations cannot be considered as state aid under article 107(1).[204] However, so as not to come under the qualification as state aid, a compensation must meet the following four conditions:[205]

- the recipient undertaking is actually entrusted to discharge clearly defined public service obligations;
- the parameters for the calculation of the compensation have been established beforehand in an objective and transparent manner;
- the compensation does not exceed what is necessary to cover the costs incurred in discharging the public service obligations;
- if the undertaking is not selected pursuant to a public tendering procedure, the level of compensation has to be determined on the basis of the costs which a typical, well run and adequately resourced company would have incurred.

The Commission has examined compensation granted for the performance of public duties in the energy branch, especially those under the Electricity and Gas Directives, in light of these conditions.[206] For instance, in a case regarding the construction of new electricity generation capacity in Ireland which was necessary for the security of supply, it held the *Altmark* criteria to be applicable.[207] Consequently, the Commission did not consider the compensation intended for the companies undertaking the construction as state aid. By contrast, in a case concerning long-term power purchase agreements (PPAs) used in Hungary, it found that these criteria were not met.[208] Among other things, the Commission pointed out that the power generators involved could not show that they had been entrusted with clear-cut services of general economic interest neither by the Hungarian state nor through the PPAs. Even though power generators, in general, make a contribution to security of supply, this fact in itself does not mean that the performance of such services has been officially assigned to them.

ii)   *Capacity mechanisms*

With a view to ensure the availability of a sufficient amount of electricity at all times and so as to avoid black-outs in particular, a number of member

---

204 ECJ Case C-280/00 *Altmark* [2003] ECR I-7747.
205 ECJ Case C-280/00 *Altmark*, para 3.
206 See also A Johnston and G Block, *EU Energy Law*, 248.
207 Commission decision of 16 December 2003 on state aid case N 475/2003, C(2003) 4488fin.
208 Commission Decision 2009/609/EC of 4 June 2008 [2009] OJ L 225/53, para 254 et seq.

states have introduced so-called capacity mechanisms. Capacity mechanisms are generally aimed at either securing the maintenance of existing capacity or encouraging investments in new capacity, meaning new power plants. Such mechanisms often serve as precautionary measures which have become particularly necessary within the context of the transformation from traditional centralised energy systems using rather constantly available sources towards ones involving numerous small-scale and, in parts, irregular sources.

There are various forms of capacity mechanisms ranging from tenders for specific capacity or strategic reserves to quite complex market-wide mechanisms, such as the central buyer model or the de-central obligation model.[209] Capacity mechanisms often involve benefits to particular market players and must therefore be scrutinised under state aid rules, unless its qualification as state aid may already be excluded in accordance with the *Altmark* criteria.

In order to better understand the capacity mechanisms deployed in member states the Commission launched a sector inquiry in April 2015. Apart from that, the Commission has started to assess various national schemes in light of state aid rules. When doing so, it has especially taken as a basis its Guidelines on State aid for environmental protection and energy 2014–2020 (EEAG)[210] which contain specific rules on capacity mechanisms (see sec 3.9 of the EEAG). In its first decision taken in reference to the EEAG the Commission approved the so-called *UK Capacity Market*.[211] Under that scheme the United Kingdom organises centrally-managed auctions to procure the level of capacity that is necessary to guarantee sufficient energy generation, that is, generation adequacy. Successful bidders must deliver electricity at times of stress and receive in return a steady payment for the duration of their capacity agreement. Payments are financed through a levy on electricity supplies.

iii)   *Aid granted in line with the European Union's climate and sustainability agenda*

The European Union attaches particular importance to state aid designed to support member states in the attainment of the 2020 climate targets and in the building up of a sustainable and secure energy supply. In order to

---

209 For details see Commission staff working document, *Generation adequacy in the internal electricity market – guidance on public interventions* (SWD(2013) 438 final); European Commission, *Fact Sheet State Aid: sector inquiry into capacity mechanisms – frequently asked questions* (29 April 2015).

210 Communication from the Commission, *Guidelines on State aid for environmental protection and energy 2014–2020* [2014] OJ C 200/1.

211 Commission decision of 23 July 2014 on state aid C(2014) 5083 final; European Commission, *State aid: Commission authorises UK Capacity Market electricity generation scheme* (press release of 23 July 2014).

facilitate the implementation of present EU climate and energy policy, the Commission has adopted the EEAG[212] which have applied from 1 July 2014 and which replaced the previous Guidelines on State Aid for Environmental Protection.[213] Based on the EEAG, the Commission assesses and may consider as being compatible with the internal market, for instance, state aid for energy from renewable sources, for energy efficiency measures (for example, cogeneration and district heating), for CO_2 capture and storage, for energy infrastructure and for measures of generation adequacy. As regards aid for energy from renewable sources, in particular, the EEAG provides for a reorientation of state aid policy, which at present mainly rests on feed-in tariff models.[214] Given the fact that renewable energy is gradually becoming competitive on the electricity market, feed-in tariffs are supposed to be progressively replaced by bidding processes.

In addition to the EEAG, the Commission has adopted a renewed General Block Exemption Regulation (GBER)[215] applicable from 1 July 2014, according to which certain categories of state aid are freed from the obligation of prior notification. Under the specific conditions of the GBER (for example, thresholds) certain state aid measures in the field of energy, such as aid for district heating, operating aid for renewable energies and aid for energy infrastructure, may also be covered by the GBER and thus exempted from the notification requirement.

The application of both the GBER and the EEAG presupposes, however, that a given state measure comes under the concept of state aid. Especially in terms of feed-in tariff models this may be a debatable point. In its landmark judgment *PreussenElektra*, the Court of Justice held in this context that a statutory obligation as provided for in the German Law on feeding electricity from renewable energy sources into the public grid ('*Stromeinspeisungsgesetz*') to purchase electricity produced from renewable energy sources at minimum prices indeed confers an economic advantage on producers of that kind of energy.[216] Nevertheless, it did not classify this kind of advantage as state aid in the sense of EU law by recalling that only aid granted by a member state or through state resources is covered by the state aid rules. This did not apply in the case at hand since the disputed statutory obligation only

---

212 Communication from the Commission, *Guidelines on State aid for environmental protection and energy 2014-2020* [2014] OJ C 200/1.

213 Community guidelines on State aid for environmental protection [2008] OJ C 82/01).

214 See also section 3.2.3 below.

215 Commission Regulation (EU) No 651/2014 of 17 June 2014 declaring certain categories of aid compatible with the internal market in application of Articles 107 and 108 of the Treaty [2014] OJ L 187/1.

216 ECJ case C-379/98 *PreussenElektra AG v Schleswag AG* [2001] ECR I-02099.

ordered the transfer of resources between companies.[217] By contrast, in the *Vent De Colère!* case the Court found that a feed-in tariff model falls within the category of state aid if the compensation made to operators is under state control and administrated by a public body, even if the financial means originally stem from charges paid by final consumers of electricity.[218] However, in an earlier case the Court furthermore laid out that even non-public funds that draw on compulsory levies may be considered as state resources if levies are statutorily imposed, managed and apportioned pursuant to the applicable legislation.[219]

Having regard to this case law, the Commission has resumed that also the successors of the *Stromeinspeisungsgesetz*, the *German renewable energy laws of 2012 and 2014* (EEG 2012 and EEG 2014), have provided for state aid, although both laws have set out that feed-in tariffs are to be paid by net operators and the compensation scheme apportioning the additional costs to electricity customers is organised by these companies.[220] In 2015 Germany brought an action against the Commission's decision on the EEG 2012 with a view to definitively clarifying the qualification of such schemes as state aid. Apart from that, the Commission's decision gave Germany no reasons for objection as it principally confirmed the compliance of the German scheme and its originally contested surcharge reductions for energy-intensive companies with state aid rules and the Commission's Guidelines on State Aid for Environmental Protection and Energy 2014–2020, in particular.

iv)   *Carbon leakage*

Aid granted for the promotion of green energy and energy efficiency is only one building block in the European Union's climate and energy strategy. The EU Greenhouse Gas Emission Allowance Trading Scheme (EU ETS) represents another one. As explained in more detail in Chapter 5 below, under the EU ETS installations emitting greenhouse gases, which are covered by the scheme, require a certain number of allowances corresponding to their

---

217 M Roggenkamp, C Redgwell, I del Guayo and A Rønne, *Energy Law in Europe*, 283; ECJ Case C-379/98 *PreussenElektra v Schleswag*, para 59 et seq.

218 Case C-262/12 *Association Vent De Colère! Fédération nationale and Others*, paras 30 and 33.

219 Case 173/73 *Italy v Commission* [1974] ECR 709, para 16.

220 European Commission decision C(2013) 4424 final, para 74 et seq; European Commission, *State aid: Commission approves German aid scheme for renewable energy (EEG 2012), orders partial recovery* (press release of 25 November 2014, IP/14/2122); European Commission decision C(2014) 5081 final, para 147 et seq; European Commission, *State aid: Commission approves German renewable energy law EEG 2014* (press release of 23 July 2014).

emissions.[221] The EU ETS may place European industries at competitive disadvantages on the global market through ancillary costs incurred by the requirements of the scheme or through increased electricity prices (so-called 'carbon leakage'). In order to offset these disadvantages the Commission has not only set up a list of sectors eligible for additional free emission allowances, it has furthermore established guidelines allowing member states to grant under certain conditions to companies potentially affected by carbon leakage state aid for the compensation of increased electricity costs.[222] However, according to the Commission, these guidelines were nevertheless designed in a way that allows the attainment of the European Union's climate targets as well as ensuring a level playing field in the internal market.[223]

v)   *Stranded costs*

In respect of compensation for non-recoverable costs emerging from investments that energy companies have taken prior to the liberalisation of the European electricity market ('stranded costs'), the Commission established a *Methodology for analysing State aid linked to stranded costs.*[224] In light of this methodology, the Commission concluded, for instance, that compensation for stranded costs to power companies in Austria, the Netherlands and Spain indeed constituted state aid. However, given the transformation of electricity markets initiated by the Electricity Directive, the national compensations could enjoy an exemption under article 87(3)(c) of the EC Treaty (now article 107(3)(c) TFEU).[225]

By contrast, in a more recent case concerning a Hungarian state aid regime, the Commission rejected granting an exemption on the basis of the methodology in question.[226] In this case the state-owned company Magyar Villamos

---

221 See Chapter 5.3.1.

222 Communication from the Commission, *Guidelines on certain State aid measures in the context of the greenhouse gas emission allowance trading scheme post-2012* (SWD(2012) 130 final) (SWD(2012) 131 final) Text with EEA relevance [2012] OJ C 158/4. Communication from the Commission amending the Communication from the Commission Guidelines on certain State aid measures in the context of the greenhouse gas emission allowance trading scheme post-2012 Text with EEA relevance [2012] OJ C 387/5.

223 European Commission, *State aid: Commission adopts rules on national support for industry electricity costs in context of the EU Emission Trading Scheme* (press release, IP/12/498).

224 Commission Communication relating to the methodology for analysing State aid linked to stranded costs of 26 July 2001.

225 European Commission, *Commission gives green light to 'stranded costs' compensation by Spain, Austria and The Netherlands* (press release of 25 July 2001, IP/01/1079).

226 European Commission, *State aid: Commission requests Hungary to end long-term power purchase agreements and recover state aid from power generators* (press release of 04 June 2008, IP/08/850); Commission Decision 2009/609/EC of 4 June 2008 [2009] OJ L 225/53. See also K Talus, *EU Energy Law and Policy – A Critical Account* (2013 Oxford University Press) 150 et seq.

Művek (MVM), being responsible for selling two-thirds of the electricity produced in Hungary that time, was obligated to buy a fixed quantity of generated electricity at a fixed price on the basis of long-term power purchase agreements (PPAs). In this way Hungary wished to give incentives for power generators to modernise the power generation infrastructure. However, the Commission nevertheless found that the PPAs in question did not help the transition to a competitive market, particularly as they were deployed irrespective of actual market developments.[227] Considering this, the Commission held that the PPAs rather shielded certain generators from real competition. Finally, the Commission required Hungary to terminate these contracts and recover unjustified earnings from the generators. Actions for annulment of the decision of the Commission were dismissed by the General Court in 2012 and 2014.[228]

vi)   *State aid for the construction and operation of new nuclear power plants*

EU member states pursue different strategies as regards their national energy mix, an approach that fundamentally conforms to article 194(2) TFEU. While a number of countries bank on the further extension of renewable energies, others are sticking to or indeed rediscovering traditional energy sources, especially nuclear power and coal power. As seen above, member states wishing to subsidise the promotion of renewable energy may invoke the EEAG, though the Commission has already raised the prospect of a reorientation with renewable energy becoming competitive. However, the question arises whether member states counting on traditional and, thus, fundamentally mature energy sources may also have recourse to any exemptions, for instance, those following from article 107(3) TFEU.

The hotly disputed *Hinkley Point case* is illustrative in this context. In this case the British government plans to support a new nuclear power plant in South-West England for a period of 35 years.[229] The support scheme particularly provides for the payment of a guaranteed purchase price to the operator of the plant, protecting it from any price volatility in the electricity market. The European Commission finally gave the green light to the planned package in October 2014 by referring to article 107(3)(c) TFEU as a basis for the derogation. In particular it saw a market failure in the lack of financial instruments

---

227 Commission Decision 2009/609/EC of 4 June 2008 [2009] OJ L 225/53, paras 423 et seq.

228 General Court, Joined Cases T-80/06 and T-182/09, *Budapesti Erőmű Zrt. v European Commission*; Case T-179/09, *Dunamenti Erőmű Zrt. v European Commission*.

229 Commission Decision (EU) 2015/658 of 8 October 2014 on the aid measure SA.34947 (2013/C) (ex 2013/N) which the United Kingdom is planning to implement for support to the Hinkley Point C nuclear power station (notified under document C(2014) 7142) [2015] OJ L 109/44.

hedging against the enormous risks of investing in nuclear energy.[230] In its further deliberations it also quoted additional investment risks when considering the possibility of changing political attitudes towards nuclear energy. Altogether the Commission held the contemplated state intervention as being necessary. In 2015 two pleas for annulment were lodged against the decision at the European Court of Justice. Critics particularly doubt the existence of a market failure when after decades of being on the market there is still no viable investment model for nuclear energy.[231] Fouquet expressed it candidly when noting that we do not face a market failure here but the result of a learning process on the market.[232] Investment risks appear because nuclear energy is not considered profitable and not because it constitutes a new type of energy generation. Moreover, by hinting at the possibly political nature of the Commission's decision, it was furthermore underlined with justification that subsidising nuclear energy cannot be compared with the support of renewable energy as the extension of the latter is explicitly required by present EU legislation, namely Directive 2009/28/EC.[233]

vii)   *Other categories of cases*

This introductory textbook provides merely an insight into the categories of state aid cases the Commission or the Court of Justice have dealt with in relation to the energy sector. Apart from the cases listed here, there are of course more conceivable situations in which member states wish to resort to state support. In order to get a more comprehensive overview it is necessary to consult specialised literature[234] and the pertinent databases of the Commission and the Court of Justice.[235] The categories of cases not

---

230 Commission Decision (EU) 2015/658 of 8 October 2014, paras 375 et seq.

231 See release by law firm Becker Büttner Held, 'State aid for Hinkley Point nuclear power plant: BBH to prepare a lawsuit against the EU Commission' (12 March 2015) http://www.beckerbuettnerheld. de/en/article/state-aid-for-hinkley-point-nuclear-power-plant-bbh-to-prepare-a-lawsuit-against-the-eu-commission/ accessed 29 April 2016. Dörte Fouquet, 'Erarbeitung eines Antwortkataloges im Hauptprüfverfahren der Europäischen Kommission, Staatliche Beihilfe SA.34947 (2013/C) (ex 2013/N) – Investitionsvertrag' (legal opinion submitted to the Austrian Ministry of Agriculture, Forestry, Environment and Water Management on 5 March 2014) p 37.

232 Dörte Fouquet, ibid.

233 See release by law firm Becker Büttner Held, 'State aid for Hinkley Point nuclear power plant: BBH to prepare a lawsuit against the EU Commission'.

234 See, for instance, K Bacon (ed.), *European Union Law of State Aid* (2nd edn, Oxford University Press 2013); L Hancher, T Ottervanger and P J Slot, *EU State Aids* (4th edn, Sweet & Maxwell 2012); E Szyszczak (ed.), *Research Handbook on European State Aid Law* (Edward Elgar Publishing 2011); Jones (ed.), *EU Energy Law: Volume II, EU Competition Law and Energy Markets*; Cameron, *Competition in Energy Markets: Law and Regulation in the European Union*.

235 For cases the Commission dealt with see http://ec.europa.eu/competition/elojade/isef/index.cfm, accessed on 29 April 2016. For rulings of the Court see http://curia.europa.eu/jcms/jcms/j_6/, accessed on 29 April 2016.

mentioned so far include, by way of example, support for stricken companies and aid to the coal sector. As regards the latter, please see the respective outline given in Chapter 4.4 below. The other category, namely state aid to financially stricken companies, generally remains a hotly disputed political issue at national and European level. A prime example of how the Commission deals with such support in the energy sector is the case of the large French conglomerate Alstom which initially led to some discontent between Brussels and Paris. The package envisaged by the French government aimed at supporting the industrial restructuring of Alstom. After detailed investigations, the Commission ultimately approved the support under strict conditions, including divestment and market-opening measures.[236]

2.3 Treaty law on taxation

2.3.1 General remarks

Essentially it is still up to the member states to determine to what extent they burden citizens and undertakings with taxes. However, this principle bears the risk of different taxation and thus of jeopardising the functioning of the single market. For this reason, EU law sets out a general framework for taxation consisting of treaty rules and legislative acts. The latter in particular include the Energy Taxation Directive[237] which will be outlined in Chapter 5 below.[238] Relevant treaty rules relating to taxation comprise articles 110 to 113 TFEU. These provisions complete the body of rules necessary to avert distortions of competition through member states. The treaty rules particularly provide for a ban on tax-related discrimination, as laid down in article 110 paragraphs 1 and 2. Paragraph 1 establishes that member states may not impose on products imported from other member states any internal taxation in excess of that imposed on similar domestic products. Moreover, paragraph 2 prohibits any taxation of products from other member states of such a nature as to afford indirect protection to other products.

The ban on tax discrimination must be distinguished from the prohibition of custom duties on imports and exports and of charges having equivalent effect (article 30 TFEU). One and the same charge cannot be subject to both prohibitions at the same time.[239] As the Court of Justice has established, article

---

236 European Commission, *Aid for Alstom approved, subject to conditions* (press release of 07 July 2004), IP/04/859.

237 Council Directive 2003/96/EC of 27 October 2003 restructuring the Community framework for the taxation of energy products and electricity [2003] OJ L 283/51.

238 Cf section 5.1.3.

239 E.g. Case C-234/99 *Nygård v Svineafgiftsfonden* [2002] ECR I-3657, para 17.

30 covers charges imposed on goods by reason of the crossing of a frontier.[240] By contrast, article 110 concerns charges which relate to a 'general system of internal dues applied systematically to categories of products in accordance with objective criteria irrespective of the origin or destination of the products'.[241]

2.3.2 Energy-related cases

The Court of Justice has also dealt with the distinction between internal taxes and custom duties within the context of the energy branch.[242] In the *Haahr Petroleum case*, it held that an import surcharge levied on a general goods duty payable for the use of a member state's commercial port is to be considered in the light of the tax provisions.[243] The Court referred to the general system of internal dues, which applied without regard to the origin of the products. The surcharge formed part of the duty itself since it was expressed as a percentage of the duty and both the duty and the surcharge were levied on the same legal basis in accordance with the same criteria and by the same authorities. By contrast, in the case *Commission v Italy* the Court decided that a Sicilian environmental tax on methane gas imported from Algeria is subject to the provisions on custom duties and not subject to the tax provisions.[244] The Court argued that the tax was actually a pecuniary charge, which was imposed unilaterally on goods by reason of the fact that they cross the Italian border. The designation of the charge and also its mode of application were of no significance. Ultimately, in the *Air Liquide case*, the Court held that neither the provisions on custom duties nor those on taxation were applicable to a tax on motive force, levied on motors used for transporting industrial gas through very high pressure pipes.[245] The Court reasoned that the tax in question applies to economic activities carried out by industrial, commercial, financial or agricultural undertakings and not to products as such as required by the provisions on taxation.[246]

In addition to the determination that the national measure at issue constitutes an internal taxation rather than a custom duty, an assessment in light of article 110 paragraph 1 particularly requires assessment as to whether the

---

240 E.g. Case C-234/99 *Nygård v Svineafgiftsfonden*, para 19.
241 ECJ Case C-517/04 *Visserijbedrijf v Productschap Vis* [2006] OJ C 178/4, para 16; see also C-234/99 *Nygård v Svineafgiftsfonden*, para 19.
242 E.g. ECJ Cases C-90/94 *Haahr Petroleum* [1997] ECR I-04085; C-213/96 *Outokumpu Oy* [1998] ECR I-01777; C-206/06 *Essent Netwerk Noord v Aluminium Delfzijl* [2008] ECR I-5497.
243 ECJ case C-90/94 *Haahr Petroleum*.
244 Case C-173/05 *Commission v Italy* [2007] ECR I-04917.
245 Joined Cases C-393/04 and C-41/05 *Air Liquide* [2006] OJ C212/6.
246 Joined Cases C-393/04 and C-41/05 *Air Liquide*, para 57.

measure poses a tax-related discrimination, or more precisely, whether it imposes on imported products internal taxation in excess of that levied on domestic ones. In this context it is worth having a look at the *Outokumpu case* brought before the Court of Justice.[247] In this case a Finnish system of taxation provided for different tax rates for electricity of domestic origin. Electricity produced by an environmentally-friendly method was subject to a lower tax than electricity from polluting sources. By contrast, as regarded imported electricity the Finnish scheme did not draw such a distinction; instead a flat rate applied calculated so as to correspond to the average rate levied on domestic electricity. As a consequence, polluting electricity from abroad gained an edge over polluting homemade electricity, while the flat rate placed imported electricity from an environmentally friendly source at a disadvantage vis-à-vis that of a domestic origin. In its defence the Finnish government argued that given the characteristics of electricity, its method of production cannot be ascertained once it has entered the network. However, the Court refused this line of argumentation and found that the Finnish scheme constituted an unequal treatment of imported green electricity in the sense of article 95 of the EC Treaty, the current article 110 of the TFEU. Indeed the Court conceded that it may be extremely difficult to identify the method of production of electricity from a source abroad. However it ultimately countered the Finnish objection with the fact that the given taxation system did not even provide for the opportunity for importers to demonstrate the environmentally-friendly origin of their electricity with a view to qualify it for the lower tax rate. Today, it is even clearer that the argument as then put forward by the Finnish government is in principle not tenable.[248] The current EU legislation on the internal electricity market and on renewable energy just requires transparency regarding the origin of electricity. Electricity suppliers have to break down the composition of their energy mix[249] and for that purpose member states must particularly ensure the issuance of guarantees of origin upon request from a producer of renewable electricity.[250]

 REVIEW QUESTIONS

1. What are the four freedoms intended to ensure? *See section 2.1.*
2. In what situations is recourse to the four freedoms possible? *See section 2.1.*
3. In terms of the energy sector, give examples of legislative acts that can potentially block recourse to article 34 of the TFEU? *See section 2.1.1 b) i).*
4. As regards the energy sector, what type of reasons can potentially serve as a basis for a justification of a national measure violating article 34? *See section 2.1.1 b) iv).*

---

247 C-213/96 *Outokumpu Oy.*
248 See also A Johnston and G Block, *EU Energy Law*, 341.
249 Article 3(9)(a) of Directive 2009/72/EC.
250 Article 15(1) and (2) of Directive 2009/28/EC.

5. Which three momentous cases of the Court of Justice dealt with questions of justification concerning the renewable energy sector? *See section 2.1.1 b) iv)*.
6. What forms of competition practices and governmental measures come under EU competition law? *See section 2.2 (introductory notes)*.
7. Does EU competition law apply to the whole energy branch? *See section 2.2 (introductory notes)*.
8. The prohibition of cartels and related practices as established by article 101 TFEU presupposes that a relevant conduct affects trade and competition to an appreciable extent. What publications give guidance in the assessment as to whether this is the case in terms of an individual practice? *See section 2.2.1 a)*.
9. As regards the energy sector, what conduct at horizontal level and at vertical level typically requires scrutiny under article 101 TFEU? *See section 2.2.1 b)*.
10. What categories of cases are discussed under article 102 TFEU when it comes to the energy sector? *See section 2.2.2 b)*.
11. What are features of long-term supply contracts that can discourage competitors, potentially resulting in an infringement of article 102 TFEU by an incumbent energy supplier? *See section 2.2.2 b) iii)*.
12. Why does article 106 TFEU feature prominently in the energy sector? *See section 2.2.3 b)*.
13. Is recourse to article 106 TFEU still conceivable as regards undertakings operating in the electricity and gas sectors? *See section 2.2.3 b)*.
14. What kind of mergers fall within the European Union's remit and what kind of mergers fall within that of member states? *See section 2.2.4*.
15. What categories of cases relating to the energy sector are discussed under article 107 TFEU? *See section 2.2.5 b)*.
16. What does the *Altmark* judgement of the European Court of Justice generally say? *See section 2.2.5 b) i)*.
17. What do capacity mechanisms generally aim at and what guidelines does the European Commission apply when assessing such mechanisms? *See section 2.2.5 b) ii)*.
18. What kinds of state aid are for instance covered by the EEAG? *See section 2.2.5 b) iii.*

 FURTHER READING

Kelyn Bacon (ed.), *European Union Law of State Aid* (2nd edn, Oxford University Press 2013)
Adrian de Hauteclocque, *Market Building through Antitrust: Long-Term Contract Regulation in EU Electricity Markets* (Edward Elgar Publishing 2013)
Leigh Hancher, Tom Ottervanger and Piet Jan Slot, *EU State Aids* (4th edn, Sweet & Maxwell 2012)
Christopher Jones (ed.), *EU Energy Law: Volume II*, EU Competition Law and Energy Markets (3rd edn, Claeys & Casteels Publishing 2011)
Alison Jones and Brenda Sufrin, *EU Competition Law: Text, Cases, and Materials* (5th edn, Oxford University Press 2014)
Angus Johnston and Guy Block, *EU Energy Law* (Oxford University Press 2013)
Ulrich Scholz and Stephan Purps, 'The Application of EU Competition Law in the Energy Sector' (2013) 4(1) Journal of European Competition Law & Practice 63–82
Kim Talus, *EU Energy Law and Policy – A Critical Account* (Oxford University Press 2013)

3

Objectives and strategies of European energy policy and law

Considering their dependency on fossil fuels, in the decades to come EU member states will face huge energy-related challenges, requiring well-reasoned and balanced strategic planning and action. While member states hunger for more and more energy resources, fossil fuels will run short on a global scale. Nevertheless the energy supply must remain secure, just as energy prices must be affordable for the purpose of facilitating economic growth and social welfare. Moreover, the progression of climate change requires appropriate counteraction and calls for the continuous expansion of low-carbon technologies, renewable energy sources and high-efficiency appliances. Nothing short of rethinking and reorganising the traditional energy supply system is needed.

Given the complexity of challenges, a European energy policy, to be success-ful, requires a sufficient degree of forward-looking planning. This is particu-larly true when considering that the legislation of 28 member states has to be synchronised in an area of significant strategic importance. Against this back-ground, the present chapter aims to look behind the scenes and cast some light on the planning framework underlying and connecting individual legal acts.

The given planning framework exhibits some complexity. Broadly speaking, it consists of overall objectives and a range of strategies and roadmaps that show the way forward for European energy policy. Before focusing attention on these strategies in section 3.2 it is useful to take a brief look at the overall objectives guiding the common energy policy.

3.1 Overall objectives

The European Union relies on the transfer of competences by member states. This concession of responsibilities happens in primary law and is connected to certain general aims. These aims are of course authoritative for all EU institutions and, thus, form the top level of objectives the European Union pursues. As we have seen in chapter 1, such aims especially arise from article 194 TFEU when it comes to the common energy policy.

As the institution in charge of adopting the general political directions of the European Union, the European Council has prioritised and substantiated the general aims relevant to energy policy.[1] Taking the corresponding European Council determinations into account, the prioritised overall objectives pursued by the European energy policy can be summed up as follows:

- ensuring and increasing the security of the energy supply;
- availability of affordable energy for companies and citizens (especially by establishing and completing an integrated and competitive energy market);
- promoting environmental sustainability and combating climate change.

The Commission has seized upon these aims in the course of strategic planning by especially stressing the centrality of security of supply, competitiveness and sustainability within the context of European energy policy (see, for instance, the 2020 Energy Strategy).[2] Based on these overall objectives, the Commission has identified in its Communications general long-term and short-term goals guiding the European Union's energy agenda throughout the years. Such goals include, for instance, building an integrated EU-wide energy market, expanding energy networks, promoting energy efficiency, fostering renewable energy and reducing the European Union's dependence on imported fuels.[3] This wider planning framework thereby hinted at, and its evolution in recent years will constitute, the main focus of the subsequent section.

3.2 Strategies and roadmaps

3.2.1 A brief look back

European energy policy and respective legislation have been framed on the basis of different treaty provisions for decades and consequently lacked

---

1 See in particular European Council 23/24 March 2006, *Presidency Conclusions* (doc 7775/1/06 REV1) no 46; European Council 8/9 March 2007, *Presidency Conclusions* (doc 7224/1/07 REV1) no 28; European Council 26/27 June 2014, *Conclusions* (EUCO 79/14) annex I, no 3.

2 European Commission, *Energy 2020 – A strategy for competitive, sustainable and secure energy* (COM(2010) 639 final).

3 See, for instance, European Commission, *Energy 2020 – A strategy for competitive, sustainable and secure energy* (COM(2010) 639 final); European Commission, *Energy Roadmap 2050* (COM(2011) 885 final).

a coherent general concept. However, over the years the need for a more sophisticated approach has become apparent. Ultimately, in 2006 the Commission set the ball rolling for a reorientation with its *Green Paper on Energy*.[4] In this paper EU officials defined a general framework for a common coherent European energy policy by identifying six key issues to be jointly tackled. Topics covered ranged from internal EU affairs (for example, completing the internal electricity and gas markets, and enhancing energy efficiency) to questions of external policy. The new orientation was approved by the European Council and eventually also given a new legal foundation by the incorporation of article 194 into the TFEU in 2007.

Ultimately, the task of elaborating a true European energy policy was virtually clinched when the EU Heads of State and Government determined the European Union's 20-20-20 climate and energy targets in 2007 leaving no alternative to joint energy action.[5] These goals include:

- EU greenhouse gas emissions reduction (20% by 2020 compared to 1990)
- Increasing the share of renewable energy (20% of EU energy consumption by 2020)
- Reduction of EU energy consumption by increasing energy efficiency (20% of consumption compared to projections for 2020).

In addition to this, the Heads of State and Government decided in 2009 to reduce EU greenhouse gas emissions by 80–95% by 2050 compared to 1990, requiring a shift to a low-carbon economy if meant seriously.[6]

All three, the 2006 Green Paper on Energy, the 20-20-20 targets and the 2050 low-carbon economy goal have presented the cornerstones for progressive development of EU energy policy and the adoption of concrete legislative packages in subsequent years.[7] As regards the European Union's general energy agenda, enduring efforts have resulted in numerous strategic documents and proposals published by the European Commission, such as the communications on an 'Energy Policy for Europe' (2007),[8] 'European Strategic Energy

---

4 European Commission, *Green Paper on a European Strategy for Sustainable, Competitive and Secure Energy* (COM (2006) 105 final).
5 See European Council 8/9 March 2007, *Presidency Conclusions* (doc 7224/1/07 REV1).
6 See European Council 29/30 October 2009, *Presidency Conclusions* (doc 15265/09).
7 For an overview see also B Delvaux, *EU Law and the Development of a Sustainable, Competitive and Secure Energy Policy: Opportunities and Shortcomings* (Intersentia 2013) 15 et seq.
8 Doc COM (2007) 1 final.

Technology Plan (SET-Plan)' (2007),[9] 'Energy for a Changing World: 20 20 by 2020 – Europe's Climate Change Opportunity' (2008),[10] 'Second Strategic Energy Review' (2008),[11] 'A resource-efficient Europe – Flagship initiative under the Europe 2020 Strategy' (2011),[12] and 'European Energy Security Strategy' (2014).[13] All these publications led to a more comprehensive and forward-looking general planning, even though the European Union still seems to have just begun to open the window upon an extended common policy.

The fundamental direction of European energy policy as envisaged for the present decade and for the decades to come is laid down in several medium-term and long-term strategies and roadmaps which include:

- the '2020 Energy Strategy';[14]
- the '2030 Climate and Energy Policy Framework';[15]
- the 'Roadmap for moving to a competitive low-carbon economy in 2050';[16]
- the 'Energy Roadmap 2050';[17] and
- the 'Roadmap to a Single European Transport Area' envisaging a 60% cut in transport emissions by 2050'.[18]

3.2.2 The '2020 Energy Strategy'

The 2020 Energy Strategy addresses the planning horizon until 2020 and builds on five priorities that have been shaping energy action in recent years, and will continue to do so in the next years to come. These priorities can be broken down as follows:

- **Strengthening energy efficiency**
  In the first place, priority is given to the increase in energy efficiency. Achieving greater energy efficiency is expected in relation to all relevant

---

9 See press releases from 22 November 2007: IP/07/1750, MEMO/07/493, MEMO/07/494.

10 Doc COM (2008) 30 final.

11 Doc COM (2008) 781 final.

12 Doc COM (2011) 21.

13 European Commission, *European Energy Security Strategy* (COM/2014/0330 final).

14 European Commission, *Energy 2020 – A strategy for competitive, sustainable and secure energy* (COM (2010) 0639 final); see also European Council 4 February 2011, *Conclusions* (EUCO 2/11).

15 European Council 24 October 2014, *Conclusions* (EUCO 169/14).

16 European Commission, *A Roadmap for moving to a competitive low carbon economy in 2050* (COM (2011) 0112 final).

17 European Commission, *Energy Roadmap 2050* (COM (2011) 0885 final).

18 European Commission, *White Paper, Roadmap to a Single European Transport Area – Towards a competitive and resource efficient transport system* (COM (2011) 0144 final).

policy fields in order to attain the 20% energy saving target by 2020. The focus is set on the whole energy chain, from production, through transmission and distribution, to final energy consumption. The biggest potential is seen in the building and transport sector, but the industrial sector and energy intensive products are also covered by the plan. However, the '2020 Energy Strategy' settles for an enumeration of instruments to be introduced or reinforced, while details remain reserved for the separate 'Energy Efficiency Plan 2011'[19] and concrete legislation.

- **Establishment of a genuinely integrated internal energy market**
  The track record of the European Union's efforts to establish an internal energy market is quite sobering in terms of remaining national market fragmentation and the dominance of a small number of market players. On the one hand the Commission plans to solve this problem by an intensified enforcement of existing competition rules and internal market legislation. On the other hand, grid infrastructure is to be improved in order to better connect national systems and to pave the way for an enhanced use of renewable energy sources. Particular provision is made for more favourable legislative and financial frameworks fostering grid expansion. Further details were, for instance, published in the Commission's communication on energy infrastructure priorities for 2020 and beyond.[20]

- **Secure, safe and affordable energy**
  The 2020 Energy Strategy lays increased focus on the energy consumer side. Despite rising prices for natural resources and increasing costs for grid expansion, energy prices are to remain affordable for citizens and businesses. For that reason, the Commission once again calls for a reinforced implementation of competition policy and internal market legislation, namely that tied up in the '3rd Energy Package'. Respective legislation is particularly aimed at safeguarding the principle that customers may easily change their electricity or gas supplier and receive all necessary consumption data. Moreover, special attention is to be paid to safety and security on the production and transmission sides. Accordingly, the Commission has a focus on safety measures in relation to the extraction of oil and gas, nuclear energy generation and waste management, and the deployment of new energy technologies, such as CO_2 storage.

---

19 European Commission, *Energy Efficiency Plan 2011* (COM (2011) 0109 final).

20 European Commission, *Energy infrastructure priorities for 2020 and beyond – A Blueprint for an integrated European energy network* (COM (2010) 677 final).

- **Technological shift**
  It is clear that the European Union's ambitious decarbonisation goals necessitate the development and deployment of new technologies, which above all call for technological rethinking by the industry. In this respect the Commission is banking on inducing respective processes through incentive systems comprising the EU Emissions Trading System (ETS) and various support and funding schemes. Funding sources relevant to energy technology are mainly coordinated by the European Strategic Energy Technology Plan (SET Plan) and its individual initiatives, such as those on solar and wind technologies, electricity grids, bio-energy and Smart Cities.

- **Strengthening external energy policy**
  Considering the European Union's high dependency on external energy resources, the Commission attaches particular importance to the foreign dimension of EU energy policy. Efforts are to be especially concentrated on involving the neighbourhood into the EU energy concept. This includes, for instance, the integration of EU and neighbouring energy markets and the approximation of regulatory frameworks where possible. Particular ties are envisaged with key energy suppliers and transit countries. Apart from that, the Commission expects the European Union to play a pioneering role in the dissemination of low-carbon energy concepts. Another main line of action will be the promotion of legally binding standards in terms of nuclear safety, security and non-proliferation.

The 2020 Energy Strategy covers the period from 2010 until 2020. Within this timeframe programming takes place on a multi-annual and annual basis in due consideration of the strategic guidelines adopted by the European Council. The latest strategic agenda set by the European Council applies to the current institutional cycle from 2014 until 2019 and elevates a secure future for energy and climate to become one out of five overarching priorities of the European Union in the coming years.[21] In this context the European Council underscored that energy and climate policies must aim at an affordable, secure and sustainable energy supply. Mindful of the enormous dependency on oil and gas imports, the European Council placed special emphasis on the issue of security of supply and on the necessity to build an 'Energy Union' which particularly focuses on this issue. As regards the envisaged Energy Union, the Commission presented more concrete

---

21 See European Council 26/27 June 2014, *Conclusions* (EUCO 79/14) annex I: 'Strategic agenda of the Union in times of change'.

plans in early 2015[22] which were endorsed by the European Council shortly afterwards.[23]

However, contrary to what might be expected from an auspicious term such as 'Energy Union', the concept neither provides for essential institutional changes, nor does it present clear ideas of reshaping major governance procedures.[24] Ultimately it neither matches an obviously principal element of the original concept of an Energy Union as framed by Jerzy Buzek and Jacques Delors and which was adopted later on by the Polish Prime Minister Donald Tusk. This main constituent was seen in 'a single interface' in the European Union's relations with energy producing and transit countries, meaning a joint purchasing of gas from outside suppliers in particular.[25] However, apart from the apparently misleading term of the Energy Union which was obviously coined in order to give the common energy policy fresh impetus,[26] the Commission plans, if implemented, would nevertheless bring about enhanced coordination and cooperation among member states and also among Commission directorates responsible for energy and climate. Furthermore, considering the roadmap accompanying the Commission's proposal, the plans will very likely lead to a revision of numerous legislative acts outlined in this textbook. Of course, the concrete shape of reforms remains to be seen.

3.2.3 The '2030 Climate and Energy Policy Framework'

Whereas the 2020 Energy Strategy covers the period until 2020, pathways beyond that horizon are illustrated in the '2030 Climate and Energy Policy Framework'[27] which was adopted by the European Council in 2014. The 2030 framework is set to provide regulatory certainty for investors and

---

22 European Commission, *Energy Union Package, A Framework Strategy for a Resilient Energy Union with a Forward-Looking Climate Change Policy* (COM(2015) 80 final), see annex one for related roadmap.

23 European Council 20 March 2015, *Conclusions* (EUCO 11/15).

24 The Commission has remained rather vague in this context when formulating that it 'will launch a dynamic governance process for the European Energy Union'. See also D Buchan and M Keay, 'Europe's "Energy Union" plan: a reasonable start to a long journey' (March 2015) Oxford Energy Comment.

25 See J Buzek and J Delors, 'Towards a new European Energy Community' (5 May 2010) http://www. notre-europe.eu/media/en_buzek-delors_declaration.pdf?pdf=ok accessed 3 May 2016; euractive, 'Poland hopes Tusk will create an EU Energy Union' (10 September 2014) http://www.euractiv.com/sections/ poland-ambitious-achievers/poland-hopes-tusk-will-create-eu-energy-union-308333 accessed 3 May 2016; S Andoura, L Hancher and M van der Woude, 'Towards a European Energy Community: A policy proposal' (March 2010) http://www.delorsinstitute.eu/011-2155-Towards-a-European-Energy-Community-A-Policy-Proposal.html accessed 3 May 2016; D Buchan and M Keay, 'Europe's "Energy Union" plan: a reasonable start to a long journey', 5.

26 Cf D Buchan and M Keay, 'Europe's "Energy Union" plan: a reasonable start to a long journey', 5.

27 European Council 24 October 2014, *Conclusions* (EUCO 169/14).

safeguard continued concerted action among member states in the medium term. Consequently the Commission has also taken the 2030 Framework into account when drafting its plans for the Energy Union.

In substance, the 2030 Framework seems to confirm a creeping paradigm shift diverting the European Union from the global forerunner role it sought to occupy in earlier years in terms of climate and energy policies.[28] Economic and debt crisis, negative experiences connected with the international climate change negotiations,[29] the discord among member states as to the role of coal, nuclear energy and renewable energy sources in electricity generation and some member states' difficulty in attaining the renewable targets for 2020 have all left marks on the ambitiousness and determination of both the European Council and the Commission. As to whether the so-called Paris Agreement, adopted in December 2015 by the UN Climate Change Conference with the aim of limiting global warming, will have an impact on the planning for the 2030 horizon was not clear when finalising this textbook. Core points of the original version of the 2030 framework may, however, be summarised as follows:

- Corresponding to the 2030 framework, the European Union is setting its sights on a reduction of at least 40% in greenhouse gas emissions by 2030 relative to emissions in 1990. Prior to the adoption of the 2030 framework, the Commission had already seen no merit in a more ambitious target without profound reduction commitments from other world regions.[30] Against this backdrop, the Commission had not considered it appropriate either to set new emission targets for the transport sector after 2020.[31]
- The 2030 framework furthermore provides for an increase in the overall share of renewable energy in the European Union to at least 27% by 2030, whereas no binding targets for renewable energy going beyond those for 2020 are imposed on member states. The 2030 framework remains rather vague as to the extent to which the European Union will foster member states in realising more ambitious targets.[32] By contrast, the Commission

---

28 See also O Geden and S Fischer, 'Moving Targets, Die Verhandlungen über die Energie- und Klimapolitik-Ziele der EU nach 2020' (January 2014) SWP-Studie.

29 See also O Geden and S Fischer, 'Moving targets, Die Verhandlungen über die Energie- und Klimapolitik-Ziele der EU nach 2020'.

30 European Commission, *A policy framework for climate and energy in the period from 2020 to 2030* (COM (2014) 015 final) sec 2.1.

31 European Commission, *A policy framework for climate and energy in the period from 2020 to 2030* (COM (2014) 015 final) sec 2.2.

32 Cf European Council 24 October 2014, *Conclusions* (EUCO 169/14) sec 3.

has already made it plain that it is contemplating revising its present subsidies policy promoting the market penetration of renewable energy sources[33] – a path it has begun to pursue with its Guidelines on State Aid for Environmental Protection and Energy 2014–2020 (EEAG).[34] Aside from this, the Commission signalled in a heavily criticised decision from October 2014 that it is ready to accept state aid for the construction and operation of new nuclear power plants under certain conditions.[35] As a result, the European Union's new orientation might ultimately rather accommodate the member states banking on nuclear energy and to curb those willing to more ambitiously expedite the development of renewable energy sources and to phase out nuclear power.[36]

● As a third headline target, the European Council is planning to improve energy efficiency at EU level by at least 27% by 2030 compared to current projections. However, heads of state explicitly ruled out translating this indicative goal into binding targets for member states.[37]

3.2.4 Long-term planning horizon

The long-term planning horizon until 2050 is addressed by three further roadmaps which include:

● the 'Roadmap for moving to a competitive low carbon economy in 2050';[38]
● the 'Energy Roadmap 2050';[39] and
● the 'Roadmap to a Single European Transport Area' envisaging a 60% cut in transport emissions by 2050'.[40]

---

33 Cf European Commission, *A policy framework for climate and energy in the period from 2020 to 2030* (COM (2014) 015 final) sec 2.5.

34 European Commission, *Guidelines on State aid for environmental protection and energy 2014–2020* [2014] OJ C 200/1. See also above section 2.2.5 b) iii).

35 European Commission, *State aid: Commission concludes modified UK measures for Hinkley Point nuclear power plant are compatible with EU rules* (press release of 8 October 2014). See also commentary at Spiegel-online, 'Hinkley Point C: EU billigt Milliardenhilfen für britisches Atomkraftwerk' http://www.spiegel.de/wirtschaft/unternehmen/atomkraftwerk-eu-billigt-beihilfen-fuer-hinkley-point-c-a-996073.html accessed 3 May 2016.

36 See also S Fischer and O Geden, 'Die Energieziele sind nicht besonders ehrgeizig' (Handelsblatt 26 January 2014) http://www.handelsblatt.com/meinung/gastbeitraege/klima-und-eu-die-energieziele-sind-nicht-besonders-ehrgeizig/9369846.html accessed 3 May 2016.

37 Cf European Council 24 October 2014, *Conclusions* (EUCO 169/14) sec 3.

38 European Commission, *A Roadmap for moving to a competitive low carbon economy in 2050* (COM (2011) 0112 final).

39 European Commission, *Energy Roadmap 2050* (COM (2011) 0885 final).

40 European Commission, *White Paper, Roadmap to a Single European Transport Area – Towards a competitive and resource efficient transport system* (COM (2011) 0144 final).

Both the 'Roadmap for moving to a competitive low carbon economy in 2050'[41] and the 'Energy Roadmap 2050'[42] are geared towards reducing greenhouse gas emissions by 80–95% by 2050. In the 'Roadmap for moving to a competitive low carbon economy in 2050' the Commission marks out a cost-effective pathway of transition, including milestones, measures and technologies necessary to be implemented. In addition to this, the Commission presents different decarbonisation scenarios and consequences of an almost carbon-free energy system in the 'Energy Roadmap 2050'.

3.2.5 Cross-cutting EU strategies

The planning instruments mentioned in this section are not the result of area specific reflection alone, but also follow, of course, more general political considerations, convictions and principles. General guidelines arise particularly from strategies spanning various areas with a view to giving European Union policies a coherent direction. The present overarching frameworks of the European Union particularly include the Europe 2020 Strategy, following the Lisbon Strategy, and the EU Sustainable Development Strategy (EU SDS).

Both the Europe 2020 Strategy and the EU SDS cover and, consequently, impinge on energy related policies. This is not surprising given that energy occupies a central role for the functioning of economy and society and for the adjustment of the latter to sustainability criteria. The Europe 2020 Strategy constitutes the European Union's present growth strategy and particularly aims at attaining sustainable growth through the establishment of a low-carbon economy. This general orientation is emphasised by the EU SDS which sketches out a long-term vision of sustainability reconciling economic growth, social cohesion and environmental protection.[43] Both cross-cutting strategies have influenced the determination of the chief targets and priorities in the broader field of energy policy but also the shaping of concrete legislation in relation to energy. The EU climate and energy objectives, the 20-20-20 targets, resoundingly belong to the groundbreaking commitments the Union has adopted in this respect.

---

41 European Commission, *A Roadmap for moving to a competitive low carbon economy in 2050* (COM (2011) 0112 final).

42 European Commission, *Energy Roadmap 2050* (COM (2011) 0885 final).

43 See European Commission, *Mainstreaming sustainable development into EU policies: 2009 Review of the European Union Strategy for Sustainable Development* (COM/2009/0400 final).

3.3 Legislative packages

Based on the planning instruments, especially those for the 2020 horizon, the European Union has adopted and revised a range of legal acts introducing numerous regulatory, financial and market-based instruments in most of the energy sectors. Many instruments have been tied up in bundles, so called legislative packages. These packages have served one or more of the overall energy objectives by using a set of various approaches. These packages in particular include the 'Energy and Climate Change Package', the 'Energy Efficiency Package' and the '3rd legislative package on EU Electricity and Gas markets' (3rd Energy Package). The packages are frequently cited in literature so that it makes sense to briefly sum up some key aspects in the following subsections, whereas specific details about individual instruments included in these packages will be the object of consideration in Chapters 4 and 5 below. The same goes for instruments which have been adopted or revised outside the package structures.

3.3.1 Energy and Climate Change Package

The 'Energy and Climate Change Package' or 'Climate Package' constitutes one of the most demanding energy milestones of recent years.[44] The package was adopted by the Council and the European Parliament in December 2008 in order to implement the 20-20-20 targets. It focused primarily on the reduction of EU greenhouse gas emissions and raising the share of renewable energy. The package envisaged furthermore the improvement of energy efficiency but it did not include concrete binding rules to tackle this issue. The topic was addressed in a separate Energy Efficiency Package in 2009 and 2010, which will be summarised in the following subsection.

The Energy and Climate Change Package comprised mainly four essential and legally binding components:

- Revision, strengthening and extending the EU Greenhouse Gas Emission Trading System (EU ETS), which was introduced in 2005 to help EU Member States comply with the commitments under the Kyoto Protocol. In this context the European Parliament and the Council adopted Directive 2009/29/EC to amend the original ETS-Directive 2003/87/EC.
- Agreement on national emissions limitation targets for 2020 in sectors

---

44 For details see also R Hinrichs-Rahlwes, *Sustainable Energy Policies for Europe* (CRC Press 2013) 21 et seq.

not included in the EU Emission Trading System (EU ETS), for example, transport, buildings, agriculture and waste. Emissions in these sectors represent about 60% of total greenhouse gas emissions in the European Union. National targets depend on a member state's relative wealth ranging from −20% for richer member states to +20% for poorer member States. This agreement was adopted in the form of the Effort Sharing Decision of the European Parliament and Council in April 2009, Decision 406/2009/EC. In the same context, agreement was reached on binding targets for emissions from new passenger cars to assist member states in complying with their emissions targets in the non-ETS sectors. Details were laid down in Regulation (EC) No 443/2009.

- Mandatory national targets for renewable energy, in order to establish a common framework for the promotion of renewable energy and increasing its share so that 20% of EU energy consumption will come from renewable resources by 2020. The targets and framework are laid down in Directive 2009/28/EC of the European Parliament and of the Council amending and subsequently repealing Directives 2001/77/EC and 2003/30/EC (Renewable Energy Directive). The Directive strengthens the share of renewable energy and thus contributes to reducing greenhouse gas emissions and to decreasing the dependence on energy imports.

- A legal framework for carbon capture and storage (CCS). CCS represents a way to prevent negative effects of carbon dioxide emissions on climate through trapping the gas underground. In this regard the European Parliament and the Council adopted Directive 2009/31/EC on the geological storage of carbon dioxide.

Some further actions accompanied the core elements of the Energy and Climate Change Package such as Directive 2008/101/EC to include aviation activities in the EU ETS and Directive 2009/30/EC regarding the specification of petrol, diesel and gas-oil and introducing a mechanism to monitor and reduce greenhouse gas emissions mainly in respect of road vehicles, and non-road mobile machinery.

3.3.2 Energy Efficiency Package

The 'Energy Efficiency Package' from 2009 and 2010 constitutes another key component of the EU strategy to achieve the 20-20-20 targets. The objective of the Energy Efficiency Package was to get market actors and consumers to behave more energy-efficiently, particularly when making or using buildings, appliances and means of transport. The three measures included in the package were:

- A regulation on the labelling of tyres in order to promote fuel efficiency[45]
- An update and extension of the Energy Performance of Buildings Directive[46]
- An update and extension of the Energy Labelling Directive.[47]

Meanwhile legislation applicable to energy efficiency has been further developed and especially supplemented by the so-called Energy Efficiency Directive introducing a common framework for the promotion of energy efficiency.[48]

3.3.3 3rd Legislative Package on EU Electricity and Gas Markets

Whereas the Energy and Climate Change Package and the Energy Efficiency Package were primarily adopted to tackle the issue of reducing negative effects on the environment, the '3rd Legislative Package on EU Electricity and Gas Markets' (3rd Energy Package) was put together to address the issues of an open and fair energy market, a secure energy supply and affordable energy prices.[49] The European Parliament and the Council adopted the 3rd Energy Package in 2009, which came into force in March 2011. This package included the following components:

- Regulation (EC) No 713/2009 establishing an Agency for the Cooperation of Energy Regulators
- Regulation (EC) No 714/2009 on conditions for access to the network for cross-border exchanges in electricity and repealing Regulation (EC) No 1228/2003
- Regulation (EC) No 715/2009 on conditions for access to the natural gas transmission networks and repealing Regulation (EC) No 1775/2005
- Directive 2009/72/EC concerning common rules for the internal market in electricity and repealing Directive 2003/54/EC

---

45 Regulation (EC) No 1222/2009 of the European Parliament and of the Council of 25 November 2009 on the labelling of tyres with respect to fuel efficiency and other essential parameters.
46 Directive 2010/31/EU of 19 May 2010 on the energy performance of buildings (recast) [2010] OJ L 153/13.
47 Directive 2010/30/EU of the European Parliament and of the Council of 19 May 2010 on the indication by labelling and standard product information of the consumption of energy and other resources by energy-related products [2010] OJ L 153/1.
48 Directive 2012/27/EU of the European Parliament and of the Council of 25 October 2012 on energy efficiency, amending Directives 2009/125/EC and 2010/30/EU and repealing Directives 2004/8/EC and 2006/32/EC [2012] OJ L 315/1.
49 For further details see also C Jones (ed.), *EU Energy Law: Volume I, The Internal Energy Market: The Third Liberalisation Package* (3rd edn, Claeys & Casteels Publishing 2010); A Johnston and G Block, *EU Energy Law* (Oxford University Press 2013) 23 et seq.

- Directive 2009/73/EC concerning common rules for the internal market in natural gas and repealing Directive 2003/55/EC

? REVIEW QUESTIONS

1. Where do the overall objectives of the European energy policy arise from? *See section 3.1.*
2. What do the European Union's 20-20-20 climate and energy targets as adopted in 2007 provide for? *See section 3.2.1.*
3. Which medium-term and long-term strategies address the planning horizons 2020 and 2030? *See section 3.2.*
4. Why may the term 'Energy Union' be considered as misleading? *See section 3.2.2.*
5. Which sectors have been targeted by the so-called 3rd Energy Package? *See section 3.3.3.*

4

Sector-specific legislation

The creation of a single market as a barrier-free zone for business and consumers across Europe is one of the European Union's main goals. Despite all achievements of recent decades, the process of establishing the single market has not yet been accomplished. This is especially true for the internal energy market. The European Union still aims at a more extensive integration of the formerly encapsulated national energy markets, which have long been dominated by state monopolies and their successors. Today, the European Union is concentrating its efforts particularly on increasing competition and improving the energy infrastructure, in order to improve the functioning of the single energy market within all its sectors and in order to secure the availability of affordable energy.

As seen in Chapter 2 above, the Treaty on the Functioning of the European Union (TFEU), the Euratom Treaty and respective court decisions form the cornerstones of a single energy market. The treaty rules and court decisions generally guarantee that energy, energy sources, energy-related services, energy investments and energy-related payments can freely be transferred and people working in the energy sector can freely move across the European Union. Moreover, the TFEU provides basic rules for competition, state aid and taxation in order to prevent distortions and national restraints of the internal energy market.

But these quite general rules would not be sufficient to create a completely integrated market in the foreseeable future and they alone hardly permit the shaping of the internal market in accordance with a number of other goals pertaining to, for instance, security of supply, climate change and energy prices. Therefore the EU and Euratom institutions have been provided with a set of legislative powers to complete and maintain the internal energy market and to provide it with a form that fits all the European Union's and Euratom's overall objectives (see Chapter 1.4). In the past decades the EU and Euratom institutions have made ample use of their powers and they have adopted a number of acts introducing various instruments, including regulatory instruments and market-based instruments. Member states were required to fully implement key legislation by 2014.[1] In the following chapters, relevant legislation and instruments will be outlined, whereby a distinction is maintained between legislative acts concerning individual sub-sectors of the energy market (see this Chapter 4) and those having a bearing on several sub-sectors (see Chapter 5).

4.1 The electricity sector

To begin with, the European Community and the European Union, respectively, have been deeply engaged in integrating the electricity sector since 1996. Since then, the internal market for electricity has been progressively implemented through several legislative packages ('energy packages'), which, to be precise, focus on both the electricity sector and the gas sector.[2] These packages and accompanying acts have introduced and increasingly refined rules on the internal electricity market, on security of supply in the branch and on the cooperation of national energy regulators.

After the implementation of the first two packages, the Commission identified a number of remaining malfunctions.[3] Considering the modest success of these packages, the European Union has relied on several strategies in order to consolidate the internal electricity and gas markets. First, the Commission has reinforced its efforts to apply the EU competition rules, namely those on cartels and dominant positions (articles 101, 102 and 106 TFEU), the rules on merger control (Council Regulation (EC) No 139/2004) and those on state aid control (articles 107–109 TFEU) (see above, chapter 2.2). Second, the Commission has initiated a number of infringement procedures against

1 See European Commission, *Making the internal energy market work* (COM (2012) 663 final) sec 1.
2 First Electricity and Gas Directives from 1996 and 1998: Directive 96/92/EC concerning common rules for the internal market in electricity and Directive 98/30/EC concerning common rules for the internal market in natural gas; *2nd package*: Directive (EC) 2003/54/EC concerning common rules for the internal market in electricity and repealing Directive 96/92/EC, Directive 2003/55/EC concerning common rules for the internal market in natural gas and repealing Directive 98/30/EC, Regulation (EC) No 1228/2003 on conditions for access to the network for cross-border exchanges in electricity, Regulation (EC) No 1775/05 on conditions for access to the natural gas transmission network; *3rd package*: Directive 2009/72/EC concerning common rules for the internal market in electricity and repealing Directive 2003/54/EC, Directive 2009/73/EC concerning common rules for the internal market in natural gas and repealing Directive 2003/55/EC, Regulation (EC) No 714/2009 on conditions for access to the network for cross-border exchanges in electricity and repealing Regulation (EC) No 1228/2003, Regulation (EC) No 715/2009 on conditions for access to the natural gas transmission networks and repealing Regulation (EC) No 1775/2005 and Regulation (EC) No 713/2009 establishing an Agency for the Cooperation of Energy Regulators.
3 See European Commission, *Prospects for the internal gas and electricity market* (COM (2006) 0841 final). As regards the first and second Electricity Regulation in particular, see also T von Danwitz, 'Regulation and liberalization of the European electricity market – A German view' (2006) 27 Energy Law Journal 435 et seq; M Roggenkamp, C Redgwell, I del Guayo and A Rønne, *Energy Law in Europe* (2nd edn, OUP 2007) 356.

member states, which have not correctly implemented the 2nd Energy Package. Third, the European Union has adopted the 3rd Energy Package, which has not only refined the common market rules, but has also established an Agency for the Cooperation of Energy Regulators.

The progress in creating the internal market through all of these measures is monitored by the Commission in yearly benchmarking reports. In 2012 the Commission still ascertained that the European Union was lagging behind its goals as member states continued to be slow in transforming relevant national legislation and maintained inward-looking policies.[4] Against this background, the Commission adopted a package of measures with its communication on 'Making the internal energy market work', which, inter alia, furthermore sought to pursue infringement procedures against member states lagging behind in the transposing of the 3rd Energy Package Directives into national law, and also sought to enforce EU competition law.[5]

In the following sections, the rules and instruments relevant to the electricity sector as introduced mainly through the 3rd Energy Package will be scrutinised under the following three different headings: common market rules (section 4.1.1), security of supply and infrastructure investments (section 4.1.2), as well as regulation and monitoring of the market (section 4.1.3).

4.1.1 Common market rules

The energy packages have progressively established the architecture of the internal energy market. At present key elements follow from Directive 2009/72/EC (Electricity Directive) which forms an essential part of the 3rd Energy Package and repeals the previous Directive 2003/54/EC by amending, extending and, in parts, taking over from previously effective rules.[6]

The present Electricity Directive addresses a number of market issues and defines specific common rules for the generation, transmission, distribution and supply of electricity. It banks on various instruments which mainly include the following: the exclusion of supply price regulation; an unbundling regime; a system on third-party access to transmission and distribution networks; an *ex ante* regulation of transmission and distribution tariffs; and the right of customers to freely choose their electricity supplier

---

4 See European Commission, *Making the internal energy market work* (COM (2012) 663 final).
5 Ibid.
6 Directive 2009/72/EC concerning common rules for the internal market in electricity and repealing Directive 2003/54/EC [2009] OJ L 211/55.

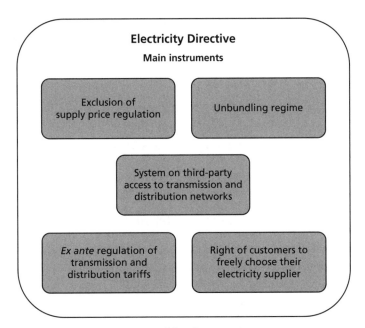

Figure 4.1 Main instruments of the Electricity Directive

(see Figure 4.1). Apart from these determinations, which primarily serve the strengthening of competition and consumer protection, the Electricity Directive sets forth further determinations with a view to improve security of supply, environmental protection and consumer protection.

Member states were required to transpose into national law the Electricity Directive and the common market rules contained within this by March 2011.[7] However, even though the third Electricity Directive has further curtailed the room for national manoeuvre, it continues to permit member states exemptions under certain circumstances. Pursuant to article 3 paragraph 14 the directive allows member states not to apply certain of its provisions including those on third party access to the transmission and distribution systems. A non-application may come into consideration insofar as the application of the provisions specified in paragraph 14 would prevent electricity undertakings from fulfilling obligations imposed on them in the general economic interest. Moreover, in the event of a sudden crisis in the market or where the safety of persons or system integrity is threatened, a member state may temporarily take the necessary safeguard measures (see article 42 Electricity Directive). Furthermore, pursuant to article 44 of the Electricity Directive

---

7 See art 49 Directive 2009/72/EC.

member states may under certain conditions apply for derogations from specific provisions of the directive in the event of substantial problems for the operation of small isolated systems.

In order to be able to provide as complete a picture as possible, the instruments mentioned above and further rules will be grouped into and explained within categories reflecting more or less the whole value chain from electricity generation to electricity supply (see subsections b) to e)). Beforehand, in the following subsection an outline of the general rules for the organisation of the electricity sector will be given.

a)   General rules for the organisation of the electricity sector

Chapter II of the Electricity Directive forms the general framework for the organisation of the electricity sector defining a number of basic aims, precise objectives and requirements relating to public service obligations, consumer protection and especially the protection of vulnerable customers (for example, the elderly and handicapped), security of supply, technical rules and regional cooperation.

Before shedding some more light on these determinations, it should be noted that one of the fundamental principles underlying the common electricity market lacks an explicit mention in chapter II or in any other part of the Electricity Directive. Ultimately, the Electricity Directive proceeds on the assumption that the internal electricity market will basically operate on the principle of supply and demand. This concept excludes an all-encompassing regulation by member states, otherwise a market liberalisation as aspired to by the Directive remains unattainable. On account of this, the Electricity Directive in particular bars governments from setting up or adjusting end-user electricity prices (for exemptions under article 3(2) see the next paragraph).[8] Based on this assumption, the Commission has already found fault with some member states' schemes designed to regulate end-user prices.[9] By contrast, the Electricity Directive makes a general exemption from the principle of supply and demand in regard to network access charges. As will be shown below, the Directive explicitly foresees national regulation of access fees in order to prevent system operators from abusing their incumbent position through excessive pricing.[10]

---

8 Cf *Federutility Judgement* of the European Court of Justice regarding the comparable Gas Directive: ECJ, Case C-265/08 *Federutility* [2010] ECR I-03377, paras 18 et seq.

9 Cf European Commission, press release IP/11/414 of 6 April 2011.

10 See section 4.1.1 c) v) below.

In addition, the Electricity Directive defines a range of further rules shaping the common electricity market. Article 3(2) makes clear, inter alia, that member states may impose on electricity undertakings public service obligations which can relate to security of supply, regularity, quality and price of supplies and environmental protection. However, such obligations must be clearly defined, transparent, non-discriminatory and have to guarantee equality of access for electricity undertakings to consumers. As decribed in Chapter 2 above, with a view to enable undertakings to fulfil public service obligations imposed on them, member states may intervene in the market.[11] Against this background national authorities may, for instance, be allowed to regulate end-user prices,[12] grant financial compensation or confer exclusive rights.[13]

Article 3(3) establishes one of the key principles of European electricity policy, the guarantee of a minimum supply.[14] Pursuant to paragraph 3, member states shall make sure that at least all private households are appropriately supplied with electricity. Private customers shall enjoy universal service, meaning they have to be provided with electricity of a specified quality at reasonable, easily and clearly comparable, transparent and non-discriminatory prices. For that reason, member states may appoint a supplier of last resort and shall impose on distribution companies an obligation to connect consumers to their system. Even for carrying out such obligations, financial compensation or exclusive rights may be conferred under the conditions of article 3(6).

Another vital element of European electricity policy accrues from article 3(5). Accordingly member states must safeguard that all customers have the right to freely choose their electricity supplier, to change their supplier within three weeks and to receive all relevant consumption data. In order to strengthen consumer rights and to enable customers to carefully choose their supplier, member states must also ensure that electricity suppliers specify the contribution of each energy source to the overall fuel mix of the supplier, information on the environmental impact, at least in terms of CO_2 emissions and the radioactive waste resulting from the electricity produced, as well as information concerning customers' rights in the event of a dispute.[15]

---

11 See above section 2.2.3.

12 Cf ECJ, Case C-265/08 *Federutility* [2010] ECR I-03377, paras 21–24; European Commission, press releases IP/11/414 of 6 April 2011 and IP/11/590 of 19 May 2011.

13 See also art 3(6) Directive 2009/72/EC.

14 See also T von Danwitz, 'Regulation and liberalization of the European electricity market – A German view' 439.

15 Cf art 3(9) Directive 2009/72/EC.

b) *Electricity generation*

As regards the generation of electricity, chapter III of the Electricity Directive creates a legal framework for relevant authorisation procedures and tendering. Whereas article 7 defines basic requirements for the authorisation of the construction of new generating capacity, article 8 determines basic prerequisites as to the tendering procedure for new generating capacity and energy efficiency/demand-side management measures. The precise definition of pertinent procedures remains at the discretion of member states. However, article 8(1) and (2) also make clear that member states in general have to leave the creation of new capacity, in particular, to market forces.[16] For that reason they have to establish the authorisation procedure as the normal case while tendering may only be provided for in the exceptional cases defined in paragraphs (1) and (2). Apart from that, if a tender includes plans for a subsidy to attract bidders, which is typically the case when the new capacity is to serve security of supply in times of stress, it must be observed that the envisaged scheme may also come under the EU state aid rules requiring additional assessment and approval by the Commission.[17]

c) *Transmission and distribution*

i) *Transmission: transmission system operators and unbundling at transmission level*

Chapters IV and V of the Electricity Directive provide rules on energy transmission defining the tasks of transmission system operators (TSOs), the requirement of certification of TSOs and requirements of the unbundling of transmission systems and TSOs.

Definition, certification and tasks of TSOs: Pursuant to article 2(4) of the Electricity Directive transmission system operator (TSO) means a natural or legal person responsible for operating, maintaining and developing the transmission system in a given area. Transmission systems primarily consist of extra high-voltage and high-voltage interconnected power lines carrying electricity from generating power plants to the distribution systems near consumption centres. Before being officially designated as a TSO, an undertaking must first be certified according to the procedures provided for in article 10.

---

16 See also A Johnston and G Block, *EU Energy Law* (Oxford University Press 2013) 262.
17 See above section 2.2.5 (particularly under subsection b) ii)) and Johnston and Block, *EU Energy Law*, 264.

In case a third-country transmission system owner or a third-country TSO desires certification, article 11 must be observed.

In order to fulfill their salient role in maintaining energy supply, TSOs must discharge certain tasks. Their duties accrue from article 12 of the Electricity Directive. Accordingly TSOs must especially secure the long-term ability of the system to meet reasonable demands for the transmission of electricity, contribute to security of supply through adequate transmission capacity, grant and manage third-party access and provide system users with the information they need to efficiently access the system.

Unbundling of TSOs – general remarks: The unbundling regime for transmission systems and TSOs, represents one of the building blocks of the Electricity Directive.[18] The unbundling regime aims at separating transmission activities from production and supply activities. The goal is to avoid the distortion of competition through discrimination against competitors and cross-subsidisation of their own activities by undertakings which simultaneously control, on the one hand, the transmission of electricity and, on the other hand, its generation or supply.

The present unbundling regime applicable to TSOs has been gradually developed over the three generations of the Electricity Directive. Whereas the First Electricity Directive was content in unbundling as to management, information and accounts, the second version of the directive went further by introducing minimum requirements of legal and functional unbundling. Accordingly, TSOs had to be independent at least in terms of their legal form, organisation and decision-making. However, the tightening of the unbundling framework has nevertheless been revealed to be toothless and has triggered off discussion on the introduction of the most incisive form of unbundling, which is ownership unbundling. EU institutions contemplated ownership unbundling as the most effective tool for driving forward market integration.[19] Critics have called the benefits of full ownership separation into question and raised particular objections regarding the infringement of property rights guaranteed by both European law and national constitutional law.[20]

---

18 For details see also C Jones (ed.), *EU Energy Law: Volume I, The Internal Energy Market: The Third Liberalisation Package* (3rd edn, Claeys & Casteels Publishing 2010) chapter 4; A Johnston and G Block, *EU Energy Law*, 35 et seq; K Talus, *EU Energy Law and Policy – A Critical Account* (Oxford University Press 2013) 77 et seq.

19 See, for instance, Recital 11 of Directive 2009/72/EC; A Piebalgs, 'Towards a Single European Gas and Electricity Market' (speech held at the VDEW Congress Berlin on 24 May 2007, European Commission Speech/07/335, 24/05/2007).

20 Cf, for example, A Johnston and G Block, *EU Energy Law*, 67 et seq; J Haucap, 'The costs and benefits

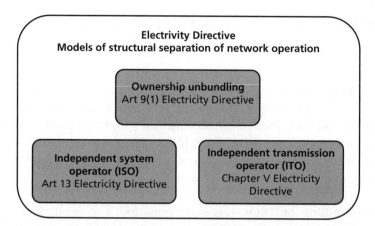

Figure 4.2 Models of structural separation of network operation

Taking account of the two opposing views, the European legislature has ultimately decided in favour of a compromise solution. Accordingly, the European Union has adopted a concept of ownership unbundling but allowed member states to exempt any transmission systems that belonged to vertically integrated undertakings on 3 September 2009. Thus, the compromise settlement renders the protection of previous ownership possible and may therefore decisively restrict the practical effect of the new path taken. Even though exempted grids are subject to other rules of unbundling, it remains to be seen whether this solution proves to be a flaw in the Third Electricity Directive.

To be precise, the new approach adopted with the Third Electricity Directive comprises three different models of structural separation of network operation from production and supply activities: ownership unbundling, independent system operator (ISO) and independent transmission operator (ITO) (see Figure 4.2).[21]

In general, member states must transpose into national law and apply the rules on ownership unbundling as set out in article 9(1). However, as

---

of ownership unbundling' (November/December 2007) Intereconomics 304; von Danwitz, 'Regulation and liberalization of the European electricity market – A German view' (2006) 27 Energy Law Journal 436 et seq; Piebalgs, 'Towards a Single European Gas and Electricity Market'; J Pielow, G Brunekreeft and E Ehlers, 'Legal and economic aspects of ownership unbundling in the EU' (2009) 2(2) Journal of World Energy Law & Business 96 et seq.

21 Cf art 9(1) and (8) Directive 2009/72/EC. For detailed guidance see European Commission, *Commission staff working paper, Interpretative note on Directive 2009/72/EC concerning common rules for the internal market in electricity and Directive 2009/73/EC concerning common rules for the internal market in natural gas, the unbundling regime* (22 January 2010).

indicated, in cases where the transmission system already belonged to a verti-cally integrated undertaking on 3 September 2009, a member state is free to opt for the application of ownership unbundling pursuant to article 9(1) or apply one of the other two models.[22] A 'vertically integrated undertaking' means one or more undertakings which are controlled by the same person or persons and where the undertaking or undertakings perform at least one of the functions of transmission or distribution, and at least one of the func-tions of generation or supply of electricity.[23]

If a member state opts against article 9(1), it may either designate an inde-pendent system operator (ISO) as laid down in article 13 or comply with the provisions of Chapter V of the Electricity Directive relating to an inde-pendent transmission operator (ITO).[24] However, member states may not in any event prevent vertically integrated undertakings owning a transmis-sion system from complying with the provisions on ownership unbundling.[25] Against this background, all member states had to transpose the rules on own-ership unbundling into national law at least for such companies. Additionally, it also follows clearly from the Electricity Directive that member states have to transpose into national law, and must apply, the rules on ownership unbun-dling in terms of transmission systems which did not belong to a vertically integrated undertaking on 3 September 2009 or which did not exist at all at that date. Besides, it should be noted that new direct current interconnectors may be exempted, for a limited period, from the requirements of article 9 under certain conditions (see article 17 Regulation (EC) No 714/2009).

Ownership unbundling (article 9 Electricity Directive): The first model, ownership unbundling, is defined by the cumulative requirements of article 9(1), which are further described in the following paragraphs. In particular article 9(1) sets forth the following provisions:

- First, member states must make sure that each undertaking which owns a transmission system acts as a TSO and therefore meets all of the require-ments of a TSO.
- Second, member states shall ensure that the same person or persons, meaning private individuals, companies or any other public or private

---

22 Cf art 9(8) Directive 2009/72/EC.

23 Cf art 2(21) Directive 2009/72/EC.

24 Cf art 9(8) Directive 2009/72/EC.

25 Cf art 9(11) Directive 2009/72/EC. See also European Commission, *Commission staff working paper,* Interpretative note on Directive 2009/72/EC concerning common rules for the internal market in electricity and Directive 2009/73/EC concerning common rules for the internal market in natural gas, the unbundling regime (22 January 2010), p 5.

entities, are not entitled to exercise control over an undertaking performing any of the functions of generation or supply, and to exercise control or
any right over a TSO or over a transmission system.[26] The same prohibition applies to the alternative situation of a person or persons exercising
control over a TSO or over a transmission system, and exercising control
or any right over an undertaking performing any of the functions of generation or supply.[27] The definition of 'control' follows from article 2(34)
of the Electricity Directive and Council Regulation (EC) No 139/2004
(Merger Regulation).[28] In short, 'control' includes all means which,
directly or indirectly, separately or in combination, confer the possibility of exercising 'decisive influence' on an undertaking. Decisive influence may, for instance, accrue from ownership or from rights or contracts
conferring crucial influence on the voting or decisions of the organs of
an undertaking.[29] For further details on the interpretation of the concepts of 'control' and 'rights', see article 3(2) of the Merger Regulation,
article 9(2) of the Electricity Directive and the pertinent notes of the
Commission.[30]

- The third and fourth cumulative requirements of article 9(1) cover the
  issue of conflict of interest through the appointment of board members
  and through multiple board memberships. Member states must ensure
  that the same person may not appoint members of the supervisory board,
  the administrative board or bodies legally representing the undertaking,
  of a TSO or a transmission system, and exercise control or exercise any
  right over an undertaking performing any of the functions of generation
  or supply. Moreover, the same person may not be a member of the supervisory board, the administrative board or bodies legally representing the
  undertaking, of both an undertaking performing any of the functions of
  generation or supply and a TSO or a transmission system.

According to these determinations, ownership unbundling means in effect
two things: first, a prohibition to acquire a TSO or a transmission system
contrary to the unbundling rules and, second, the requirement to discharge a
TSO or a transmission system if the unbundling criteria are met.[31]

---

26 See art 9(1)(b)(i) Directive 2009/72/EC; European Commission, *Commission staff working paper*, ibid,
p 8.
27 See art 9(1)(b)(ii) Directive 2009/72/EC.
28 See recital 13 of Directive 2009/72/EC.
29 Cf art 3 Regulation (EC) No 139/2004 (Merger Regulation).
30 See, for instance, European Commission, *Commission staff working paper, Interpretative note on Directive
2009/72/EC concerning common rules for the internal market in electricity and Directive 2009/73/EC concerning
common rules for the internal market in natural gas, the unbundling regime* (22 January 2010), pp 8 et seq.
31 Cf M Schmidt-Preuß, 'OU – ISO – ITO: Die Unbundling-Optionen des 3. EU-Liberalisierungspakets'

As regards the latter (the discharge of an integrated TSO or transmission system), member states may, with a view to safeguarding the interests of shareholders of a vertically integrated undertaking, choose whether the separation shall be brought about by direct divestiture or by splitting the shares of the integrated undertaking into shares of the network undertaking and shares of the remaining supply and generation undertaking.[32] In case a member state uses the second option, the said unbundling requirements must nevertheless be complied with, meaning that shareholders taking stakes in both the network undertaking and the remaining supply and generation undertaking, may not be in a position to exercise control simultaneously over these two undertakings. Eventually neither the transmission system nor the TSO may remain within the originally vertically integrated undertaking. Instead, transmission must be organised by a separate company, which owns the transmission system, acts as the TSO and fulfils all the tasks of a TSO. Any control over the created TSO by the formerly vertically integrated undertaking must be precluded.

The requirement of separation applies in all instances if a vertically integrated undertaking solely owns a TSO or a transmission system or if it holds a majority shareholding in one of them.[33] In case such an undertaking is in the possession of a minority shareholding, it may keep this stake provided that, in relation to the TSO or the transmission system, it does not exercise any voting rights and powers to appoint members of organs and does not have any form of direct or indirect control.[34] Under these preconditions it should also be possible for a generation and supply undertaking not possessing a TSO or transmission systems so far to acquire minority stakes in these.[35]

Independent system operator (ISO) (article 13 Electricity Directive): In terms of transmission systems which belonged to a vertically integrated undertaking on 3 September 2009, member states may opt against the application of the rules of ownership unbundling as laid down in article 9. Instead member states may opt for the model of an independent system operator (ISO), as follows from article 13 of the Electricity Directive. Under the ISO

("et" Energiewirtschaftliche Tagesfragen, September 2009) http://www.et-energie-online.de/AktuellesHeft/Topthema/tabid/70/Year/2009/Month/9/NewsModule/423/20099.aspx accessed 3 May 2016.

32 Recital 18 of Directive 2009/72/EC; R Pisal, *Entflechtungsoptionen nach dem Dritten Energiebinnenmarktpaket* (Nomos 2011) 173.

33 Cf European Commission, *Commission staff working paper, Interpretative note on Directive 2009/72/EC concerning common rules for the internal market in electricity and Directive 2009/73/EC concerning common rules for the internal market in natural gas, the unbundling regime* (22 January 2010), p 9.

34 Cf European Commission, *Commission staff working paper,* ibid.

35 Cf M Schmidt-Preuß, 'OU – ISO – ITO: Die Unbundling-Optionen des 3. EU-Liberalisierungspakets'.

model, a transmission system owner may keep property in the transmission assets, especially the grid, keep the assets on its balance sheet and generate returns on them.[36] Apart from this, all other unbundling requirements as provided for in article 9(1)(b) to (d) remain applicable.[37] This means that transmission must be organised by a fully independent and therefore separate company outside the integrated undertaking, the ISO, which acts as the TSO and is in charge of all tasks of TSOs, such as granting and managing third-party access to the system. Moreover, article 13 affirms that independence of the ISO is also required in terms of investment decisions pertaining to the transmission system. Accordingly, the system owner is responsible for financing investments, but investment planning and taking respective decisions remain the tasks of the ISO.[38]

Under the ISO model both the ISO and the transmission system owner have to comply with individual unbundling schemes. Whereas the ISO must meet all requirements set out in article 9(1)(b) to (d), as mentioned above, the transmission system owner which is part of a vertically integrated undertaking must itself fulfil obligations of legal and functional unbundling, which result from article 14. Accordingly, the transmission system owner is required to be independent at least in terms of its legal form, organisation and decision- making from other activities which do not relate to transmission.

Independent transmission operator (ITO) (Chapter V of the Electricity Directive): As regards transmission systems which belonged to a vertically integrated undertaking on 3 September 2009, member states may also choose a third option: the independent transmission operator (ITO). In this case all responsibilities of the transmission system operator (TSO) must be exercised by the ITO.[39] In contrast to full ownership unbundling and the formation of an ISO (options one and two), no change in ownership as regards the ITO is required, meaning the ITO may remain part of the vertically integrated undertaking[40]. Nevertheless, the Electricity Directive provides for ample unbundling requirements which are designed to ensure the autonomy of the ITO:

First, it must be safeguarded that the ITO is provided with all human, technical, physical and financial resources essential for the fulfilment of the tasks

---

36 Haucap, 'The Costs and Benefits of Ownership Unbundling' 301.

37 Cf art 13(2)(a) Directive 2009/72/EC.

38 See art 13(5)(b) Directive 2009/72/EC; European Commission, *Commission staff working paper*, ibid, pp 12 et seq.

39 Cf art 17(2) and 12 Directive 2009/72/EC. More tasks are for instance laid down in arts 17(2), 21, 22 and 23.

40 Cf M Schmidt-Preuß, 'OU – ISO – ITO: Die Unbundling-Optionen des 3. EU-Liberalisierungspakets'.

conferred to it (article 17). This means in particular that the ITO must own the transmission system and that it has to be equipped with appropriate financial resources for investment projects by the integrated undertaking.[41] Second, articles 18 and 19 determine the level of independence the ITO must be granted in relation to the vertically integrated undertaking. These provisions lay down for instance the requirements of independence in respect of maintaining and developing the transmission system, raising money on the capital market, the day-to-day competitive behaviour of the ITO and its staff and management. Apart from that, article 18(3) excludes shareholdings in the ITO by subsidiaries of the integrated undertaking performing functions of generation or supply. Third, for the ITO a supervisory body must be installed which basically assembles representatives of the vertically integrated undertaking and of third party shareholders.[42] The supervisory body assumes responsibility for decisions which potentially have a significant impact on the value of the assets of the shareholders within the ITO, for example decisions regarding the level of indebtedness. However, decisions of the supervisory body must not be involved in any way with the day-to-day business of the ITO and the management of the network.

ii)   *Cross-border transmission*

Considering the formerly isolated energy supply systems in member states, the strengthening of cross-border exchange in electricity is a focal point for the creation of a true trans-European energy market. In order to intensify cross-border competition the Electricity Directive has been supplemented by Regulation (EC) No 714/2009 (Electricity Regulation)[43] which also forms part of the 3rd Energy Package. The Electricity Regulation shall primarily augment transmission of electricity between states. For that reason, it establishes a common regulatory framework providing for, in particular, the cooperation of TSOs at Union level, a compensation mechanism for transfrontier flows of electricity and harmonised principles on transmission charges, on capacity allocation and on congestion management.[44]

Granting adequate transmission capacity and fair management of congestion constitute preconditions for an essential increase in cross-border flows of electricity. As a general principle in this context the Electricity Regulation

---

41 Cf art 17(1)(a), (d).
42 Cf art 20 Directive 2009/72/EC.
43 Regulation (EC) No 714/2009 of the European Parliament and of the Council of 13 July 2009 on conditions for access to the network for cross-border exchanges in electricity and repealing Regulation (EC) No 1228/2003 [2009] OJ L 211/15.
44 See art 1 Regulation (EC) No 714/2009.

determines that system operators must make available the maximum capacity of transnational interconnections and transmission networks affecting cross-border flows to market participants, under due regard of safety standards.[45] This means that system operators may not withhold capacity in relation to cross-border flows or refuse the transmission of electricity originating from other member states, respectively. This core concept is backed by the basic principle of congestion management saying that congestion problems have to be resolved on a non-discriminatory market-based manner.[46] To that extent, in the case of congestions, cross-border flows may not be treated less favourably than domestic flows. Further specifications as to capacity allocation and congestion management are set out in articles 15 and 16 of the Electricity Regulation. In addition to these provisions, Annex I of that regulation stipulates detailed guidelines on the management and allocation of transfer capacity of interconnections between national systems.

Carrying electricity across borders involves additional costs for TSOs. With a view to balancing out these additional expenses, article 13 of the Electricity Regulation introduces a compensation mechanism (Inter-Transmission System Operator Compensation (ITC)) which provides for payments to TSOs rendered by the so-called ITC Fund.[47] The ITC fund collects contributions made by system operators from which cross-border flows of electricity originate and system operators where these flows end. Guidelines on the ITC are laid down in the Commission Regulation (EU) No 838/2010.[48]

Basic principles on charges for network access follow from article 14 of the Electricity Regulation. Thus, access charges in particular must be transparent, non-discriminatory, take into account the need for network security, reflect actual costs and they must not be distance-related. Furthermore, when fixing these charges, among others, payments and receipts from the ITC fund have to be considered.

Cooperation between national TSOs is to take place within the so-called ENTSO-E, the European Network of Transmission System Operators for Electricity. ENTSO-E represents the successor of six regional TSO

---

45 Article 16(3) Regulation (EC) No 714/2009.
46 Article 16(1) Regulation (EC) No 714/2009.
47 See annex – part A of Commission Regulation (EU) No 838/2010 of 23 September 2010 on laying down guidelines relating to the inter-transmission system operator compensation mechanism and a common regulatory approach to transmission charging [2010] OJ L 250/5.
48 Commission Regulation (EU) No 838/2010 of 23 September 2010 on laying down guidelines relating to the inter-transmission system operator compensation mechanism and a common regulatory approach to transmission charging [2010] OJ L 250/5.

associations and is set up to facilitate the proper management, operation and technical evolution of the European electricity transmission network through cooperation. The remit of ENTSO-E, inter alia, comprises the elaboration of network codes, for instance, relating to network security, network interconnection rules and third-party access rules; working out non-binding EU-wide network development plans; and the adoption of recommendations as to the coordination of technical cooperation between EU and third-country TSOs. However, the founding of ENTSO-E does not detract from the fact that the Commission, which is assisted by the Electricity Cross-Border Committee assembling member states' representatives,[49] and the Agency for the Cooperation of Energy Regulators, have the leading role to play when carrying out the Electricity Regulation. ENTSO-E should also not be confused with the Electricity Regulatory Forum (the Florence Forum) that brings together stakeholders to discuss, among other topics, issues of cross-border electricity exchange and interconnection capacity.[50]

iii)   *Distribution: distribution system operators and unbundling at distribution level*

Whereas chapters IV and V of the Electricity Directive and the Electricity Regulation set out rules on the transmission of electricity, chapter VI of the Electricity Directive concerns the next link in the supply chain: the distribution of electricity. Chapter VI primarily addresses the issues of designation, tasks and the unbundling of distribution system operators, the so-called DSOs.

Definition, designation and tasks of DSOs: A distribution system operator (DSO) is a natural or legal person in charge of operating, maintaining and developing a distribution system in a certain region. The DSO also bears responsibility for the long-term ability of the system to satisfy reasonable demands for distributing electricity.[51] Distribution systems mainly consist of high-voltage, medium-voltage and low-voltage power lines which carry electricity from transmission systems towards consumers. However, under the Electricity Directive, distribution just means the transport of electricity and does not include its final supply to consumers.[52] DSOs must be designated by member states or by undertakings which are requested to do so by member states in conformity with article 24. The tasks of DSOs are set forth in article

---

49 See art 46 Electricity Directive (Directive 2009/72/EC) and art 23 Electricity Regulation (Regulation (EC) No 714/2009).

50 The Florence Forum is composed of representatives of the European Commission, Member States, national regulatory authorities, TSOs, network users, consumers etc.

51 Article 2(6) Directive 2009/72/EC.

52 Article 2(5) Directive 2009/72/EC.

25 including, in particular, the responsibility for operating a secure, reliable and efficient electricity distribution system in its area and ensuring access to users on a non-discriminatory basis.

Unbundling of DSOs – general remarks: The Electricity Directive also provides for the unbundling of DSOs.[53] In contrast to the unbundling requirements for TSOs, the Directive principally adheres to the regime of the previous 2nd Energy Directive.[54] Accordingly the requirements of legal and functional unbundling are fundamentally laid down in article 26 which stipulates that where the DSO is part of a vertically integrated undertaking, it must be independent at least in view of its legal form, organisation and decision-making from other activities not relating to distribution. Furthermore article 26 makes clear that the directive does not impose any obligation on the vertically integrated undertaking to separate ownership of assets of the DSO, meaning the grid in particular. Besides, DSOs also have to comply with the confidentiality obligations provided for in article 27 and the rules of accounting unbundling contained in article 31.

Legal unbundling of DSOs: Legal unbundling under article 26 means that a separate company must be created which accomplishes the task of electricity distribution. However, this obligation only covers the network business. The production of electricity and its supply to consumers can be further operated by a single company.[55]

Functional unbundling of DSOs: Article 26 also provides for minimum requirements for functional unbundling. 'Minimum requirements' means that member states may determine additional obligations to ensure effective unbundling. According to article 26, the DSO must be independent in terms of its organisation and decision-making from the other activities not related to distribution. This means that the management staff of the DSO may not participate in company structures of the integrated undertaking responsible for the day-to-day operation of the generation, transmission or supply of electricity. In addition, it must be ensured that the management of the DSO can act independently. Furthermore, the DSO must have effective decision-making rights, independent from the inte-

---

53 For details see also C Jones (ed.), *EU Energy Law: Volume I, The Internal Energy Market: The Third Liberalisation Package.*

54 In terms of the previous regime, see, for instance, Roggenkamp, Redgwell, del Guayo and Rønne, *Energy Law in Europe,* 343 et seq.

55 See European Commission, *Commission staff working paper,* Interpretative note on Directive 2009/72/EC concerning common rules for the internal market in electricity and Directive 2009/73/EC concerning common rules for the internal market in natural gas, the unbundling regime (22 January 2010), p 23.

grated electricity undertaking, in regard to assets required for operating, maintaining or developing the network. For this reason, the DSO shall be equipped with the necessary resources including human, technical, physical and financial resources. But this does not mean that the assets must belong to the DSO and that the parent company may not approve the annual financial plan of the DSO and set global limits on the levels of indebtedness.[56] However, it must be safeguarded that the parent company does not instruct the DSO in terms of the day-to-day business and decisions concerning the construction or upgrading of distribution lines that do not exceed the terms of the approved financial plan.[57] Finally, the DSO must draw up a compliance programme which shall ensure that the DSO as a whole, as well as its employees and management, operate in conformity with the principle of non-discrimination.[58]

Exemptions from legal and functional unbundling: Article 26(4) of the Electricity Directive provides for possible exceptions from the requirements above. Accordingly member states may abstain from the application of the provisions on legal and functional unbundling to undertakings serving less than 100,000 connected customers, or serving small isolated systems. Pursuant to article 2(26) a small isolated system is 'any system with consumption of less than 3000 GWh in the year 1996, where less than 5% of annual consumption is obtained through interconnection with other systems'.

iv)   *Accounts of electricity undertakings: accounting unbundling*

Article 31 of the Electricity Directive sets out rules on accounting unbundling that are applicable to all electricity undertakings. These provisions ultimately also aim at avoiding cross-subsidisation between transmission and distribution activities and the generation or supply of electricity. Under article 31 each electricity undertaking is obliged to keep separate accounts for each of its transmission and distribution activities. Article 31 defines the minimum unbundling requirements each network operator has to satisfy, meaning even DSOs which are exempted from legal and functional unbundling under article 26(4).[59]

---

56 Article 26(2)(c) Directive 2009/72/EC; European Commission, *Commission staff working paper*, ibid, p 25.
57 Article 26(2)(c) Directive 2009/72/EC.
58 Article 26(2)(d) Directive 2009/72/EC; European Commission, *Commission staff working paper*, ibid, p 26.
59 European Commission, *Commission staff working paper*, ibid, p 28.

v)   *Organisation of access to transmission and distribution systems*

Aside from the unbundling obligations at transmission and distribution levels, safeguarding non-discriminatory third-party access to the transmission and distribution networks represents one further building block of a fair internal energy market and is therefore also an essential element of the Electricity Directive.[60] In actual fact, third-party access could at least under certain circumstances be effected under EU competition law (the 'essential facilities doctrine').[61] The European Union, however, decided on detailed legislation as the way of EU competition law has proved to be too cumbersome and, therefore, not sufficient to cover the crucial issue of network access. Thus EU competition law only provides for a safety net in case the rules of the Electricity Directive fall short.[62]

Under article 32(1) of the Electricity Directive, member states are required to ensure the introduction of a system of third-party access to transmission and distribution systems on the basis of published tariffs. The system of third-party access shall apply to all eligible customers and must be implemented on objective criteria without discrimination between system users.[63] The tariffs, or the methodologies underlying their calculation, must be approved by the respective national regulatory authority and published prior to their entry into force. Certain exemptions may be granted to new direct current interconnectors in respect of tariff approval and regulation.[64] In case the transmission or distribution system operator does not dispose of the necessary capacity, it may refuse access to the network, specifying substantiated reasons for the refusal (see article 32(2)). Furthermore, the rejection must be grounded on objective and technically and economically justified criteria, which are to be consistently applied. The regulatory authorities must also make sure, where appropriate, that the system operator provides information on how to reinforce the network.

Ultimately, the rules of article 32(1) of the 3rd Electricity Directive as just mentioned confirm the exclusion of member states' leeway in deciding how

---

60 For details see also C Jones (ed.), *EU Energy Law: Volume I, The Internal Energy Market: The Third Liberalisation Package*, chapter 3; Johnston and Block, *EU Energy Law*, 73 et seq; Talus, *EU Energy Law and Policy – A Critical Account*, 70 et seq.

61 See section 2.2.2 above; ECJ Case C-7/97 *Bronner* [1998] ECR I-07791.

62 Cf M de Rijke, 'Third-party access: Implementing EU legislation' (08 November 2004) http://www.internationallawoffice.com/Newsletters/detail.aspx?g=dbc384ba-54af-4770-9083-6a1ed81e8fa1 accessed 3 May 2016.

63 Since 1 July 2007 'eligible customers' in terms of art 32 para 1 shall comprise all customers; see art 33 para 1.

64 Cf art 17 Regulation (EC) No 714/2009.

to generally organise third-party access. While the 1st Electricity Directive still allowed member states to choose between three different options, encompassing a negotiated access to networks (*ex post* control of network access charges), a regulated access to networks (*ex ante* regulation of network access charges) and a single buyer procedure, the 2nd Electricity Directive has already required member states to implement the second model (regulated access) as the only acceptable way to generally grant network access.[65] Ultimately, this determination has been carried over to the 3rd Electricity Directive. Apart from these general stipulations, some discretion on how to implement the regulated access model subject to the conditions of the Electricity Directive remains within the hands of member states.[66]

d)   *Supply*

The Electricity Directive attempts to rearrange the electricity markets by impinging on all segments of the supply chain. It does not only focus on questions related to the generation, transmission and distribution of electricity. Ultimately, it also aspires to trigger transformation at the level of electricity supply.[67] Respective rules are primarily designed to strengthen the position of customers. The key requirements as laid down in article 3 of the Electricity Directive have already been outlined above:[68] article 3(3) requires member states to guarantee that all private households are appropriately supplied with electricity, that is, enjoy universal service. Universal service particularly encompasses consumers' right to be supplied with electricity at reasonable, easily and clearly comparable, transparent and non-discriminatory prices. Besides, article 3(5) obliges member states to make sure that all customers have the right to freely choose their supplier and to change it within three weeks. Apart from that, the Electricity Directive in article 3(7) demands particular measures to protect vulnerable customers (for example, elderly and handicapped people) and customers in remote areas. As shown above, the Electricity Directive also presupposes that end-user prices are established by the operation of supply and demand only. Correspondingly, regulation of supply prices is, at least in general, prohibited. Ultimately, in terms of the protection of household customers member

---

65 For details, see von Danwitz, 'Regulation and liberalization of the European electricity market – A German view' 435 et seq and 438 et seq; A Johnston and G Block, *EU Energy Law*, 21 et seq.

66 See, for instance, European Commission, *Commission staff working paper*, Interpretative note on Directive 2009/72/EC concerning common rules for the internal market in electricity and Directive 2009/73/EC concerning common rules for the internal market in natural gas, the regulatory authorities (22 January 2010), p 14.

67 See also A Johnston and G Block, *EU Energy Law*, 198 et seq.

68 See section 4.1.1 a).

states have to make special provision particularly concerning minimum requirements for electricity supply contracts and the implementation of intelligent metering systems.[69]

Transparency of prices, terms and conditions applied in the market represents another prerequisite of effectively functioning energy markets, which article 3 of the Electricity Directive and some other provisions address. In the context of consumer protection, article 3 assigns a special role to transparency. Member states shall particularly guarantee that prices, terms and conditions and dispute settlement mechanisms are transparent.[70] Furthermore, pursuant to article 3 customers shall have the right to receive all relevant consumption data and electricity bills must contain a range of other specific information (for example, the fuel mix of the supplier).[71] As regards the transparency of prices charged to industrial end-users, Directive 2008/92/EC must also be taken into account. This directive, which also applies to the gas sector, requires electricity or gas suppliers to submit to Eurostat, the Statistical Office of the European Union, prices and terms of sale of electricity and gas to industrial end-users, the pricing systems, the breakdown of consumers and the corresponding volumes by category of consumption. Based on this data, Eurostat publishes biannually (in May and November) electricity and gas prices for industrial end-users and the used pricing systems.

The Electricity Directive and other legislative acts deal with further questions directly or indirectly concerning the level of electricity supply. This is, for instance, true for article 41 of the Electricity Directive focusing on the general functioning of retail markets and Directive 2005/89/EC pertaining to measures of security of supply. Both shall be subject to further consideration in the following subsections.

e)   Wholesale and retail markets

The liberalisation of European energy markets results in an increase in market players and energy-related transactions and, thus, in the creation of new, and the extension of existing, wholesale and retail markets. The European Union also sees a need to regulate and monitor these trading markets considering the fact that appropriate energy prices for household and industrial customers presuppose the proper and fair functioning of these markets. However, at European level the legislator is satisfied with rather broad provisions.

---

69 Article 3(7) sentence 7 in conjunction with annex I of the Electricity Directive.
70 See art 3(3) and (7) Electricity Directive.
71 See art 3(5) and (9) Electricity Directive.

As for wholesale markets, Regulation (EU) No 1227/2011 on wholesale energy market integrity and transparency (REMIT) represents the European Union's relevant legislation which seeks to prevent distortions of wholesale energy prices through market abuse.[72] The regulation covers all wholesale energy trading, meaning it pertains to supply and transportation contracts and derivatives in both the electricity sector and the gas sector. REMIT, which is as a regulation directly applicable in member states, explicitly prohibits insider trading (particularly the use of inside information when acquiring or disposing of wholesale energy products) and market manipulation.[73] With a view to creating transparency on the market and on the establishment of prices, it furthermore provides for several notification and disclosure requirements. Accordingly, market participants are obliged in particular to publish inside information, which may for instance relate to the capacity and use of facilities for production, storage, transmission or consumption of electricity.[74] Moreover, market participants need to register and report their wholesale energy market transactions, including orders to trade, and specifics on them, such as identity of the traded product, price and quantity.[75] The transparency requirements, for instance, also cover information concerning infrastructures, such as those related to capacity and use of facilities for production, storage, consumption or transmission of electricity or natural gas.[76] The competence to implement REMIT principally rests with the Agency for the Cooperation of Energy Regulators (ACER) and national regulatory authorities (NRAs). While the enforcement of the prohibitions on insider trading and market manipulation and of the obligation to publish inside information rests with NRAs, the ACER in particular assumes responsibilities for market monitoring and data collection.

As regards retail markets for electricity, article 41 of the Electricity Directive sets out some basic regulative requirements which are to contribute to the proper and transparent functioning of retail markets. Ultimately, article 41 aims at making access to networks easier for customers and suppliers. Against this background, the provision requires member states to safeguard

---

72 Regulation (EU) No 1227/2011 of the European Parliament and of the Council of 25 October 2011 on wholesale energy market integrity and transparency [2011] OJ L 326/1. For further details see, for instance, R Feltkamp, 'Insider trading and market manipulation in wholesale energy markets: The impact of REMIT' in B Delvaux, M Hunt and K Talus (eds), *EU Energy Law and Policy Issues, vol 4* (Intersentia 2014) 307 et seq; J Ratliff and R Grasso, *EU Energy Law: Volume X, Insider Trading and Market Manipulation in the European Wholesale Energy Markets – REMIT* (Claeys & Casteels Publishing 2015).

73 See arts 3(1) a and 5 REMIT.

74 See art 4 REMIT.

75 See art 8(1) REMIT.

76 See art 8(5) REMIT.

that retail markets are transparently structured, namely, that the responsibilities and roles of market participants, particularly those of TSOs, DSOs and supply undertakings, are clearly defined especially in terms of contractual arrangements, commitment to customers, data exchange and meter responsibility.

4.1.2 Security of supply and infrastructure investments

Back in 2006, power outages in the European Union and United States illustrated the susceptibility of present electricity supply systems to breakdown. These events made clear the vital necessity of enhancing the safety of the electricity supply by appropriate action and to expand electricity infrastructures, in particular. A range of legislative acts and political initiatives deal with the issue, be it acts or initiatives with special focus on the electricity sector or those with a scope covering various sectors.

Security of the electricity supply even represents one of the main objectives pursued in the Electricity Directive.[77] Ultimately, the efficient functioning of the internal electricity market, as aspired to by the Electricity Directive, represents a precondition for secure electricity supply throughout Europe.[78] However, the Electricity Directive does not only promote security of supply through its general focus but also in very specific terms, for instance, by allowing member states to impose on undertakings, in the general economic interest, public service obligations relating to security of supply[79] and by clearly putting TSOs and DSOs in charge of ensuring the long-term transmission and distribution capacity of systems.[80]

Further to the Electricity Directive, the European Union has adopted Directive 2005/89/EC which specifically addresses action to safeguard the security of electricity supply and infrastructure investment.[81] Directive 2005/89/EC establishes a rather broad framework for respective measures at member states' level. Accordingly, with a view to achieving a high level of security of supply, member states must clearly determine the roles and responsibilities of competent authorities and relevant market players (for example, electricity generators, TSOs and DSOs) and they have to ensure a stable investment climate, especially in relation to investments made by

---

77 In this context see also A Johnston and G Block, *EU Energy Law*, 259 et seq.
78 Cf recital 25 Directive 2009/72/EC.
79 Article 3(2) Directive 2009/72/EC.
80 Articles 12(a) and 25(1) Directive 2009/72/EC.
81 Directive 2005/89/EC of the European Parliament and of the Council of 18 January 2006 concerning measures to safeguard security of electricity supply and infrastructure investment [2006] OJ L 33/22.

TSOs and DSOs.[82] When implementing these general obligations, member states must especially consider the importance of safeguarding the continuity of supplies and ensuring sufficient transmission and generation reserve capacity.[83] A range of other issues have to be taken into account when adopting any security-related measure, such as the requirements of the internal market, the impact of measures on electricity prices for consumers and the importance of promotion of renewable energy sources.[84] Furthermore, member states' action may not be discriminatory or place an unreasonable burden on market players. As regards operational network security in particular, TSOs shall be required to set the minimum operational rules and obligations on network security.

Numerous other EU initiatives with cross-sector focus affect security of supply and infrastructure investments in the electricity sector. For an overview, see the respective remarks in Chapter 5 (sections 5.5 and 5.6) and Chapter 6.

4.1.3 Regulation and monitoring of the market

Responsibilities as to the regulation and monitoring of the European electricity market are mainly divided between the Commission, national regulatory agencies and the Agency for the Cooperation of Energy Regulators (ACER).[85] As the guardian of EU law, the Commission is generally responsible for monitoring and ensuring the application of legislation creating and guaranteeing the common electricity market. Thus the Commission assumes overall responsibility for observing the implementation of common market rules. Apart from that, individual pieces of legislation, such as the Electricity Directive and the Electricity Regulation, also allocate other specific powers to the Commission. Thus, the Commission may, inter alia, adopt guidelines relating to the cross-border transmission of electricity and it determines the amounts of compensation payments payable to TSOs hosting cross-border flows.[86]

Member states remain responsible for implementing the common market rules on their territory. As regards regulatory tasks, the Electricity Directive

---

82 Cf recital 15 and art 3(1) Directive 2005/89/EC.
83 Article 3(2) Directive 2005/89/EC.
84 Article 3(2), (4) and (5) Directive 2005/89/EC.
85 As to the roles of NRAs and ACER see also M Simm, 'The interface between energy, environment and competition rules of the European Union' (Institutional Report to the FIDE Congress 2012) pp 4 et seq http://www.fide2012.eu/General+and+EU+Reports/id/217/ accessed 3 May 2016.
86 See arts 18 and 13(4) Regulation (EC) No 714/2009.

requires member states to designate a single National Regulatory Authority (NRA).[87] NRAs must work independently, meaning without receiving governmental instructions. They have to be entrusted with all regulatory tasks specified in the Electricity Directive, which does not allow for the splitting of duties between NRA and national ministries.[88] Accordingly, NRAs are especially in charge of fixing or approving transmission or distribution tariffs or the methodologies underlying their calculation. They shall also ensure that electricity undertakings comply with their obligations under the Electricity Directive and that there are no cross-subsidies between transmission, distribution and supply activities. Furthermore, NRAs have to monitor investment plans of TSOs, compliance with network security and reliability rules, levels of transparency, and the effectiveness of market opening and competition on wholesale and retail markets. NRAs may also be entrusted with the monitoring of issues relating to security of supply.[89] Individual legislative acts allocate further tasks to NRAs, which cannot be listed here. Accordingly, NRAs should, for instance, ensure compliance with the Electricity Regulation and the Wholesale Market Regulation and they should contribute to promoting efficiency in the supply of electricity and gas pursuant to the Energy Efficiency Directive.[90]

The 3rd Energy Package has also provided for the creation of ACER.[91] ACER has been established as the EU agency to assist National Regulatory Authorities and to coordinate their action.[92] The remit of ACER also comprises the monitoring of the two European Networks of TSOs (ENTSO-Electricity and ENTSO-Gas), the observance of energy market developments and the participation in the establishment of network codes. Moreover, it may take binding decisions on terms and conditions for access to and operational security of cross-border infrastructure where national regulators are not able to reach an agreement.[93] ACER was established in 2009 with its head office in Ljubljana, Slovenia and continues the work of the European Regulators' Group for Electricity and Gas (ERGEG). ACER

---

87 For details see also Jones (ed.), *EU Energy Law: Volume I, The Internal Energy Market: The Third Liberalisation Package*, chapter 6.

88 See European Commission, *Commission staff working paper*, Interpretative note on Directive 2009/72/EC concerning common rules for the internal market in electricity and Directive 2009/73/EC concerning common rules for the internal market in natural gas, the regulatory authorities (22 January 2010).

89 Article 4 Directive 2009/72/EC.

90 See recital 25 of Regulation (EC) No 714/2009, recital 26 of Regulation (EU) No 1227/2011 and art 15 Directive 2012/27/EU.

91 See Regulation (EC) No 713/2009 of the European Parliament and of the Council of 13 July 2009 establishing an Agency for the Cooperation of Energy Regulators [2009] OJ L 211/1.

92 See art 1(2) Regulation (EC) No 713/2009.

93 See art 7(7) and 8 Regulation (EC) No 713/2009.

must be distinguished from the Council of European Energy Regulators (CEER). The CEER constitutes a voluntary association of national regulators, which used to be a preparatory body for the advisory body ERGEG and is now primarily engaged in issues falling outside the remit of ACER (for example, international energy issues).

4.2 The gas sector

On top of its efforts in the electricity sector, the European Union has been particularly engaged in past decades to induce an ever-closer integration of the European gas market. Developments in the gas sector have also taken place gradually in the wake of the implementation of the three generations of legislative energy packages.[94] As compared with the legal framework applicable to the electricity sector, the body of legislative acts governing the gas sector features the same complexity and, in parts, even provides for similar provisions. Present key legislation is tied up in the 3rd Energy Package and comprises the Gas Directive,[95] the Gas Regulation[96] and the ACER Regulation.[97] These three legislative acts have been accompanied with several other acts, including especially Directive 2008/92/EC introducing transparency rules relating to prices charged to industrial end-users, Regulation (EU) No 994/2010 concerning security of gas supply, the Wholesale Market Regulation (EU) No 1227/2011 (REMIT) and the Hydrocarbons Licensing Directive 94/22/EC laying down rules on authorisations for the prospection, exploration and production of hydrocarbons.

As is true for the electricity sector, legislation pertinent to the gas sector mainly provides for rules fostering the common market, ensuring security of supply and enhancing the cooperation of national energy regulators.

---

94 See, in particular, Directive 98/30/EC concerning common rules for the internal market in natural gas (part of 1st package); Directive 2003/55/EC concerning common rules for the internal market in natural gas and repealing Directive 98/30/EC, Regulation (EC) No 1775/05 on conditions for access to the natural gas transmission network (part of 2nd package); Directive 2009/73/EC concerning common rules for the internal market in natural gas and repealing Directive 2003/55/EC, Regulation (EC) No 715/2009 on conditions for access to the natural gas transmission networks and repealing Regulation (EC) No 1775/2005 and Regulation (EC) No 713/2009 establishing an Agency for the Cooperation of Energy Regulators (all part of 3rd package).

95 Directive 2009/73/EC concerning common rules for the internal market in natural gas and repealing Directive 2003/55/EC [2009] OJ L 211/94.

96 Regulation (EC) No 715/2009 of the European Parliament and of the Council of 13 July 2009 on conditions for access to the natural gas transmission networks and repealing Regulation (EC) No 1775/2005 [2009] OJ L 211/36.

97 Regulation (EC) No 713/2009 of the European Parliament and of the Council of 13 July 2009 establishing an Agency for the Cooperation of Energy Regulators [2009] OJ L 211/1.

4.2.1 Common market rules

EU legislation particularly concentrates on safeguarding the internal gas market by laying down more or less specific rules as to the production, transmission, storage, distribution, supply and trade of gas. The latest Gas Directive (Directive 2009/73/EC), which applies to natural gas, including liquefied natural gas (LNG), but also to other types of gas (for example, biogas and gas from biomass) represents the central plank among pertinent legislative acts as regards the establishment, organisation and preservation of the internal gas market. As is the case with the Electricity Directive in the electricity sector, the Gas Directive builds on several tools, including specifically the general ban on end-user price regulation; an unbundling regime; an arrangement for third-party access to transmission and distribution networks; an *ex ante* regulation of transmission and distribution tariffs; and the right of customers to freely change their gas supplier.

a) *General rules for the organisation of the gas sector*

First, the Gas Directive sets out in articles 3 to 8 essential rules for the organisation of the gas sector. Accordingly member states are to generally ensure the creation of a competitive, secure and environmentally sustainable gas market where no discrimination between undertakings takes place. In order to induce or foster specific developments, article 3(2) allows member states to impose on gas companies public service obligations comparable to those provided for in the electricity sector. Such obligations may be used, for instance, to safeguard security of supply, ensure a certain quality of supplies and promote energy efficiency.

Furthermore, article 3 requires member states to introduce a high level of customer protection, whereas special safeguard measures must be taken in terms of vulnerable customers, such as final customers in remote areas who are connected to the system. Apart from that, the Gas Directive entitles customers to freely choose their gas supplier, to change their supplier easily within three weeks and to receive all relevant consumption data.[98]

In its *Federutility Judgement*, the European Court of Justice has also made clear that the Gas Directive is based on the assumption that end-user prices shall be determined by the operation of supply and demand only.[99] Accordingly, the Court of Justice has confirmed that at least in general the regulation of

---

98 See art 3 para 3 and 6 Gas Directive (Directive 2009/73/EC).
99 ECJ, Case C-265/08 *Federutility* [2010] ECR I-03377, para 18.

supply prices is prohibited at national level, even though exemptions from that principle may appear conceivable with reference to article 3(2) of the Gas Directive.[100]

Articles 4 to 8 of the Gas Directive contain a range of further rather general requirements that member states must meet. Article 4, for example, lays down principles that member states have to comply with when authorising the construction or operation of natural gas facilities. Article 6 provides for member states' cooperation in terms of security of supply, especially in emergency situations. Furthermore article 8 obliges member states to ensure the determination of technical safety criteria and technical rules defining minimum requirements for the connection to the system of LNG and storage facilities and gas lines.

b) Gas production

In terms of gas production, the so-called Hydrocarbons Licensing Directive must be taken into account.[101] It specifies general conditions for issuing und using licenses as to the prospection, exploration and production of hydrocarbons. The Directive covers not only the gas sector, but also other energy sectors and will therefore be outlined below in Chapter 5 (section 5.1.2).

c) Transmission, storage, LNG and distribution

Both the Gas Directive and the Gas Regulation cover various other issues concerning individual links of the gas supply chain, whereas the rules provided leave member states quite different room for manoeuvre.

Transmission system operators: As regards the transmission of gas, the Gas Directive defines the procedure of certification of transmission system operators (TSOs), which must be conducted before their official designation.[102] Besides, article 11 establishes special provisions for third-country system owners and third-country system operators seeking certification as a TSO. Once TSOs are designated as such they occupy a key position within the supply chain. In order to make sure that TSOs fulfil their role, article 13 allocates certain responsibilities to TSOs. Accordingly, transmission system operators are primarily in charge of operating, maintaining and developing

---

100 ECJ, ibid, paras 21 and 25.
101 Directive 94/22/EC of 30 May 1994 on the conditions for granting and using authorisations for the prospection, exploration and production of hydrocarbons [1994] OJ L 164/3.
102 Article 10 Gas Directive (Directive 2009/73/EC).

transmission systems. While doing so they must particularly ensure that systems work securely, reliably and efficiently and that no discrimination takes place between system users.

Storage and LNG system operators: The Gas Directive also requires member states to arrange the appointment of one or more storage and LNG system operators (article 12 Gas Directive). Storage and LNG system operators have to discharge statutory tasks, which are similar to those of TSOs. They bear, in particular, responsibility for operating, maintaining and developing their facilities for the benefit of a secure and open market. Furthermore, they have to provide such information to other system providers and to system users that the interconnected system may function well and may be used efficiently.

Unbundling at transmission level: Gas undertakings are subject to an unbundling regime comparable to that applicable to electricity undertakings. Accordingly, the Gas Directive also distinguishes between three models of structural separation of network operation from production and supply activities:[103]

- Ownership unbundling (article 9 Gas Directive);
- Independent system operator (ISO) (article 14 Gas Directive);
- Independent transmission operator (ITO) (Chapter IV Gas Directive).

Under article 9 of the Gas Directive, member states have to transpose into national law the rules on the unbundling of transmission systems and TSOs.[104] However, in cases where on 3 September 2009, the transmission system already belonged to a vertically integrated undertaking a member state is free to opt for the ISO model or the ITO model.[105] Major new gas infrastructure, such as interconnectors, LNG and storage facilities, may under certain conditions apply for an exemption from the requirements of article 9 of the Gas Directive (see article 36 Gas Directive). Derogations from article 9 may also be considered in cases of emergent and isolated markets (cf article 49 Gas Directive). For further details pertaining to the applicable

---

103 See also European Commission, *Commission staff working paper*, Interpretative note on Directive 2009/72/EC concerning common rules for the internal market in electricity and Directive 2009/73/EC concerning common rules for the internal market in natural gas, the unbundling regime (22 January 2010). For details see also Jones (ed.), *EU Energy Law: Volume I, The Internal Energy Market: The Third Liberalisation Package*, chapter 4; Johnston and Block, *EU Energy Law*, 38 et seq.

104 See also European Commission, *Commission staff working paper*, ibid, p 5.

105 See art 9(8) Gas Directive (Directive 2009/73/EC). The meaning of 'vertically integrated undertaking' is defined in art 2 para 20 Gas Directive.

unbundling regime see above section 4.1.1 c) i) regarding unbundling in the electricity sector and articles 9, 14,15, 16 and 31 as well as chapter IV of the Gas Directive.

Distribution system operators and unbundling at distribution level: Pursuant to article 24 of the Gas Directive, member states have to ensure the designation of one or more distribution system operators (DSOs). The statutory tasks of DSOs result from article 25. The Gas Directive also provides for an unbundling regime for DSOs which is comparable to that applicable in the electricity sector (see article 26 and section 4.1.1 c) iii) above). Accordingly, DSOs are not subject to ownership unbundling, but they are governed by requirements of legal and functional unbundling. Thus, DSOs which are part of a vertically integrated undertaking have to be independent in terms of their legal form, organisation and decision-making.[106] However, member states may exclude smaller gas companies from the application of these obligations as long as gas undertakings serve less than 100,000 connected customers.[107] Apart from the obligation of legal and functional unbundling, DSOs must also comply with the confidentiality requirements set out in article 27 and the rules of accounting unbundling laid down in article 31.

Organisation of Access to Transmission and Distribution Systems: Third-party access to transmission and distributions systems is primarily governed by chapter VII of the Gas Directive and by the Gas Regulation.[108] The Gas Directive defines member states' general duty to ensure the introduction and maintenance of a system of third-party access to transmission and distribution systems and LNG facilities (see article 32). Under the respective scheme customers must be granted access on the basis of published tariffs under the application of objective criteria and without any discrimination. The tariffs, or the methodologies underlying their calculation, require approval by the regulator and must be published before entering into force. In other words, as regards access to transmission and distributions systems the European legislator has also opted for the model of regulated access and, therefore, for an *ex ante* regulation of network access charges or the methods of their calculation. Article 32 also stipulates the possibility of TSOs to gain access to the system of other TSOs if necessary, for instance, in relation to cross-border transmission.

---

106 For details, see above section 4.1.1 c) iii); European Commission, *Commission staff working paper*, ibid, pp 23 et seq.

107 See article 26 para 4 Gas Directive (Directive 2009/73/EC).

108 For details see also C Jones (ed.), *EU Energy Law: Volume I, The Internal Energy Market: The Third Liberalisation Package* (3rd edn, Claeys & Casteels Publishing 2010) chapters 3 and 9.

In terms of access to storage facilities and line pack, member states may still choose between two different models of access regimes: negotiated access (*ex post* regulation) and regulated access (*ex ante* regulation).[109] Member states may also implement both of them. However, they must make sure that these procedures apply objectively, transparently and without discrimination. Differently treated is also the access to upstream pipeline networks, in terms of which member states must at least comply with the provisions of article 34 of the Gas Directive.

Natural gas undertakings are allowed to refuse access to the system if they lack sufficient capacity or if third-party access would compromise the performance of their public service obligations.[110] A refusal of access may furthermore be considered in case of serious economic and financial difficulties with take-or-pay contracts.[111] Ultimately, an exemption from the said provisions may be granted upon application in regard of major new gas infrastructure.[112]

In terms of access to natural gas transmission networks the provisions of the Gas Directive are complemented by Regulation (EC) No 715/2009 (Gas Regulation).[113] The Gas Regulation is another component of the 3rd Energy Package and originates in the previous Regulation (EC) No 1775/2005 and the Guidelines for Good Practice adopted by the European Gas Regulatory Forum (the Madrid Forum).

The aim of the Gas Regulation is to set fair rules for access conditions to natural gas transmission systems, LNG facilities and storage facilities. Moreover, the regulation aims at developing a well-functioning wholesale market and harmonising the network access rules for cross-border exchanges in gas. The regulation includes in particular further harmonised principles for tariffs, or the methodologies underlying their calculation, for network access (article 13), rules on third-party access services (articles 14 and 15), principles of capacity-allocation mechanisms and congestion-management procedures (articles 16 and 17), transparency requirements (articles 18 and 19), principles for balancing rules and imbalance charges (article 20), and principles for trading of capacity rights (article 22).

---

109 See art 33 Gas Directive (Directive 2009/73/EC).
110 See art 35 Gas Directive.
111 See arts 35 and 48 Gas Directive.
112 See art 36 Gas Directive.
113 Regulation (EC) No 715/2009 of the European Parliament and of the Council of 13 July 2009 on conditions for access to the natural gas transmission networks and repealing Regulation (EC) No 1775/2005 [2009] OJ L 211/36.

Besides, a principle objective of the regulation has also been to initiate the establishment of the 'European Network of Transmission System Operators for Gas' (ENTSOG or ENTSO for Gas) as a platform of cooperation and coordination among TSOs at EU level.

As the ENTSO-E in the electricity sector, the ENTSOG is particularly responsible for the elaboration of:

- network codes;
- common network operation tools;
- a non-binding EU-wide ten-year network development plan;
- recommendations relating to the coordination of technical cooperation between EU and third-country TSOs.

d) *Supply and wholesale and retail markets*

As is true for the electricity sector, EU gas legislation is spread over a range of further issues regarding, among others, the supply of gas and the regulation of wholesale and retail markets. Ultimately provisions related to the gas sector compare, in part, with those applicable to the electricity sector. For instance, this pertains to the general prohibition of end-user price regulation[114] and to the right of customers to freely choose their gas supplier, to change supplier within three weeks and to receive all relevant consumption data.[115] Household customers are also specifically protected through a range of further precautionary measures, such as the definition of specific minimum requirements for supply contracts and the implementation of intelligent metering systems.[116] In terms of gas supplies to industrial end-users, Directive 2008/92/EC applies as well. As outlined above, Directive 2008/92/EC defines a specific procedure to establish the transparency of industrial gas prices.[117]

Fair pricing on gas wholesale markets ought likewise to be ensured by Regulation 1227/2011, which is meant to prevent distortions of wholesale prices through abusive practises, such as insider trading.[118] Ultimately, article 45 of the Gas Directive stipulates some basic rules designed to foster the proper functioning of retail markets. Corresponding requirements are

---

114 See European Court of Justice, Case C-265/08 *Federutility* [2010] ECR I-03377.

115 See art 3(3) and (6) Gas Directive (Directive 2009/73/EC). See also section 4.2.1 a) above.

116 See art 3(3) sentence 7 in conjunction with annex I of the Gas Directive.

117 See section 4.1.1 d) above.

118 Regulation (EU) No 1227/2011 of the European Parliament and of the Council of 25 October 2011 on wholesale energy market integrity and transparency [2011] OJ L 326/1.

comparable to those set out in article 41 of the Electricity Directive and aim at making transparent the structuring of retail markets.[119]

4.2.2 Security of supply

Security of continuous supply is also of outstanding importance in the gas sector. The issue became abundantly clear in 2009 in face of the Russian-Ukrainian gas row and the resulting difficulties in getting gas to Eastern Europe. In 2010 the European Union introduced new rules to enable the European Union to prevent and respond to gas supply disruptions, which are laid down in Regulation (EU) No 994/2010.[120] Measures provided for in this Regulation have been supported by the European Energy Programme for Recovery, which sets out particularly to improve gas infrastructure.

Regulation (EU) No 994/2010 contains provisions concerning the following issues in particular:[121]

- responsibilities for ensuring security of supply;
- establishment and content of preventive action and emergency plans;
- infrastructure standard;
- bi-directional capacity;
- supply standard;
- risk assessment;
- EU-wide and regional emergency responses.

Coordination of measures relating to security of supply are to be enhanced by the Gas Coordination Group.[122] The Coordination Group, which is presided over by the Commission, assembles member states' officials and representatives of ACER, ENTSOG, the industry and of concerned consumers. The Group acts primarily as an advisory body to the Commission in terms of issues concerning security of supply, particularly in emergency situations, but also in respect of the assessment of preventive action and emergency plans, for example.

In addition to Regulation (EU) No 994/2010, a range of other legislative acts and initiatives serve the issue of security of gas supply. This is particularly

---

119 See also section 4.1.1 e) above.
120 Regulation (EU) No 994/2010 of 20 October 2010 concerning measures to safeguard security of gas supply and repealing Council Directive 2004/67/EC [2010] OJ L 295/1.
121 For further details see A Johnston and G Block, *EU Energy Law*, 269 et seq.
122 See art 12 Regulation (EU) No 994/2010.

true for the Gas Directive, which provides the general basis for a common gas market and therefore for an EU-wide enhancement of gas supply. But a number of cross-sector initiatives coming under internal or external EU policy also foster security of supply (see in this regard chapter 5 sections 5.5 and 5.6 and chapter 6 below).

4.2.3   Regulation and monitoring of the market

Similar to the electricity sector, responsibilities as to the regulation and monitoring of the gas market are mainly split between the Commission, national regulatory agencies (NRAs) and the Agency for the Cooperation of Energy Regulators (ACER).[123] The Commission generally oversees the proper implementation of internal market legislation throughout the European Union and observes its impact on the short, medium and long-term evolution of the market. Apart from that, secondary law assigns very specific tasks and powers to the Commission, for instance, the adoption of guidelines in the context of access to transmission networks[124] or of guidelines for regional cooperation.[125]

Member states are obliged to transpose and execute EU gas legislation. The Gas Directive obliges member states to entrust a National Regulatory Agency (NRA) with the discharge of regulatory tasks as provided for under EU legislation.[126] NRAs must function independently, that is, especially without governmental influence. According to EU gas legislation, especially the Gas Directive and the Gas Regulation, NRAs are to undertake a range of duties. They are, for example, concerned with fixing or approving transmission and distribution tariffs or methodologies underlying their calculation, with the prevention of untoward cross-subsidies, for example, between transmission and supply activities, and with the monitoring of investment plans of TSOs.[127] Member states may even assign their obligation to monitor security of supply to NRAs.[128]

The Agency for the Cooperation of Energy Regulators (ACER) represents another player in the gas sector. Its role has already been outlined above in the context of the electricity market (see section 4.1.3). ACER's ambit particularly consists in the assistance of NRAs at Community level and, if

---

123   For details see also C Jones (ed.), *EU Energy Law: Volume I, The Internal Energy Market: The Third Liberalisation Package*, chapters 6 and 7.
124   See art 23 Regulation (EC) No 715/2009.
125   See art 6(4) Directive 2009/73/EC.
126   Article 39 Directive 2009/73/EC.
127   Article 41 Directive 2009/73/EC.
128   Article 5 Directive 2009/73/EC.

necessary, in the coordination of their action.[129] Apart from that, ACER shall, for instance, also monitor the execution of particular tasks by ENTSOG[130] or deliver opinions on specified issues.[131]

In addition to the Commission, NRAs and ACER, several other entities are dedicated to developments in the gas branch, such as ENTSOG (see section 4.2.1 c) above), the Gas Coordination Group (see section 4.2.2 above), the Gas Committee, the Madrid Forum and the Berlin Forum. The Gas Committee assembles representatives of the member states and serves as an assisting entity to the Commission as provided for in both the Gas Directive and the Gas Regulation.[132] The Madrid Forum constitutes a platform to discuss questions regarding the evolution of the internal gas market, especially as to cross-border trade. The Madrid Forum brings together representatives of the Commission, member states, NRAs, TSOs, gas suppliers, consumers and of other stakeholders. The Berlin Forum (Fossil Fuels Forum) also consists of representatives of member states and stakeholders, and it represents another working group to assist the European Commission in the coal, gas and oil sectors. It is especially committed to issues of fossil fuels in the context of climate change and security of supply.

4.3 The oil sector

Due to the tremendous need for oil in the production of fuel, petrochemicals and electricity, the long-term security of the oil supply is of central importance to member states. The lack of large domestic oil reserves in many member states, the continuously growing oil demand and the necessity of reasonable oil prices, confront national governments with huge challenges, which, at least in part, can be met more effectively through action on a pan-European scale. Hence EU energy policy also comprises the oil sector, although existing legislation is far from being as complex as in the electricity and gas sectors.

4.3.1 Common market rules

The internal European oil market is based essentially on EU primary law, meaning the treaty rules contained in the TFEU (see Chapter 2 above).

---

129 Article 1(2) Regulation (EC) No 713/2009.
130 Article 9(1) Regulation (EC) No 715/2009.
131 See, e.g., art 43(1) Gas Directive (Directive 2009/73/EC).
132 See art 51 Gas Directive (Directive 2009/73/EC) and art 28 Gas Regulation (Regulation (EC) No 715/2009).

Primary law guarantees that oil and related services can freely move across borders and it seeks to provide against market distortions through cartels, incumbent suppliers, state aid or unequal taxation. Secondary law establishing and forming the oil market is confined to a rather small number of acts which, for the most part, do not solely cover the oil sector, but also other energy sectors.[133]

Exploration and production: Prospection, exploration and production of oil requires governmental authorisation which may be used to keep foreign businesses away from exploiting domestic deposits. The exclusion of foreign companies contradicts the concept of the internal market, but may, however, be deemed necessary due to national security concerns. Against this background, the European Union has adopted Directive 94/22/EC which at least in principle is aimed at avoiding discrimination and making licensing procedures transparent, even though it continues to allow for constraints in some respects, including national security concerns. See section 5.1.2 below.

When faced with the explosion of the Deepwater Horizon drilling rig in the Gulf of Mexico in April 2010 and the subsequent environmental disaster, the European Commission screened existing European and national rules applicable to oil platforms and came to the conclusion that a common and more coherent framework is needed to ensure the highest safeguard standards for European oil rigs.[134] Based on the Commission's initiative, in 2013 the European legislature adopted Directive 2013/30/EU on the safety of offshore oil and gas operations.[135] Among other issues, the Directive lays down standards and requirements relating to risk management, the granting of licenses, liability for environmental damage, the appointment and functioning of national regulatory authorities, the provision of assistance by the European Maritime Safety Agency (EMSA), cooperation between member states, transparency, internal and external emergency response plans, emergency preparedness and actual emergency response.

---

133 For instance, Directive 2004/17/EC of the European Parliament and of the Council of 31 March 2004 coordinating the procurement procedures of entities operating in the water, energy, transport and postal services sectors [2004] OJ L 134/1; and Directive 94/22/EC of the European Parliament and of the Council of 30 May 1994 on the conditions for granting and using authorizations for the prospection, exploration and production of hydrocarbons [1994] OJ L 164/3.

134 See European Commission, 'Offshore oil drilling: European Commission envisages EU safety rules' (press release of 13 October 2010, IP/10/1324).

135 Directive 2013/30/EU of the European Parliament and of the Council of 12 June 2013 on safety of offshore oil and gas operations and amending Directive 2004/35/EC Text with EEA relevance [2013] OJ L 178/66.

Market observation: A basic prerequisite for both the fair functioning of the internal market and security of supply consists in the transparency of the factors governing the oil business. With a view to informing about prevailing key conditions, the Commission regularly publishes an oil bulletin and summaries of oil stocks data. The oil bulletin, in particular, exhibits trends of crude oil supply costs, consumer prices of petroleum products as well as duties and taxes levied in member states.[136]

As a net importer of oil, the European Union attaches special importance to information regarding crude oil imports from third-countries and crude oil deliveries from other member states. Undertakings receiving such a shipment must provide information on its characteristics (for example, quantity in barrels, cif price paid per barrel).[137] Data is collected by member states and forwarded to the Commission which prepares an overview on prevailing conditions for imports and deliveries. Based on the collected data, the Commission publishes summaries of general information regarding imports and deliveries. However, details remain confidential and are shared with member states only.

4.3.2 Security of supply

Oil continues to be one of the key carriers of energy and major crude materials in the world considering its central importance for transport and the petrochemical industry. As EU members do not dispose of sufficient domestic oil resources and, therefore, resort to imports from third countries, mainly from post-Soviet States, the Middle East and Africa, an elaborated security of supply policy takes on special significance. With a view to encountering possible supply shortages due to conceivable disturbances in those regions or oil crises, the European Community already began to create an oil stocking system back in 1968. Based on Council Directive 68/414/EEC, the applicable legislation in those times, member states have built up emergency stocks which, however, differed from each other especially in terms of the entities responsible for stockholding.

In order to enhance national stocking systems and make them more convergent with each other and with the one established by the International

---

136 See overview on Commission website https://ec.europa.eu/energy/en/statistics, accessed 3 May 2016. Data collection is based on Council Decision 1999/280/EC regarding a Community procedure for information and consultation on crude oil supply costs and the consumer prices of petroleum products; and Commission Decision 1999/566/EC of 26 July 1999 implementing Council Decision 1999/280/EC.

137 Cf Council Regulation (EC) No 2964/95 of 20 December 1995 introducing registration for crude oil imports and deliveries in the Community.

Energy Agency, the original Directive has been extended and revised several times. Current requirements as to the maintenance of minimum stocks of crude oil and petroleum products arise from Directive 2009/119/EC.[138]

Accordingly, member states have to ensure the stockpiling of an emergency reserve which, at least, corresponds to 90 days of average daily net imports or 61 days of average daily inland consumption, whichever of these two quantities is higher.[139] Member states shall make sure that these stocks are at all times available and physically accessible and that relevant information, especially on the location of stocks, contained quantities and their owners are conveyed to the Commission.[140] Member states may also put in place specific oil stocks for storing ethane, LPG, aviation gasoline, diesel oil or other petroleum products. Specific stocks must be calculated in terms of the number of days of consumption and have to be owned by the respective member state or the central stockholding entity set up by it.[141] Such a central stockholding entity (CSE) may be established by a member state in the European Union for the purpose of acquiring, maintaining or selling both kinds of stocks, emergency stocks and specific stocks.[142]

With a view to ascertaining that oil stocks may indeed be deployed in the event of a major supply disruption, member states must ultimately elaborate emergency procedures allowing them to put emergency and specific reserves into circulation if necessary.

4.4 The coal sector

Coal represents another major carrier of energy throughout the European Union. Some 30% of European power generation is based on coal burning, making it still an indispensable source of energy.[143] In consequence, the European Union lies third among the world's largest consumers of coal, after China and the United States. However, coal-based power generation is hotly disputed within the European Union. Coal burning remains one of the largest contributors to the man-made increase in carbon dioxide and, thus, puts the

---

138 Council Directive 2009/119/EC of 14 September 2009 imposing an obligation on Member States to maintain minimum stocks of crude oil and/or petroleum products [2009] OJ L 265/9. As regards the history of pertinent legislation, see A Johnston and G Block, *EU Energy Law*, 253 et seq.

139 Article 3 Directive 2009/119/EC.

140 European Commission, MEMO/08/697 of 13 November 2008.

141 Article 9 Directive 2009/119/EC.

142 Article 7 Directive 2009/119/EC.

143 European Commission, *Commission staff working document, The Market for Solid Fuels in the Community in 2008 and Estimates for 2009* (SEC(2010) 996 final), p 8.

achievement of the European Union's greenhouse gas emissions reduction targets at risk. On the other hand, a number of member states rely on coal in light of their intention to reduce dependencies on oil and gas and to phase out nuclear power generation.

Against this backdrop, it becomes clear that both EU climate and environmental policy and EU energy policy have a focus on coal consumption, and the corresponding goals and instruments need proper harmonisation. Whereas climate and environmental policy aims at reducing the adverse environmental impacts of coal consumption, energy policy is, inter alia, concerned with safeguarding the functioning of the internal energy market and energy supply with recourse to coal. Measures and strategies related to the protection of climate and the environment encompass, for example, the EU Emission Trading Scheme (EU ETS) and the facilitation of clean coal technologies (CCT) and carbon capture and storage (CCS) and will be further outlined in Chapter 5 below.[144]

The common coal market is primarily safeguarded by the rules of the TFEU. Its provisions apply fully in the coal sector after the expiration of the European Coal and Steel Community Treaty (ECSC Treaty). Accordingly, coal, meaning hard coal and lignite in particular, and related services may freely cross internal EU borders under the terms of the free movement of goods and service principles (see Chapter 2 above). Furthermore, corporate transactions and governmental action in the coal sector are subject to the treaty law on competition, especially the provisions on cartels and the abuse of dominant positions.

State aid in the coal sector is a topic of particular sensitivity, especially in Germany, Poland and Spain.[145] In order to maintain a high level of energy self-sufficiency and to avoid the social impacts of mine-closures, some member states remain keen on granting state aid even to loss-making hard coal mines. Until the end of 2010, state aid to the coal industry was considered as compatible with EU competition law under the conditions of Council Regulation (EC) No 1407/2002.[146] This regulation ultimately led to a gradual reduction in production aid granted to coal businesses.[147] In

---

144 See sections 5.3 und 5.6.

145 See Council Regulation (EC) No 1407/2002 of 23 July 2002 on State aid to the coal industry, recitals 2 et seq; European Commission, *Commission staff working document, The Market for Solid Fuels in the Community in 2008 and Estimates for 2009* (SEC(2010) 996 final), pp 49 et seq.

146 Council Regulation (EC) No 1407/2002 of 23 July 2002 on State aid to the coal industry.

147 European Commission, *Commission staff working document, The Market for Solid Fuels in the Community in 2008 and Estimates for 2009* (SEC(2010) 996 final), p 49; European Commission, 'State aid: Commission

2010 the Commission presented a proposal for a new Council Regulation to end operating aid to uncompetitive hard coal mines. However, following criticism from Germany, the Council ultimately decided to extend the period of simplified aid allocation.[148] Accordingly, member states may under certain conditions continue to grant subsidies meant to cover production losses, provided that the production unit concerned is closed by the end of 2018 at the latest. Apart from that, in order to mitigate the negative impacts of mine closures, state aid to cover certain exceptional costs are considered as permissible.[149] Exceptional costs include, for instance, costs of retraining workers, additional underground safety work or surface recultivation. Ultimately, the Council Decision leads to the expiration of the aid scheme specifically designed for the coal sector, with the result that the general state aid rules as applicable to all sectors will also apply throughout the coal business.

In recent years the European Union has become increasingly dependent on hard coal imports, especially from Russia, South Africa, Australia, Columbia and the United States.[150] Diversification of energy sources in general and of coal suppliers in particular remains one of the crucial tasks of internal and external supply policy. Strategies belonging to the external dimension will be outlined further below.[151] As regards the internal dimension, the first remit consists in the observation of coal imports, allowing the European Union and member states to keep track of current supply diversification. To that end, the European Union has introduced a monitoring scheme for hard coal, which is laid down in Council Regulation (EC) No 405/2003.[152] Accordingly, undertakings importing certain crucial coal products, such as coal for the production of electricity, must notify member states of the shipment, specifying in particular, its quantity and price. Member states have to pool the data and forward to the Commission specific information on the basis of which it can monitor market developments and propose political measures as deemed necessary.

---

proposes Council Regulation on State aid to close uncompetitive coal mines' (press release of 20 July 2010, IP/10/984).

148 Council Decision of 10 December 2010 on State aid to facilitate the closure of uncompetitive coal mines (2010/787/EU).

149 See art 4 and annex of Council Decision 2010/787/EU.

150 See European Commission, *Market Observatory for Energy, report 2009, Europe's energy position – markets and supply*, p 22.

151 See Chapter 6.

152 Council Regulation (EC) No 405/2003 of 27 February 2003 concerning Community monitoring of imports of hard coal originating in third countries.

4.5 The renewable energy sector

In recent years the European Union has put an ever greater emphasis on renewable energy sources (RES), placing these sources ultimately at the heart of EU energy policy.[153] Renewables are considered a decisive factor for three reasons. First, they represent the key to crucially reduce the European Union's dependency on foreign energy sources. Second, they form the backbone of the European Union's strategy to decisively cut CO_2 emissions. Third, renewables constitute a virtually inexhaustible resource. Renewable energy sources comprise all non-fossil sources that are naturally replenished, in particular sunlight, wind, biomass, hydropower and geothermal energy. Renewables serve to generate electricity, heat and cold, and can also be used as fuel in the transport sector.

Present renewable energy policy primarily revolves around boosting the share of renewables in the overall energy mix. Back in 2007, Heads of State and Government decided to increase the share of renewable energy in EU energy consumption to 20% by 2020.[154] Since then, the European Union has adopted a variety of measures and it seems to be heading in the right direction to honour its commitment.[155] In view of the post-2020 horizon, the EU heads of state determined in October 2014 that in 2030 the share of renewable energy sources must amount to at least 27%.[156] However, in contrast to the 2020 framework, no binding targets for member states were defined, something which casts some doubt on whether the European Union will be able to achieve this target. As regards the even wider planning horizon, the Commission has pre-estimated in its Energy Roadmap 2050 that renewable energy sources must necessarily make up the largest contribution to the energy mix in 2050.[157] Otherwise, the European Union will not be in a position to reduce greenhouse gas emissions by 80 to 90% by that time as planned.

The current legal framework to boost the share of renewable energy consists of several components. Binding national targets, corresponding action plans and support schemes form the key drivers for the penetration of

---

153 The Commission already envisaged the development of renewables in a White Paper back in 1997. Subsequent developments have been based on two directives: Directive 2001/77/EC and Directive 2003/30/EC. In 2007 the European Council elevated the promotion of renewable energy sources to one of three overall objectives of recent EU energy and climate policy.

154 See European Council 8/9 March 2007, *Presidency Conclusions* (doc 7224/1/07 REV1).

155 Cf European Commission, *Renewable Energy: a major player in the European energy market* (COM/2012/0271 final).

156 Cf European Council 24 October 2014, *Conclusions* (EUCO 169/14).

157 See European Commission, *Energy Roadmap 2050* (COM/2011/0885 final).

renewables.[158] Apart from that, the expansion of renewable energies is contingent upon the smooth functioning of the internal energy market. Therefore, the proper implementation of the legislation on electricity and gas markets also plays a central role. In addition, in view of the numerous new renewable energy producers entering the market, the European Union is seeking to foster the development of requisite infrastructures. Last but not least, the European Union is banking on further promoting innovation in the renewable energy sector, especially through EU research funding.[159]

4.5.1　National targets, action plans and support schemes

The mentioned key measures are stipulated in the Renewable Energy Directive (Directive 2009/28/EC),[160] which represents the focal legislation pertaining to the renewable energy sector.[161] It was adopted in 2009 and replaced the formerly applicable regime consisting of the Renewable Electricity Directive[162] and the Biofuels Directive.[163]

a)　*Mandatory national targets and national action plans*

For the purpose of attaining the European Union's overall objective to boost the share of renewables to at least 20% by 2020, the Renewable Energy Directive determines in its article 3 and annex I individual binding targets for every member state. Accordingly, a member state is obliged to increase the share of renewable energy in its gross final consumption of energy at least to the target value specified for it. National targets vary from member state to member state and range from a 10% share in Malta to a 49% share in Sweden, taking into account each member state's different potential for increasing the share of renewable energy.[164] The share must be calculated in accordance with articles 5 to 11. In order to be able to attain its national

---

158 See also European Commission, *Renewable Energy: a major player in the European energy market* (COM/2012/0271 final).

159　See also section 5.6 below for major funding sources.

160　Directive 2009/28/EC of the European Parliament and of the Council of 23 April 2009 on the promotion of the use of energy from renewable sources and amending and subsequently repealing Directives 2001/77/EC and 2003/30/EC [2009] OJ L 140/16.

161　For details, see also T Howes, 'The EU's new Renewable Energy Directive (2009/28/EC)' in S Oberthür and M Pallemaerts (eds), *The New Climate Policies of the European Union* (VUB Press 2010) 138 et seq; P Hodson, C Jones and H van Stehen (eds), *EU Energy Law: Volume III, Book 1, Renewable Energy Law and Policy in the European Union* (Claeys & Casteels Publishing 2010); A Johnston and C Block, *EU Energy Law*, 307 et seq.

162　Directive 2001/77/EC of 27 September 2001 on the promotion of electricity produced from renewable energy sources.

163　Directive 2003/30/EC of 8 May 2003 on the promotion of the use of biofuels or other renewable fuels.

164　Recital 22 of the Renewable Energy Directive (Directive 2009/28/EC).

target, a member state may, for instance, set up support schemes, use coop-
erations with other member states and third countries, and promote energy
efficiency and energy saving.[165] In order to ensure that member states get
and remain on track, they have to elaborate and pursue individual action
plans.[166] These national schemes must specify the measures to be taken to
meet the national overall target. Furthermore, national plans must establish
individual targets for the sectors of electricity, heating and cooling, as well
as transport.

Apart from the stipulation of national overall targets, the European Union
specifically aspires to trigger a smooth transformation of energy consumption in the transport sector. In order to ensure an adequate inclusion of
energy from renewable sources in transportation, the Renewable Energy
Directive requires member states to safeguard that the share of renewable
energy in all forms of transport in 2020 will amount to at least 10% of the
final national consumption of energy in transport.[167]

Biofuels are supposed to become the main alternative to petrol used
in transport.[168] However, the increasing biomass production poses the
European Union with new possible environmental challenges (for example,
impacts on biodiversity, destruction of ecosystems, greenhouse gas emissions). In order to forestall negative environmental impacts, article 17 of
the Renewable Energy Directive defines sustainability criteria for biofuels
and bioliquids while particularly excluding those biofuels or bioliquids that
are produced from material obtained from forests, wetlands and nature protection areas. Only fuels and liquids which meet these sustainability criteria can be taken into account in respect of national targets and renewable
energy obligations. In 2010, the Commission gave further guidance to help
member states and industry with the implementation of the sustainability
provisions.[169] The Commission encourages member states and business in
particular to introduce voluntary certification schemes for biofuels.[170]

b)   National support schemes

Support schemes are considered the major measure to effect a dissemination
of renewable energy sources and, therefore, to attain the defined national

165 Article 3(1) and (3) and recital 25 of the Renewable Energy Directive (Directive 2009/28/EC).
166 Article 4 Renewable Energy Directive.
167 See art 3(4) and recital 16 of the Renewable Energy Directive.
168 European Commission, press release IP/10/711 of 10 June 2010.
169 Ibid.
170 European Commission, MEMO/10/247 of 10 June 2010.

targets.[171] Member states may deploy support schemes to reduce the costs of energy from renewable sources, to guarantee preferential prices or to fix volumes of purchase.[172] Schemes may provide for, inter alia, investment aid, tax exemptions, tax reductions, tax refunds, purchase obligations, green certificates and direct price support schemes.[173]

National support schemes place renewable energy and, thus, undertakings and private individuals generating that energy in a favourable position on the market. That said, the question arises as to whether such schemes conform to EU law.[174] Depending on the respective determinations, support schemes may be subject to specific provisions of the Treaty on the Functioning of the European Union (TFEU), especially the provisions on the free movement of goods and those on state aid. Moreover, support schemes promoting electricity produced from renewable energy sources affect the functioning of the internal electricity market and, thus, may also be covered by the Electricity Directive (Directive 2009/72/EC).[175]

Against this background support schemes fostering renewable energy may well be subject to detailed legal review and state aid control, in particular.[176] Considering that relevant treaty provisions have already been looked at more closely in Chapter 2 above,[177] the following remarks are only to recall key aspects of the corresponding legal discussion.

- **Relation to the free movement of goods principle:** With regard to the free movement of goods principle, the first question is whether recourse to it is still conceivable in relation to national support schemes for renewable energy. Possibly harmonising provisions set forth in the Renewable Energy Directive might require an assessment on their basis barring a review under primary law. However, in *Ålands Vindkraft* the Court of Justice made clear that the EU legislator did not aspire to exhaustively harmonise national support schemes for green energy production by means of that directive.[178] In the *Ålands* case the Court dealt with a

---

171 For details see also M Kahles and T Müller, 'Powerful national support systems versus Europe-wide harmonisation – assessment of competing and converging support instruments' in R Hinrichs-Rahlwes, *Sustainable Energy Policies for Europe* (CRC Press 2013) 69 et seq.

172 See art 2 k Renewable Energy Directive (Directive 2009/28/EC).

173 Ibid.

174 See European Commission, *Commission Staff Working Document, The support of electricity from renewable energy sources* (SEC(2008) 57), pp 11–13.

175 See also European Commission, ibid, pp 11 et seq.

176 See also European Commission, ibid, pp 11–13.

177 See, in particular, sections 2.1.1 and 2.2.5.

178 Case C-573/12 *Ålands Vindkraft AB v Energimyndigheten*, para 56 et seq.

Swedish support scheme the application of which was excluded for electricity produced abroad. Ultimately, the Court still reviewed the case on
the basis of the free movement of goods principle and not on that of the
Renewable Energy Directive. This may seem surprising as article 3(3)
subparagraph 2 of this directive states that, under certain conditions and
with due regard to EU state aid rules, member states may decide to what
extent they support renewable energy produced in another member
state.[179] Ultimately, the Court found that the EU legislator, in continuing to accept deviating national support schemes, did not envisage fully
harmonising the issue of territorial restrictions provided for in such
schemes.[180]

Once it is established that a national support scheme needs to be
reviewed on the basis of the free movement principle, the legal scrutiny must in particular concentrate on the question as to whether the
violation of this principle by the relevant scheme is justified. In this
context the Court of Justice stressed in a range of cases that environmental protection and the protection of the health and life of humans,
animals and plants may serve as grounds of justification. Ongoing discussion in this context particularly revolves around the landmark judgement
PreussenElektra[181] and the more recent cases *Ålands Vindkraft* and *Essent
Belgium*. For more details on these cases see Chapter 2 above.[182]

- **Relation to state aid rules:** As regards EU state aid control, the initial
  question is whether a given national support scheme does in fact involve
  state aid in the sense of EU law. One of the features required in this
  context is that support measures must be granted by a member state or at
  least through state resources. The examination of this aspect has sparked
  some debates in relation to various support schemes for renewable
  energy in the past. The Court of Justice also dealt with this topic in the
  PreussenElektra case. Here it held that at least obligations imposed on electricity supply undertakings to purchase renewable energy at minimum
  prices as provided for in the German Law on feeding electricity from
  renewable energy sources into the public grid (*Stromeinspeisungsgesetz*)
  do not constitute state aid in the sense of EU state aid law as these do not
  transfer any state resources.[183] Here the Court found that the statutory

---

179 See art 3(3) subparagraph 2 Directive 2009/28/EC; M Kahles and T Müller 'Legal assessment of
"discriminating market barriers" in national support schemes' in R Hinrichs-Rahlwes, *Sustainable Energy
Policies for Europe* (CRC Press 2013) 65 et seq.

180 Case C-573/12 *Ålands Vindkraft AB v Energimyndigheten*, para 56 et seq.

181 ECJ Case C-379/98 *PreussenElektra AG v Schleswag AG* [2001] ECR I-02099.

182 See section 2.1.1.

183 ECJ Case C-379/98 *PreussenElektra AG v Schleswag AG* [2001] ECR I-02099, para 59.

provisions under review solely require a transfer of resources between companies.[184]

However, such feed-in tariff mechanisms may also come under the concept of state aid as soon as the underlying financing turns out to be an advantage granted directly or indirectly through state resources, as the Court underlined in the *Vent De Colère!* case.[185] In its ruling the Court recalled that the concept of intervention 'through state resources' is also meant to cover advantages granted through public or private bodies appointed or established by the state to administer the aid.[186]

By referring to this case law, the Commission has found that also the successors of the said *Stromeinspeisungsgesetz*, the German renewable energy laws 2012 and 2014 (EEG 2012 and EEG 2014), have granted state aid, notwithstanding the fact that net operators pay the feed-in tariffs and the balancing mechanism apportioning the additional costs to electricity customers is privately organised.[187] The Commission held the state aid rules to be applicable because Germany established the legal framework of the compensation mechanism providing for the assignment of certain relevant duties to private companies (such as the centralisation and administration of financial flows by transmission network operators) and close monitoring of the scheme by the state.[188] In early 2015 the German government brought an action against the decision of the Commission on the EEG 2012, the outcome of which should lead to more clarity for legislators in this sensitive area of policy making.

As regards support schemes clearly coming under the concept of state aid, the Commission's new Guidelines on State Aid for Environmental Protection and Energy 2014–2020 (EEAG) replacing the previous Guidelines on State Aid for Environmental Protection, apply, which under certain conditions qualify support schemes as compatible with the European Union's state aid rules.[189] In addition, the new General Block

---

184 M Roggenkamp, C Redgwell, I del Guayo and A Rønne, *Energy Law in Europe*, 283; ECJ, Case C-379/98 *PreussenElektra AG v Schleswag AG*, paras 59 et seq.

185 Case C-262/12 *Association Vent De Colère! Fédération nationale and Others*. See also section 2.2.5 above.

186 Case C-262/12 *Association Vent De Colère! Fédération nationale and Others*, para 20.

187 European Commission, decisions C(2013) 4424 final and C(2014) 5081 final; European Commission, press releases 'State aid: Commission approves German aid scheme for renewable energy (EEG 2012); orders partial recovery' (25 November 2014, IP/14/2122) and 'State aid: Commission approves German renewable energy law EEG 2014' (23 July 2014, IP/14/867).

188 European Commission, decisions C(2013) 4424 final, paras 82 et seq and C(2014) 5081 final, para 175 et seq.

189 European Commission, *Guidelines on State aid for environmental protection and energy 2014–2020* [2014] OJ C 200/1.

Exemption Regulation (GBER) excludes under certain conditions aid from the obligation of notification to the Commission.[190]

● **Relation to further EU law:** Support for renewable energy may also appear critical in the context of other provisions of EU law. However, the European Union legislator should already have set out the necessary exemptions, giving way to the promotion of renewable energy. In this light, the Electricity Directive explicitly provides that obligations imposed on undertakings in the electricity sector relating to renewable energy sources conform to the internal energy market under certain premises.[191] Furthermore, the Energy Taxation Directive allows for exemptions from or reductions in the level of taxation to electricity from renewable sources.[192]

Given this legal framework, the Commission has dealt with a variety of national support schemes in recent years, declaring them admissible under EU law.[193] Against this background, as just indicated, the Renewable Electricity Directive also proceeds on the assumption that national schemes may at least be drafted in a way that they conform to the internal market rules. Ultimately this Directive even holds such mechanisms as being absolutely necessary to level the playing field between renewable energy sources and conventional energy sources.

However, considering the growth of the renewable energy sector, the Commission and Council have also made clear that support schemes should be gradually adapted or phased out once further penetration of renewable energy sources can also be brought about by market mechanisms.[194] Thus the legal admissibility of specific schemes will change over time with the evolution of the market. With the new Guidelines on State Aid for Environmental Protection and Energy 2014–2020, the Commission has already predetermined the way ahead, leading gradually away from the state aid approach that has applied in recent years. Accordingly, realignment already began in 2015

---

190 Commission Regulation (EU) No 651/2014 of 17 June 2014 declaring certain categories of aid compatible with the internal market in application of Articles 107 and 108 of the Treaty [2014] OJ L 187/1.

191 Article 3(2) Directive 2009/72/EC.

192 Article 15 Council Directive 2003/96/EC of 27 October 2003 restructuring the Community framework for the taxation of energy products and electricity [2003] OJ L 283/51 (Energy Taxation Directive).

193 For individual cases see the Commission's website http://ec.europa.eu/competition/index_en.html, accessed 3 May 2016.

194 European Commission, *Communication, Delivering the internal electricity market and making the most of public intervention* (C(2013) 7243 final), section IV; Council of the European Union, Council conclusions on Renewable Energy, 3204th Transport, Telecommunications and Energy Council meeting (Brussels, 3 December 2012).

with the obligation resting on member states to grant aid for at least 5% of planned new electricity capacity from renewable sources in a competitive bidding process.[195] However, the Commission also made clear that aid accruing to existing installations will not be affected by the new Guidelines.[196]

In practice, member states have deployed a range of different support mechanisms providing investment support or operating support.[197] Operating support has been more widespread and includes price-based instruments (especially feed-in tariffs) and quantity-based instruments (especially quota obligations).[198]

i)   *Feed-in tariffs model (FiT)*

The feed-in tariffs model (FiT) is a support scheme typically used in the electricity sector to boost the share of renewable energy. Under the FiT, producers of renewable energy receive fixed preferential prices on a long-term basis for electricity fed into the grid. Moreover, the network provider must guarantee preferential grid access. Most EU member states have implemented a feed-in tariffs mechanism in the electricity sector, whereas the German Erneuerbare-Energien-Gesetz (EEG) served as a model.

ii)   *Quota obligations model*

Under a quota obligations model (quota-based mechanism, RPS mechanism) a supplier of energy is obliged to deliver a certain proportion of renewable energy. Such an obligation might be imposed on suppliers of electricity or suppliers of fuel. The quota-based mechanism is frequently facilitated by tradable green certificates (TGC)/renewable energy certificates (RECs), which may be freely traded.[199] The owner of such certificates can claim to have purchased renewable energy and to comply with the quota-based mechanism.

---

195 European Commission, *Guidelines on State aid for environmental protection and energy 2014–2020* [2014] OJ C 200/1, para 126.

196 European Commission, *Energy and Environmental State aid Guidelines – Frequently asked questions* (9 April 2014).

197 For an overview see D Fouquet and C Jones (eds), *EU Energy Law: Volume III – Book Two, Renewable Energy in the Member States of the EU* (2nd edn, Claeys & Casteels Publishing 2015). As regards the transition towards renewable energy at regional level see also M Peeters and T Schomerus (eds), *Renewable Energy Law in the EU: Legal Perspectives on Bottom-Up Approaches* (Edward Elgar Publishing 2014).

198 European Commission, *Commission Staff Working Document, The support of electricity from renewable energy sources* (SEC(2008) 57), pp 4 et seq.

199 European Commission, *Commission Staff Working Document, The support of electricity from renewable energy sources* (SEC(2008) 57), p 5.

The quota obligations model is a support scheme mainly used in the European transport sector to boost the share of biofuel and therefore to reach the 10% target in the transport sector. However, quota obligations are also used in the electricity sector, whereas currently only few EU member states have recourse to this model. Among EU countries the feed-in tariffs model has become prevalent as the more effective scheme to increase the share of electricity produced from renewable energy sources.

iii)   *Other models and combinations of national support schemes*

Apart from these two main support mechanisms, member states also use other investment support schemes and operating support schemes, which mostly apply supplementary to the main schemes mentioned above. These additional support schemes particularly include investment grants, premiums, fiscal incentives, tendering and tax exemptions.[200] The respective mix of instruments depends on the sector (electricity, heating or transport) and varies from member state to member state.[201] Further information on national support schemes may be obtained from the website http://www. res-legal.eu/.[202]

c)   *Cooperation mechanisms*

Given the specific geographical location and economic capacity each member state exhibits, starting conditions for the maturing of renewable energy sources vary within the European Union. With a view to balancing out disparities, the Renewable Energy Directive defines, on the one hand, individual national target values. On the other hand, it provides for different cooperation mechanisms allowing member states to jointly develop approaches for the purpose of attaining their own national targets. Main cooperation mechanisms include statistical transfers, joint projects and joint support schemes.[203] In recent years limited use has been made by member states of these mechanisms. In order to unlock the untapped potential, the Commission gave specific guidance in 2013.[204]

---

200 European Commission, *Renewable Energy: Progressing towards the 2020 target* (COM(2011) 31 final), pp 9 et seq; European Commission, *Commission Staff Working Document, The support of electricity from renewable energy sources* (SEC(2008) 57), p 5.

201 European Commission, *Renewable Energy: Progressing towards the 2020 target* (COM(2011) 31 final), p 9.

202 Accessed 3 May 2016.

203 See arts 6 to 11 Directive 2009/28/EC.

204 European Commission, *Commission Staff Working Document, Guidance on the use of renewable energy cooperation mechanisms, accompanying the Communication from the Commission C(2013) 7243 final* (SWD(2013) 440 final).

4.5.2   Common market rules

As indicated above, the renewable energy sector comprises a variety of regenerative energy sources and forms of energy consumption. Considering the multifaceted nature of the sector, its proper functioning is not ensured by a single all-encompassing act. The internal market in renewable energy is rather based on a complex regulative framework consisting of several legislative acts which are furthermore flanked by provisions of the TFEU.

Electricity generated from renewable energy sources, such as sunlight, wind and geothermal energy, for instance, comes principally under the rules of the electricity market as laid down in the Electricity Directive.[205] This makes sense insofar as the origin of electricity can hardly be determined once it has been fed into the grid. Besides, biogas and gas from biomass are generally subject to the Gas Directive.[206] In addition, in terms of some specific forms of governmental intervention in the market, the state aid rules and the exemptions set out in the Energy Taxation Directive may apply.[207]

The Renewable Energy Directive provides for further provisions which are tailored to the specific needs of the renewable energy business and which must be seen in combination with the legal framework just outlined. For example, article 13 of the Renewable Energy Directive pertains to the authorisation, certification and licensing procedures applicable to facilities and associated grid infrastructures for the production of electricity, heating and cooling from renewable energy sources. Accordingly, member states have to ensure, inter alia, that procedures are objective, transparent and proportionate and that they do not discriminate between applicants. This means in particular that a producer from another member state wishing to erect generation capacity may not be put at a disadvantage through given administrative procedures.

Transport, that is, transmission and distribution, of electricity from renewable sources to customers poses a particular problem to member states.[208] Present network infrastructures often work at full capacity whilst more and more decentralised producers of different sizes are seeking to feed electricity into the grid. In order to prevent the further development of the renewable energy sector being curtailed against this background, the Renewable Energy

---

205 See Directive 2009/72/EC.
206 Article 1(2) Directive 2009/73/EC.
207 Article 15 Council Directive 2003/96/EC.
208 See also T Howes, 'The EU's New Renewable Energy Directive (2009/28/EC)', 138 et seq.

Directive makes some profound arrangements. First, it requires member states to take appropriate measures to develop grid infrastructures so that the net may operate properly in spite of electricity being fed in from regenerative sources.[209] Second, the Directive obliges member states to ensure that system operators transmit and distribute electricity from renewable sources.[210] Third, member states shall provide for either priority access or guaranteed access to the network of renewable electricity.[211] Priority access enables producers of renewable energy to feed electricity into the grid, whenever the source becomes available.[212] Guaranteed access concerns the integration of renewable energy into the spot market and is supposed to guarantee that all renewable energy sold and supported gains access to the net.[213]

The Renewable Energy Directive complements the Electricity Directive 2009/72/EC also in terms of customer protection. Under article 3 of the Electricity Directive electricity suppliers have to specify on or with bills issued to final customers the contribution of each energy source to the overall energy mix.[214] In order to prove to customers that a given share was produced from renewable energy sources, article 15 of the Renewable Energy Directive provides for the issuance of guarantees of origin. Member states may also determine that such guarantees are issued for heating and cooling produced from renewable energy sources. Guarantees of origin may be transferred from one holder to another. However, energy produced from renewable sources in relation to which a guarantee of origin has been transferred independently may not be sold as renewable energy.[215] Furthermore, guarantees of origin shall not be confused with the tradable green certificates (TGC) issued under a quota obligations model, as described above, or any other support scheme.[216]

4.6 The nuclear energy sector

The exploitation of certain commodities for energy production is partly subject to controversial public discussion. Nuclear energy remains surely the most disputed energy source in our time. EU member states have taken quite different paths as to the usage of nuclear fuels for electricity produc-

---

209 Article 16(1) Directive 2009/28/EC.
210 Article 16(2) a) Directive 2009/28/EC.
211 Article 16(2) b) Directive 2009/28/EC.
212 Recital 60 of Renewable Energy Directive.
213 Ibid.
214 See art 3 para 9 Directive 2009/72/EC.
215 Recital 52 of Renewable Energy Directive.
216 Ibid.

tion. While a range of member states continue to bank on nuclear power to different degrees, others have ruled it out or decided on a nuclear phase-out. To date, 14 out of 28 member states operate nuclear power plants. Taken together, these facilities produce 30% of the electricity and 15% of the energy consumed in the European Union.

Ultimately the decision on whether to include nuclear power in the energy mix lies with the member states.[217] Given its entrenchment in many countries, nuclear energy also forms a constant in European energy policy. From the European Commission's point of view, nothing should change in this respect. Within its energy roadmap for the 2050 horizon, the Commission assigned nuclear energy a key role for the distant future without even contemplating any decarbonisation scenario involving the exclusion of nuclear power.[218] This is surprising as treaty law does indeed ensure member states' right to use nuclear energy, but however it does not concede nuclear energy the status of a fixed factor. Accordingly, there is no compelling reason why the Commission did not take account of both the limited public acceptance of nuclear power in many member states and the fact that the ultimate problems it poses remain unchanged, such as residual risks and the lack of permanent repositories for nuclear waste.

Based on the Euratom Treaty, the European Union or more precisely Euratom, which is the organisation that pursues the European nuclear agenda, has adopted a complex corpus of legal acts and has concluded a range of international agreements. However, this finding alone does not give any indication of the intensity of regulation and the binding nature of individual acts. The following overview will include the most significant acts. Further measures can be found in the EUR-Lex database.[219] European engagement in the field remains necessary in several ways irrespective of whether individual member states have ruled out the use of nuclear power. First, given the relatively close proximity of nuclear facilities to neighbouring countries, high-level radiation escaping from a particular source may easily affect more than one member state. Second, radioactive materials transported across Europe present transnational safety hazards. Third, considering the fact that energy grids are already connected within Europe, electricity generated from nuclear fuels may serve energy security in a range of member states as it cannot be sequestered at state boundaries.

---

217 According to art 194(2) TFEU member states retain the right to choose between different energy sources, including nuclear energy.

218 Cf European Commission, *Energy Roadmap 2050* (COM (2011) 0885 final).

219 See website http://eur-lex.europa.eu/homepage.html, accessed 3 May 2016.

As shown in Chapter 1, the general rules applicable to the nuclear sector accrue from the Euratom Treaty.[220] The treaty lays down principles of a common nuclear supply policy, for instance, and it establishes the nuclear common market and guarantees its proper functioning. Moreover, the Euratom Treaty defines a number of legislative powers which, as indicated, Euratom has made ample use of over the years. Legislation concerns in particular the supply of nuclear fuels, sector-related investments, joint undertakings, nuclear safety, nuclear safeguards and waste management.

4.6.1 Supply of fuels

Article 52 of the Euratom Treaty establishes the basis for a common nuclear supply policy. It guarantees equal access to sources of supply and prohibits the privileging of certain users. Article 52 also provides for the establishment of the Euratom Supply Agency (ESA) which ensures equal access to as well as regular and equitable supply of nuclear fuels. The Euratom Treaty vests in ESA the right of option on ores, source materials and special fissile materials produced within the Euratom area. ESA also possesses the exclusive right to enter into contracts relating to such materials coming from inside or outside the Euratom area.

Secondary law determines further details as to the internal structure and functioning of ESA[221] and it enables ESA to obtain necessary information on the situation of the market (users' estimated requirements and producers' estimated available supplies).[222] In addition, secondary law, strictly speaking Commission Regulation (Euratom) No 66/2006, provides for exemptions from the treaty rules on supplies in regard of transfers of small quantities of ores, source materials and special fissile materials.[223]

4.6.2 Investments, support programmes and joint undertakings

Under article 40 of the Euratom Treaty, the Commission is encharged with promoting private investments in the nuclear sector and their coordination.

---

220 See section 1.5 above.

221 Council Decision 2008/114/Euratom of 12 February 2008 establishing Statutes for the Euratom Supply Agency [2008] OJ L 41/15.

222 Rules of the Supply Agency of the European Atomic Energy Community of 5 May 1960 determining the manner in which demand is to be balanced against the supply of ores, source materials and special fissile materials ([1960] OJ P 32/777–9). These rules were modified by Regulation of the Supply Agency of the European Atomic Energy Community amending the rules of the Supply Agency of 5 May 1960 determining the manner in which demand is to be balanced against the supply of ores, source materials and special fissile materials ([1975] OJ L 193/37–8).

223 Commission Regulation (Euratom) No 66/2006 of 16 January 2006 exempting the transfer of small quantities of ores, source materials and special fissile materials from the rules of the chapter on supplies.

For that reason, on a regular basis it has to publish programmes stating nuclear energy production targets and the types of investment which are required to meet these targets. With a view to enabling the Commission to elaborate respective programmes, undertakings engaged in the sector have to inform the Commission about investment projects relating to new installations, replacements or conversions. Projects covered by this obligation are defined more closely by Council Regulation (Euratom) No 2587/1999.[224]

Apart from this rather indirect form of promotion, Euratom may also directly fund investment projects in the sector by issuing loans.[225] Details on the pertinent financing scheme are laid down in Council decisions 77/270/Euratom, 77/271/Euratom and 94/179/Euratom.[226] The foundation of joint undertakings represents another type of direct project facilitation. Under articles 45, 47 and 49 of the Euratom Treaty, the Council may decide to establish joint undertakings and to provide partial financing if undertakings are of fundamental importance to the development of the nuclear sector. Joint undertakings which have been established so far include the 'Société d'énergie nucléaire franco-belge des Ardennes' (SENA), the 'Hochtemperatur-Kernkraftwerk GmbH (HKG)' and the 'Schnell-Brüter-Kernkraftwerksgesellschaft mbH' (SBK).

In addition, various support programmes are available to foster research and training in the nuclear field, nuclear safety, nuclear decommissioning and also the development of fusion energy as a conceivable alternative to fission power.[227]

---

224 Council Regulation (Euratom) No 2587/1999 of 2 December 1999 defining the investment projects to be communicated to the Commission in accordance with article 41 of the Treaty establishing the European Atomic Energy Community. See also Commission Regulation (EC) No 1209/2000 of 8 June 2000 determining procedures for effecting the communications prescribed under article 41 of the Treaty establishing the European Atomic Energy Community; and Commission Regulation (Euratom) No 1352/2003 of 23 July 2003 amending Regulation (EC) 1209/2000 determining procedures for effecting the communications prescribed under article 41 of the Treaty establishing the European Atomic Energy Community.
225 See article 2 c) Euratom Treaty.
226 Council decision 77/270/Euratom of 29 March 1977 empowering the Commission to issue Euratom loans for the purpose of contributing to the financing of nuclear power stations; Council Decision 77/271/ Euratom of 29 March 1977 on the implementation of Decision 77/270/Euratom empowering the Commission to issue Euratom loans for the purpose of contributing to the financing of nuclear power stations; Council decision 94/179/Euratom of 21 March 1994 amending decision 77/270/Euratom, to authorize the Commission to contract Euratom borrowings in order to contribute to the financing required for improving the degree of safety and efficiency of nuclear power stations in certain non-member countries.
227 See also section 5.6 below for an overview on EU support programmes.

4.6.3 Nuclear safety, nuclear safeguards and radioactive waste management

Given the significant hazards arising from nuclear substances, taking safety precautions remains the crucial issue of nuclear energy policy. Based on the Euratom Treaty, Euratom has also been engaged in this field. Legislation concerns in particular nuclear safety, so-called nuclear safeguards and nuclear waste management. In the following summary, the currently applicable legislation is listed. However this legislation will be repealed, at least in part, and brought together in a new directive, namely Directive 2013/59/Euratom, with effect from 6 February 2018.[228]

Nuclear safety in general: In principle, ensuring nuclear safety falls within the remit of member states. However, in order to ensure common standards throughout the European Union, the Euratom Treaty confers on Euratom in particular the power to establish basic safety standards, to draw up recommendations and to pass opinions on specific issues. Basic safety standards as considered in article 30 of the Euratom Treaty, have been introduced with the so-called Basic Safety Standards Directive (BSS Directive). After its initial adoption in 1959 the BSS Directive has undergone several revisions and was eventually repealed by Directive 96/29/Euratom.[229] This current version of the BSS Directive applies to all practices which involve a risk from ionising radiation.[230] The present BSS Directive defines, inter alia:

- obligations for member states to introduce reporting requirements and authorisation requirements in respect of practices which involve a risk from ionising radiation (subject to some exceptions);
- an age limit for workers exposed to ionising radiation (age of 18);
- dose limits for exposed workers and for the public;
- exposure prevention measures;
- requirements of medical surveillance of exposed workers;
- the establishment of systems of inspection;

---

228 Council Directive 2013/59/Euratom of 5 December 2013 laying down basic safety standards for protection against the dangers arising from exposure to ionising radiation, and repealing Directives 89/618/Euratom, 90/641/Euratom, 96/29/Euratom, 97/43/Euratom and 2003/122/Euratom.

229 Council Directive 96/29/Euratom of 13 May 1996 laying down basic safety standards for the protection of the health of workers and the general public against the dangers arising from ionising radiation.

230 As a non-binding reference document see the Communication from the Commission concerning the implementation of Council Directive 96/29/Euratom of 13 May 1996 laying down basic safety standards for the protection of the health of workers and the general public against the dangers arising from ionising radiation, COM/98/0087 final.

- measures in respect of natural radiation sources leading to a significant increase in the exposure of workers or the public.

The Basic Safety Standards Directive has been supplemented by a range of further acts, which will partly be outlined below. This legislation particularly concerns nuclear installations, nuclear materials, transport, nuclear emergency, protection of outside workers,[231] quality of drinking water,[232] medical examinations[233] and nuclear waste management. The present BSS Directive and in parts also directives linked to it belong to the legislation which will be repealed and brought together in Directive 2013/59/Euratom, with effect from 6 February 2018.

Nuclear installation safety: The safety of nuclear installations is specifically addressed by Council Directive 2009/71/Euratom.[234] The Directive underscores the responsibility of member states for law-making in the field of nuclear installation safety, but provides for various specifications with which member states have to comply in this context. Indeed, Directive 2009/71/Euratom is confined to rather basic questions. It requires member states to establish a national framework for nuclear installation safety concerning, in particular, the adoption of national nuclear safety requirements, a system of licensing and one of safety supervision.[235] Furthermore, pursuant to Directive 2009/71/Euratom, member states shall, for instance, establish a competent regulatory authority in the area of nuclear installation safety and they have to make sure that the prime responsibility for installation safety rests with the licence holder.[236]

The accident at the nuclear power plant in Fukushima (Japan) in early 2011 gave rise to rethink the safety of EU nuclear plants. Still in March 2011 the Heads of States and Governments of the EU Member States agreed to introduce stress tests for nuclear power plants. Stress tests concerned their security against both natural and man-made hazards (that is, earthquakes, flooding, extreme heat and cold, terrorist attacks, air crashes) as well as the safety

---

231 Council Directive 90/641/Euratom of 4 December 1990 on the operational protection of outside workers exposed to the risk of ionising radiation during their activities in controlled areas.
232 See 2013/51/Euratom of 22 October 2013 laying down requirements for the protection of the health of the general public with regard to radioactive substances in water intended for human consumption.
233 In terms of medical examination, see Council Directive 97/43/Euratom of 30 June 1997 on health protection of individuals against the dangers of ionising radiation in relation to medical exposure, and repealing Directive 84/466/Euratom 106. See also European Commission, *Communication from the Commission to the European Parliament and the Council on medical applications of ionising radiation* (COM/2010/0423).
234 Council Directive 2009/71/Euratom establishing a Community framework for the nuclear safety of nuclear installations.
235 See art 4 Directive 2009/71/Euratom.
236 See arts 5 and 6 Directive 2009/71/Euratom.

and stability of technical facilities (that is, coolant systems, backup power supplies).[237] The test specifications (criteria and ways of assessment) were elaborated by WENRA, a network of chief regulators, and then concluded by the European Commission and the European Nuclear Safety Regulators Group (ENSREG) in May 2011. The European Commission published the results of the stress tests in October 2012.[238] Accordingly, national authorities concluded that there is no need to close any nuclear power plant. However, the Commission also revealed that safety standards as established by the International Atomic Energy Agency (IAEA) and international best practices are partially not applied in member states. Against this background, the Commission sought to tighten up the stipulations of Directive 2009/71/Euratom.

Negotiations on the Commission's proposal for an amending directive were concluded in May 2014. Ultimately, in July 2014 the Council adopted Directive 2014/87/Euratom to amend the currently applicable scheme as established by Directive 2009/71/Euratom.[239] Directive 2014/87/Euratom has to be transposed into national law by member states by 15 August 2017. The amending directive provides for, among other things, initial assessments and periodic safety reassessments for every nuclear power plant (at least every 10 years), effective independence of national regulatory authorities, self-assessments and peer reviews of national nuclear safety frameworks and regulatory authorities, and transparency obligations particularly pertaining to regulatory authorities and operators.

Euratom is also committed to fostering the implementation of international safety standards as laid down in the Convention on Nuclear Safety. This international convention applies to civil installations used for nuclear power generation, namely nuclear power plants and related storage, handling and treatment facilities for radioactive materials. The aims of the Convention are to achieve and maintain a high level of nuclear safety worldwide, to establish and maintain effective defences in nuclear installations against potential radiological hazards and to prevent accidents and to mitigate their consequences.[240] Euratom acceded to the Convention in the year 2000.

---

237 See European Commission, *Nuclear stress tests* (25 May 2011, MEMO/11/339).

238 European Commission, *Communication on the comprehensive risk and safety assessments ('stress tests') of nuclear power plants in the European Union and related activities* (COM/2012/571); European Commission, *Nuclear stress tests: confirmation of high safety standards but need for further improvement* (press release of 4 October 2012).

239 Council Directive 2014/87/EURATOM of 8 July 2014 amending Directive 2009/71/Euratom establishing a Community framework for the nuclear safety of nuclear installations.

240 Cf art 1 of the Convention on Nuclear Safety.

Nuclear materials, shipment of nuclear materials and nuclear safe-guards: Specific legislation has furthermore been enacted in the field of safety of nuclear materials. With Council Directive 2003/122, Euratom has adopted provisions especially designed to prevent the exposure of workers and the public to ionising radiation arising from inadequate control of high-activity sealed radioactive sources and orphan sources.[241] Regulation No 1493/93 concerns the shipment of radioactive substances between member states.[242] It is supposed to ensure the establishment of a system for controlling shipments within the European Union. Regulation No. 302/2005 puts the provisions of the Euratom Treaty on safeguards in more concrete terms.[243] Nuclear safeguards shall ensure that nuclear materials are not diverted from their intended uses.

Apart from these legislative acts, Euratom acceded to the international 'Convention on the Physical Protection of Nuclear Material' (CPPNM). The CPPNM aims primarily at ensuring protection of nuclear materials used for peaceful purposes while in international transport. Euratom has also approved its accession to an amendment to the CPPNM, which has not become effective yet.[244]

Radiological emergency: A number of obligations are also imposed on member states in the context of radiological or nuclear accidents. Council Decision 87/600 introduces an early notification and exchange of information system, called Urgent Radiological Information Exchange (ECURIE), according to which member states must inform other member states and the European Commission in case of a nuclear accident.[245] Council Directive 89/618 requires member states to inform the general public about protection measures to be applied in the event of a radiological emergency.[246] Council Regulation No 2219/89 concerns the export of foodstuffs and feeding stuffs in case of an accident and imposes an export ban if radioactive contamination

---

241 Article 1(1) of Council Directive 2003/122/Euratom of 22 December 2003 on the control of high-activity sealed radioactive sources and orphan sources.
242 Council Regulation (Euratom) No 1493/93 of 8 June 1993 on shipments of radioactive substances between Member States; see also Commission Communication 2009/C 41/02 concerning Council Regulation (EURATOM) No 1493/93 on shipments of radioactive substances between Member States.
243 Commission Regulation (Euratom) No 302/2005 of 8 February 2005 on the application of Euratom safeguards.
244 See Council Decision 2007/513/Euratom of 10 July 2007.
245 Council Decision 87/600/Euratom on urgent information exchange in case of a radiological emergency (ECURIE).
246 Council Directive 89/618/Euratom of 27 November 1989 on informing the general public about health protection measures to be applied and steps to be taken in the event of a radiological emergency.

exceeds given maximum permitted levels.[247] Maximum permitted levels of radioactive contamination are laid down in Council Regulation No 3954/87 and Commission Regulations No 944/89 and No 770/90.[248] The import of foodstuffs and feeding stuffs possibly affected by the accidents in Chernobyl and Fukushima is subject to special regulation.[249]

Management of radioactive waste and spent fuel: The management of radioactive waste and spent fuel represents one of the core issues of nuclear policy. Radioactive waste is produced in various sectors, such as energy production, industry, medicine and research, and its quantity is continually rising. Ultimately every member state is therefore faced with the question of how to deal with nuclear waste. Tackling the problem falls generally within the ambit of member states. Notwithstanding that, in view of the fact that responsible treatment of radioactive waste and spent fuel remains a transnational concern, articles 2(b) and 30 of the Euratom Treaty call for the establishment of uniform safety standards that member states have to comply with.

Legislation adopted by Euratom institutions in this respect features some complexity. To begin with, several of the general legislative acts mentioned previously also comprise the handling of nuclear waste or spent fuel, respectively, and must therefore be taken into account. This holds especially true for:

- the Basic Safety Standards Directive 96/29/Euratom (BSS Directive);
- Council Decision 87/600/Euratom and Council Directive 89/618/ Euratom on information management in the event of a radiological emergency;
- Council Regulation (Euratom) No 1493/93 on shipments of radioactive substances between Member States;
- Council Directive 2003/122/Euratom on the control of high-activity sealed radioactive sources and orphan sources;

---

247 Council Regulation (EEC) No 2219/89 of 18 July 1989 on the special conditions for exporting foodstuffs and feeding stuffs following a nuclear accident or any other case of radiological emergency.
248 Council Regulation (Euratom) No 3954/87 of 22 December 1987 laying down maximum permitted levels of radioactive contamination of foodstuffs and of feeding stuffs following a nuclear accident or any other case of radiological emergency (modified by Council Regulation (Euratom) No 2218/89); Commission Regulation (Euratom) No 944/89 of 12 April 1989 laying down maximum permitted levels of radioactive contamination in minor foodstuffs following a nuclear accident or any other case of radiological emergency; Commission Regulation (Euratom) No 770/90 of 29 March 1990 laying down maximum permitted levels of radioactive contamination of feeding stuffs following a nuclear accident or any other case of radiological emergency.
249 For further details see European Commission, *Questions and Answers: Safety of food products imported from Japan* (8 April 2011, MEMO/11/225).

- Council Directive 2009/71/Euratom on the safety of nuclear installations.

In addition, Euratom institutions have adopted some binding and non-binding instruments with specific focus on the management of radioactive waste and spent fuel:

- Council Directive 2006/117/Euratom on the supervision and control of shipments of radioactive waste and spent fuel;[250]
- Council Directive 2011/70/Euratom establishing a Community framework for the responsible and safe management of spent fuel and radioactive waste;
- Commission Recommendation 2006/851/Euratom on the management of financial resources for the decommissioning of nuclear installations, spent fuel and radioactive waste;
- Commission Recommendation 2008/956/Euratom on criteria for the export of radioactive waste and spent fuel to third countries;
- Commission Recommendation 2010/635/Euratom on the application of article 37 of the Euratom Treaty.

In Council Directive 2011/70 ('Radioactive Waste and Spent Fuel Management Directive') Euratom sets forth a trans-European framework for ensuring the proper management of radioactive waste and spent fuel. The Directive recalls, inter alia, that member states have ultimate responsibility for the management of spent fuel and radioactive waste produced on their territory. This also applies in cases where radioactive waste or spent fuel is shipped for processing or reprocessing to another member state or a third country. Furthermore, pursuant to Directive 2011/70, member states have to establish national programmes specifying a concrete plan and schedule for the construction of disposal facilities, while two or more member states may also jointly use a facility in one of them. Exports to non-EU countries may take place under very restrictive conditions only. The destination country must, in particular, have a disposal facility in operation prior to shipment.[251] In case of highly radioactive waste disposal facility means a deep geological repository. To date, there is no such final repository for highly radioactive waste in any country in the world. In addition, Council Directive 2006/117

---

250 See also Commission decision 2008/312/Euratom of 5 March 2008 establishing the standard document for the supervision and control of shipments of radioactive waste and spent fuel referred to in Council Directive 2006/117/Euratom. Council Directive 92/3/Euratom has been repealed by Council Directive 2006/117/Euratom.

251 See also European Commission, 'Nuclear waste: Commission welcomes adoption of radioactive waste directive' (press release IP/11/906 of 19 July 2011).

completely prohibits shipments to African, Caribbean and Pacific countries and to Antarctica. Moreover, exports are ruled out to other countries without the capacity and structure necessary to safely manage radioactive waste.

Finally, in addition to the adoption of the legislation mentioned, Euratom acceded in 2005 to the international 'Joint Convention on the Safety of Spent Fuel Management and on the Safety of Radioactive Waste Management' (Joint Convention). The Joint Convention fosters safety in spent fuel and radioactive waste management on a global scale. Euratom seeks to promote the implementation of this international treaty throughout Europe, for instance, by Directive 2011/70/Euratom. The same applies to the safety standards elaborated by the International Atomic Energy Agency (IAEA). Directive 2011/70/Euratom reflects key principles and requirements of the Joint Convention and the IAEA Safety Standards.[252]

 REVIEW QUESTIONS

1. What general kind of actions does the Commission envisage in order to eliminate malfunctions in the working of the internal electricity market? *See section 4.1, preliminary remarks.*
2. What are the chief instruments provided for by the Electricity Directive and the Gas Directive? *See sections 4.1.1 and 4.2.1.*
3. Why do both the Electricity Directive and the Gas Directive principally bar member states from setting up or adjusting end-user electricity prices? *See sections 4.1.1 a) and 4.2.1 a).*
4. What does the unbundling of TSOs aim at under the Electricity Directive and the Gas Directive? *See section 4.1.1 c) i) under 'Unbundling of TSOs – general remarks'.*
5. How is third-party access to transmission and distribution systems ensured in the European Union? *See sections 4.1.1 c) v) and 4.2.1 c).*
6. What does REMIT aim at? *See sections 4.1.1 e) and 4.2.1 d).*
7. Which instruments and measures does the current legal framework provided for to boost the share of renewable energies? *See section 4.5, preliminary remarks.*
8. Where are national targets for renewable energy determined and what do they mean for member states? *See section 4.5.1 a).*
9. Which provisions of EU primary law may become particularly relevant when it comes to a legal review of national support schemes for renewable energy? *See section 4.5.1 b).*
10. What role do the Guidelines on State Aid for Environmental Protection and Energy 2014–2020 (EEAG) play? *See section 4.5.1 b).*
11. By what general features can the Feed-in Tariffs Model (FiT) be characterised? *See section 4.5.1 b) i).*

---

252 Cf Report of the European Atomic Energy Community on the implementation of the obligations under the Joint Convention on the Safety of Spent Fuel Management and on the Safety of Radioactive Waste Management, Fifth Review Meeting of Contracting Parties, Vienna, May 2015, p 38.

FURTHER READING

Bram Delvaux, Michaël Hunt and Kim Talus (eds), *EU Energy Law and Policy Issues, vol. 4* (Intersentia 2014)

Rainer Hinrichs-Rahlwes, *Sustainable Energy Policies for Europe* (CRC Press 2013)

Angus Johnston and Guy Block, *EU Energy Law* (Oxford University Press 2013)

Christopher Jones (ed.), *EU Energy Law: Volume I, The Internal Energy Market: The Third Liberalisation Package* (3rd edn, Claeys & Casteels Publishing 2010)

Kim Talus, *EU Energy Law and Policy – A Critical Account* (Oxford University Press 2013)

Jean-Arnold Vinois, (ed.), *EU Energy Law: Volume VIII, The Energy Infrastructure Policy of the European Union* (Claeys & Casteels Publishing 2014)

5

Cross-sector legislation

Alongside sector-specific legislative instruments as outlined in Chapter 4, the European Union is equipped with numerous instruments affecting more than one energy sector. As with sector-specific measures, most cross-sector instruments pursue various objectives pertaining to, for instance, competitiveness of industry, security of energy supply, climate change, consumer protection and innovation. Depending on their primary aim and main addressees, cross-sector legislation and instruments provided for therein belong to different areas of policy-making. Within the framework of this book they will be classed under the following fields: EU energy market; energy efficiency; environmental protection; consumer protection; energy security; and support programmes (for instance, for development, technology and innovation).

Technically speaking, cross-sector instruments may also be classified as market-based instruments and regulative instruments. In recent years market-based measures have taken on greater significance and with its 'Green Paper on market-based instruments for environment and related policy purposes' the European Commission is aiming at an even greater use of these measures.[1] Whereas regulative instruments directly impose certain obligations on market participants, market-based instruments provide economic incentives in order to induce market participants to act in support of a given political objective. Market-based instruments, for instance, make use of tradeable permits, taxes, charges, subsidies, licenses, deposit systems or eco-labelling. The EU Emission Trading Scheme and the EU Ecolabel are prime examples of this approach.

---

1 European Commission, *Green Paper of 28 March 2007 on market-based instruments for environment and related policy purposes* (COM(2007) 140 final).

5.1 Legislation and instruments related to the functioning of the internal energy market

5.1.1 Public procurement and the award of concession contracts

a) *Public procurement*

Public procurement (also called government procurement) means the act by which government agencies or their dependent bodies purchase goods and services from the private sector. Public procurement accounts for about 16% of EU market GDP, making it a significant instrument of economic policy. In order to guarantee equal treatment of all tenderers and the opening of national markets, public procurement is subject to a complex regulatory framework consisting of national, European and international rules.[2] EU law particularly aims at preventing national protectionism and creates a legal setting for procurement in EU member states with which national law has to comply. The EU legal framework pertinent to public procurement is formed by rules of primary law (the fundamental freedoms as laid down in the TFEU, see above Chapter 2) and secondary law. Primary law with its fundamental rules as substantiated by the European Court of Justice takes effect in terms of contracts which fall outside the scope of secondary law[3] (for example, contracts below the threshold for application of the pertinent EU directives) or where specific issues are not covered by secondary law.[4] Fundamental principles of primary law include, in particular, the principle of non-discrimination on the grounds of nationality and the obligation of transparency. The European Commission has released special guidance on EU primary law as well as on case law of the Court of Justice applicable to contract awards that are not or not fully subject to secondary law.[5]

Secondary law relevant to public procurement comprises several legislative acts.[6] The 'Special Sectors' Directive (Directive 2004/17/EC on public

---

2 M Bungenberg and C Nowak, 'Europäische Umweltverfassung und EG-Vergaberecht – zur Berücksichtigung von Umweltschutzbelangen bei der Zuschlagserteilung' (2003) Zeitschrift für Umweltrecht (ZUR) 10.

3 European Court of Justice, Cases C-324/98 *Telaustria Verlags GmbH and Telefonadress GmbH v Telekom Austria AG* [2000] ECR I-10745; C-234/03 *Contse SA and Others v Instituto Nacional de Gestión Sanitaria (Ingesa)* [2005] ECR I-09315.

4 European Court of Justice, Case C-92/00 *Hospital Ingenieure Krankenhaustechnik Planungs-Gesellschaft mbH (HI) v Stadt Wien* [2002] ECR I-05553.

5 European Commission, *Commission interpretative communication on the Community law applicable to contract awards not or not fully subject to the provisions of the Public Procurement Directives* ([2006] OJ C 179/02).

6 For details see also C Bovis, *EU Public Procurement Law*, (2nd edn, Edward Elgar Publishing 2012).

procurement in the water, energy, transport and postal services sectors)[7] and the so-called 'Traditional' Directive (Directive 2004/18/EC on public works contracts, public supply contracts and public service contracts)[8] are central to public procurement.[9] Both directives are complemented by Directives 89/665/EEC,[10] 92/13/EEC[11] and 2007/66/EC[12] which concern review procedures and remedy mechanisms. Both the Special Sectors Directive and the Traditional Directive were amended in respect of their application thresholds by Regulation 1251/2011.[13] Furthermore, in order to standardise the references used by contracting authorities to describe the subject of contracts, Regulation (EC) No. 2195/2002 establishes a Common Procurement Vocabulary (CPV), which must be used across EU countries.[14] Moreover, the Commission has elaborated special guidance on how to apply the Public Procurement Directives to institutionalised public-private partnerships (IPPP).[15]

Public procurement in the energy sector comes under the Special Sectors Directive 2004/17/EC in particular. The directive applies to all contracting authorities and public undertakings which pursue certain activities in the energy sector. It pertains furthermore to all those entities which operate on the basis of special or exclusive rights granted by competent authorities. 'Activities in the energy sector', governed by Directive 2004/17/EC, are specified in articles 3 and 7. Accordingly, Directive 2004/17/EC concerns, in

---

7 Also called Utilities Directive; Directive 2004/17/EC of the European Parliament and of the Council of 31 March 2004 coordinating the procurement procedures of entities operating in the water, energy, transport and postal services sectors [2004] OJ L 134/1.

8 Directive 2004/18/EC of the European Parliament and of the Council of 31 March 2004 on the coordination of procedures for the award of public works contracts, public supply contracts and public service contracts [2004] OJ L 134/114.

9 Besides, Directive 2009/81/EC is primarily applicable to public procurement in the fields of defence and security.

10 Council Directive 89/665/EEC of 21 December 1989 on the coordination of the laws, regulations and administrative provisions relating to the application of review procedures to the award of public supply and public works contracts.

11 Council Directive 92/13/EEC of 25 February 1992 coordinating the laws, regulations and administrative provisions relating to the application of Community rules on the procurement procedures of entities operating in the water, energy, transport and telecommunications sectors.

12 Directive 2007/66/EC of the European Parliament and of the Council of 11 December 2007 amending Council Directives 89/665/EEC and 92/13/EEC with regard to improving the effectiveness of review procedures concerning the award of public contracts.

13 Commission Regulation (EU) No 1251/2011 of 30 November 2011 amending Directives 2004/17/EC, 2004/18/EC and 2009/81/EC of the European Parliament and of the Council in respect of their application thresholds for the procedures for the awards of contract.

14 Regulation (EC) No 2195/2002 of the European Parliament and of the Council of 5 November 2002 on the Common Procurement Vocabulary (CPV), amended by Regulation (EC) No 596/2009.

15 European Commission, *Commission interpretative communication on the application of Community law on Public Procurement and Concessions to institutionalised PPP (IPPP)* ([2008] OJ C 91/02).

principle, the following activities: the provision or operation of gas, heat and electricity grids; the supply of gas, heat and electricity to such grids; and the exploration for or the extraction of oil, gas, coal or other solid fuels.[16]

The Special Sectors Directive applies to contracts which reach a certain threshold value only. Thresholds result from article 16 and have already undergone several changes. As mentioned above, current thresholds arise from Regulation 1251/2011 and may be readjusted by the Commission. Apart from that, articles 19 to 26 and article 30 totally exclude specific contracts from the scope of the Special Sectors Directive (see also Commission Decision 2005/15/EC on rules for the application of article 30).[17] This holds especially true for works and service concessions, for contracts awarded for the purposes of resale or lease to third parties, and for service contracts awarded on the basis of an exclusive right.

The process of awarding contracts falling within the scope of the Special Sectors Directive is subject to a number of detailed rules pertaining, for instance, to award procedures (open, restricted and negotiated procedures), publication and transparency, the selection of suitable participants and, finally, contract award criteria. Contract award criteria arise from article 55. Accordingly, the contracting entities are to award the contract to the tender with the lowest price or to the one with the most economical advantage. Where the contract is awarded to the most economically advantageous tender, contracting entities shall apply criteria linked to the subject-matter of the contract in question (for example, delivery or completion date, running costs, cost-effectiveness, quality, aesthetic and functional characteristics or environmental characteristics). Directives 92/13/EEC[18] and 2007/66/EC[19] ensure the effective application of Directive 2004/17/EC. The directives require member states to make certain that the awarding of a contract may be reviewed effectively on the grounds that a procurement decision has violated EU procurement law or national rules implementing that law.

---

16 See for exemptions art 3 paras 2 and 4.

17 Commission Decision of 7 January 2005 on the detailed rules for the application of the procedure provided for in article 30 of Directive 2004/17/EC of the European Parliament and of the Council coordinating the procurement procedures of entities operating in the water, energy, transport and postal services sectors (2005/15/EC).

18 Council Directive 92/13/EEC of 25 February 1992 coordinating the laws, regulations and administrative provisions relating to the application of Community rules on the procurement procedures of entities operating in the water, energy, transport and telecommunications sectors.

19 Directive 2007/66/EC of the European Parliament and of the Council of 11 December 2007 amending Council Directives 89/665/EEC and 92/13/EEC with regard to improving the effectiveness of review procedures concerning the award of public contracts.

In 2008 the Commission published a basic concept of Green Public Procurement (GPP) aiming at adjusting the European procurement regime to climate and energy efficiency targets and harmonising the various environmental criteria used in the framework of member states' procurement schemes.[20] GPP means that public authorities shall procure 'goods, services and works with a reduced environmental impact throughout their life cycle when compared to goods, services and works with the same primary function'.[21] Technically speaking, authorities will be encouraged to include environmental considerations in their procurement decisions, which furthermore falls into line with Directives 2004/17/EC and 2004/18/EC. Both allow for the consideration of environmental characteristics as contract award criteria.[22] The Commission has developed environmental criteria for a range of product types and services over the years, including the purchase of electricity by public authorities, for instance.[23]

GPP is a voluntary scheme, meaning that member states may decide how and to what extent they apply it. However, it should be kept in mind that in various respects EU legislation explicitly provides for obligations to observe specific environmental criteria. This holds true, for example, in the acquisition of office equipment[24] and road transport vehicles.[25] Furthermore, the Energy Efficiency Directive determines that at least central governments under certain conditions are required to purchase only products, services and buildings with high energy-efficiency performance, while public bodies are only encouraged to do the same.[26]

The Commission has sought to update the EU procurement regime for some considerable time.[27] In 2014 the EU legislature adopted Directives 2014/24/

---

20 European Commission, *Communication from the Commission to the European Parliament, the Council, the European Economic and Social Committee and the Committee of the Regions, Public procurement for a better environment* (COM(2008) 0400 final).

21 Section 3.1 of Commission Communication COM(2008) 0400 final.

22 See art 55 Directive 2004/17/EC and art 53 Directive 2004/18/EC.

23 See website http://ec.europa.eu/environment/gpp/eu_gpp_criteria_en.htm, accessed 5 May 2016.

24 See art 6 of Regulation (EC) No 106/2008 of the European Parliament and of the Council of 15 January 2008 on a Community energy-efficiency labelling programme for office equipment. Article 6 was amended by art 1 of Regulation (EU) No 174/2013 of the European Parliament and of the Council of 5 February 2013 amending Regulation (EC) No 106/2008 on a Community energy-efficiency labelling programme for office equipment.

25 See art 5 of Directive 2009/33/EC of the European Parliament and of the Council of 23 April 2009 on the promotion of clean and energy-efficient road transport vehicles.

26 See art 6 Directive 2012/27/EU on energy efficiency, amending Directives 2009/125/EC and 2010/30/EU and repealing Directives 2004/8/EC and 2006/32/EC.

27 See European Commission, *Green Paper on the modernisation of EU public procurement policy – Towards a more efficient European Procurement Market* (COM(2011) 15 final).

EU[28] and 2014/25/EU[29] which form the outcome of several years' reflection. These two directives repeal the currently applicable Special Sectors Directive and Traditional Directive with effect from 18 April 2016, marking the date of the realignment of the EU procurement regime.

b)   *Award of concession contracts*

Alongside the public procurement reform directives, the EU legislature adopted furthermore a new directive on the award of concession contracts (Directive 2014/23/EU) which member states also have to transpose by 18 April 2016.[30] This directive lays down rules on the procedures for procurement by means of a works or services concession. It generally also covers the energy sector whereas especially in the areas of Directive 94/22/EC (hydrocarbons licensing, see section 5.1.2 below), Directive 2009/72/EC (Electricity Directive) and Directive 2009/73/EC (Gas Directive) exemptions apply.[31]

5.1.2   Hydrocarbons licensing

With a view to promoting the functioning of the EU energy market, the Hydrocarbons Licensing Directive (94/22/EC) lays down rules on the conditions for granting and using licences for the prospection, exploration and production of hydrocarbons.[32] The directive complements the Special Sectors Directive 2004/17/EC regarding procurement procedures in the water, energy, transport and postal services sectors. The Hydrocarbons Licensing Directive is based on the premise that member states retain sovereign rights over domestic oil, gas and other hydrocarbon resources, which particularly includes their decision over which concrete oil or gas deposits are available for tapping. Whilst taking this into account, the Hydrocarbons Licensing Directive determines principles as to licensing procedures and the usage of authorisations. In particular, member states must make certain that authorisations are granted on the basis of objective,

---

28 Directive 2014/24/EU of the European Parliament and of the Council of 26 February 2014 on public procurement and repealing Directive 2004/18/EC [2014] OJ L 94/65.

29 Directive 2014/25/EU of the European Parliament and of the Council of 26 February 2014 on procurement by entities operating in the water, energy, transport and postal services sectors and repealing Directive 2004/17/EC [2014] OJ L 94/243.

30 Directive 2014/23/EU of the European Parliament and of the Council of 26 February 2014 on the award of concession contracts [2014] OJ L 94/1.

31 See art 7(2) b) and annex III of Directive 2014/23/EU.

32 Directive 94/22/EC of the European Parliament and of the Council of 30 May 1994 on the conditions for granting and using authorisations for the prospection, exploration and production of hydrocarbons [1994] OJ L 164/3.

transparent and non-discriminatory criteria. Granting criteria must in any case include the technical and financial capability of entities and the way in which they would prospect, explore and exploit the available area.[33] Member states have the right to impose conditions and requirements on the exercise of activities of prospecting, exploring for and producing hydrocarbons, provided that such restrictions are justified by specific national concerns, such as national security, public safety, public health or protection of the environment.[34]

The procedure for granting authorisations must be open to all entities from EU member states. Undertakings from third countries are in principal treated as equal. In the event that EU companies do not enjoy a comparable treatment in a third country, the Council may authorise one or more EU member states to refuse to grant a permit to an entity controlled by this particular third country or a national of this country.[35] Apart from that, member states may refuse access for third country undertakings on grounds of national security.[36]

5.1.3 Energy taxation

Tax instruments may serve different political ends. It is not just that they represent the main financial resource of government budgets. Often states deploy tax regulation also to promote specific sectors or to create obstacles for the import of products. That said, tax instruments may also constitute a crucial factor for the regulation of the energy field. With a view to preventing national tax regimes from tarnishing the internal market in energy, EU primary and secondary law seeks to align national schemes with EU objectives. As regards primary law, national energy taxation must first be in conformity with article 110 TFEU, which prohibits tax discrimination within the internal market.[37] Second, tax exemptions favouring certain branches or companies constitute state aid in the sense of EU law and have therefore to comply with the state aid rules set forth in articles 107 to 109 TFEU.[38] Third, under article 113 TFEU, the European Union may adopt measures to harmonise indirect taxation systems in member states (turnover taxes and excise duties in particular) if necessary for the functioning of the internal market.

---

33 Cf art 5 Directive 94/22/EC.
34 Cf art 6(2) Directive 94/22/EC.
35 Cf art 8 Directive 94/22/EC.
36 Cf art 2 Directive 94/22/EC.
37 For details see above section 2.3.
38 For details see above section 2.2.5.

The European Union has made use of this competence in the area of energy, particularly through the Energy Taxation Directive 2003/96/EC.[39] The Energy Taxation Directive establishes a framework for national taxation of energy products and electricity. The Energy Taxation Directive defines minimum tax levels for motor fuel, motor fuel for industrial or commercial use, heating fuel and electricity.[40] Rates of national taxation may not come below the minimum rates provided for in the Directive. Furthermore the Energy Taxation Directive exempts certain products from taxation (for example, energy products and electricity used to produce electricity) and allows member states to apply tax exemptions and reductions in the level of taxation to a number of other products and forms of energy (for example, electricity of solar, wind, wave, tidal or geothermal origin; or electricity generated from biomass).[41] In 2011 the Commission tabled a draft to recast the Energy Taxation Directive, igniting a fierce debate on the future of the EU regime. Despite some progress achieved through various council presidencies, to date the reform continues to be stalled due to the irreconcilable positions of some member states.

5.1.4 Energy statistics and market observatory

Energy policy has developed into a prime concern of the European Union. Already today it features a highly complex structure reflecting the enormous challenges the European Union faces in the development of a sustainable European-wide energy supply. To monitor the effects of EU energy policy, the European Union requires precise data on energy generation, transformation, consumption, imports and exports. With Regulation No 1099/2008 on Energy Statistics, the European Union created a common framework for the production and compilation of such data.[42] The regulation obliges member states to convey comparable national data on energy products, that is, combustible fuels, renewable energy, electricity and so on, and on the treatment und use of such products to Eurostat, the statistical office of the European Union. National statistics collected by Eurostat are taken as a basis for EU energy figures and factsheets, which the Commission publishes on its website.[43] Aside from Regulation No 1099/2008, the European Union

39 Council Directive 2003/96/EC of 27 October 2003 restructuring the Community framework for the taxation of energy products and electricity [2003] OJ L 283/51.

40 See summary of legislation at http://europa.eu/legislation_summaries/internal_market/single_market_ for_ goods/motor_vehicles/interactions_industry_policies/l27019_en.htm, accessed 5 May 2016.

41 See art 15 Energy Taxation Directive.

42 Regulation (EC) No 1099/2008 of the European Parliament and of the Council of 22 October 2008 on energy statistics [2008] OJ L 304/1.

43 See https://ec.europa.eu/energy/en/statistics, accessed 5 May 2016.

has adopted several further pieces of legislation concerning the transmission of specific information by member states and undertakings operating in the energy sector, respectively. This applies, for example, to information on imports of hard coal from third countries,[44] crude oil supply cost,[45] the consumer prices of petroleum products,[46] and sale prices of gas and electricity charged to industrial end-users.[47]

In order to be able to draw the right conclusions from incoming data, the Commission established under its umbrella the Market Observatory for Energy. Its task entails, first and foremost, the pooling and analysing of relevant information to help the Commission monitor the market and draft legislative adjustments. For that reason, it observes, for instance, demand and supply developments, market prices, trade volumes and the expansion of infrastructures.[48]

5.2 Legislation and instruments related to energy efficiency

Energy efficiency relates to the goal of reducing the amount of energy needed for the operation of objects and for the provision of services. Given that we consume energy in almost any sphere of life, its efficient use constitutes an ubiquitous issue. Indeed, energy efficiency still represents one of the largest potential energy sources in the world and especially so in the comparatively resource-poor European Union. For that reason, the European Union attaches particular importance to the issue with the ultimate goal of essentially conserving energy.[49] According to article 194 TFEU, energy efficiency is considered among the basic objectives of EU energy policy and it has been mainstreamed into the major political strategies in that field for the planning horizons 2020,[50] 2030[51] and 2050.[52] Originally, the issue gained significantly

---

44 Cf Council Regulation (EC) No 405/2003 of 27 February 2003 concerning Community monitoring of imports of hard coal originating in third countries [2003] OJ L 62/1.

45 Cf Council Decision 1999/280/EC regarding a Community procedure for information and consultation on crude oil supply costs and the consumer prices of petroleum products.

46 Ibid.

47 Directive 2008/92/EC concerning a Community procedure to improve the transparency of gas and electricity prices charged to industrial end-users (recast) [2008] OJ L 298/9.

48 See European Commission, *2008 leaflet market observatory*.

49 For further details on EU energy efficiency policy see, for instance, J Curtin (ed.), *EU Energy Law: Volume VII, Energy Efficiency in the European Union* (Claeys & Casteels Publishing 2014).

50 See European Council 8/9 March 2007, *Presidency Conclusions* (doc 7224/1/07 REV1); European Commission, *Energy 2020, A strategy for competitive, sustainable and secure energy* (COM(2010) 0639 final).

51 European Council 24 October 2014, *Conclusions* (EUCO 169/14).

52 European Commission, *Energy Roadmap 2050* (COM(2011) 885/2).

in importance with the adoption of the 20-20-20 targets for the year 2020, which laid out the objective of reducing EU energy consumption by 20% compared to projections for 2020, to be brought about by energy efficiency.[53] With a view to attaining the 2020 energy saving and efficiency goal the European Union initially adopted an 'Energy Efficiency Package' in 2009 and 2010, which already led to an extension of the legislative framework applicable at that time.[54] However, the bundle was ultimately not deemed sufficient for achieving the 20% goal,[55] so that in spring 2011 the Commission introduced an 'Energy Efficiency Plan 2011' to expedite necessary action.[56]

Based on the strategic framework, the EU legislator has finally strengthened the regulatory structures that member states have to implement. However, despite progress made in recent years, the Commission still anticipates that the European Union will fall short of the 20% goal, so that a further tightening of existing provisions is conceivable.[57] Legislation in place today comprises, in particular, the legislative acts outlined in the following subsections. Besides, energy efficiency is promoted through some of the support programmes listed in section 5.6 below and through legislation focusing on specific energy sectors (for example, the Electricity Directive and the Gas Directive).

5.2.1 Framework for energy efficiency measures

In order to set out a common foundation for energy efficiency measures, in October 2012 the European Parliament and the Council adopted the so-called Energy Efficiency Directive (Directive 2012/27/EU).[58] The Energy Efficiency Directive or EED forms an overarching framework affecting the whole energy supply chain in order to remove market barriers which obviously hamper the attainment of the 20% target for 2020.[59] The EED requires member states to define indicative national energy efficiency targets which especially take account of the indicative 9% saving target set in the previous directive 2006/32/EC.[60] In achieving these national targets, member

---

53 See European Council 8/9 March 2007, *Presidency Conclusions* (doc 7224/1/07 REV1).
54 See section 3.3 above.
55 European Commission, *The Commission's new Energy Efficiency Directive* (press release of 22 June 2011, MEMO/11/440).
56 European Commission, *Energy Efficiency Plan 2011* (COM(2011) 109 final).
57 European Commission, *A policy framework for climate and energy in the period from 2020 to 2030* (COM(2014) 015 final) sec 2.3.
58 Directive 2012/27/EU of the European Parliament and of the Council of 25 October 2012 on energy efficiency, amending Directives 2009/125/EC and 2010/30/EU and repealing Directives 2004/8/EC and 2006/32/EC [2012] OJ L 315/1.
59 Article 1 Directive 2012/27/EU.
60 Articles 3(1), 27(1) and recital 63 of Directive 2012/27/EU.

states are particularly to deploy measures laid down in the EED. In order to enable the Commission to monitor whether member states are on track towards their efficiency targets, member states have to report on progress and draw up and submit to the Commission so-called National Energy Efficiency Action Plans (EEAP) specifying, among other things, measures still required to be taken.[61]

a)   Efficiency in energy supply

With a particular focus on increasing efficiency at energy generation level, the EED seeks to expand efficient heating and cooling systems, especially high-efficiency cogeneration and efficient district heating and cooling. Member states are to particularly identify, assess and, if benefits exceed the costs, tap the potential for the deployment of the latter two technologies (see article 14 for further details). Cogeneration is a technique to exploit the heat emitted when generating electrical or mechanical energy, whereas high-efficiency cogeneration means cogeneration meeting the criteria set out in annex II of the EED. Efficient district heating and cooling refers to a district heating or cooling system using at least 50% renewable energy, 50% waste heat, 75% cogeneration heat or 50% of a combination of such energy and heat. Article 14 on efficient heating and cooling extends and replaces the former Cogeneration Directive 2004/8/EC (CHP Directive), which member states were nevertheless obliged to transpose into national law.

In addition, in article 15, the EED provides for mechanisms to improve the efficiency in energy transformation, transmission and distribution with a view to maximising grid and infrastructure efficiency and promoting demand response.[62] Accordingly, member states, and national regulatory agencies in particular, shall foster energy efficiency especially through specific measures concerning network tariffs and regulation, demand response and the operation and design of electricity and gas infrastructure.[63] Efficiency in the transformation and distribution of electricity and gas is furthermore promoted by the Electricity Directive and the Gas Directive; both Directives and the EED complement each other.

---

61 Article 24(1) and (2) Directive 2012/27/EU.

62 See also European Commission, *Commission Staff Working Document, Guidance note on Directive 2012/27/ EU on energy efficiency, amending Directives 2009/125/EC and 2010/30/EC, and repealing Directives 2004/8/ EC and 2006/32/EC, Article 15* (SWD/2013/0450 final).

63 See also European Commission, *Commission Staff Working Document*, ibid.

b)   *Efficiency in energy use*

Chapter II of the EED (articles 4 to 13) aims to augment efficiency at the level of energy consumption. Emphasis is primarily laid on strengthening the energy efficiency of buildings. Accordingly articles 4 and 5 build on obligations already set out in the Energy Performance of Buildings Directive 2010/31/EU and require, beyond that, sophisticated national investment planning for renovation and the public sector to take the lead in the renovation of buildings by specifically undertaking to renovate each year 3% of buildings owned and occupied by central governments. Article 6 of the EED provides for, furthermore, central governments and public bodies playing an exemplary role in the purchasing of products, services and buildings with high energy-efficiency performance as defined by specific efficiency-related EU legislation, such as the Energy Labelling Directive,[64] the Eco Design Directive[65] and respective implementing measures.

Besides, article 7 requires member states to set up energy efficiency obligation schemes or use other policy measures with a view to attaining certain targeted amounts of energy savings at final consumption level. Half the energy savings the EED aspires to should be achieved on the basis of article 7, making it the centrepiece of the EED.[66] The Commission has given detailed guidance on article 7 in a separate working document.[67] In order to identify the potential for energy savings, article 8 promotes the introduction and spread of energy audits and energy management systems. Whereas small and medium-sized enterprises (SMEs) shall be encouraged to undergo an energy audit and to implement its findings, member states must oblige larger enterprises to either have carried out an energy audit by 5 December 2015 and at least every four years after the previous audit, or to implement a certified energy or environmental management system including an energy audit. Articles 9 to 11, building on the stipulations set out in the Electricity and Gas Directives, lay down requirements as to metering and billing information. Individual accurate metering and free-access to consumption data and billing information are aimed at helping customers better oversee their energy use and ultimately at inducing them to save more energy.

---

64 Directive 2010/30/EU.

65 Directive 2009/125/EC.

66 See European Commission, *Implementing the Energy Efficiency Directive – Commission Guidance* (COM/2013/0762 final).

67 European Commission, *Commission Staff Working Document, Guidance note on Directive 2012/27/EU on energy efficiency, amending Directives 2009/125/EC and 2010/30/EC, and repealing Directives 2004/8/EC and 2006/32/EC Article 7: Energy efficiency obligation schemes – Accompanying the document Communication from the Commission to the European Parliament and the Council, Implementing the Energy Efficiency Directive – Commission Guidance* (SWD/2013/0451 final).

c)   *Horizontal provisions to promote energy efficiency*

Finally, articles 16 to 21 of the EED include a range of horizontal provisions to promote energy efficiency. These provisions concern, for instance, the removal of regulatory and non-regulatory barriers to energy efficiency and the establishment of financing facilities for energy efficiency improvement measures.

5.2.2   Energy performance of buildings

A large part of EU energy consumption results from the building sector. According to the Commission's estimates, buildings account for around 40% of EU energy consumption and 36% of EU CO_2 emissions.[68] Improving energy performance of buildings remains, thus, of paramount importance for attaining EU energy and climate targets. Energy performance of buildings is primarily subject to the Directive on the Energy Performance of Buildings 2010/31/EU (EPBD) which is supposed to partially recast the previous Directive 2002/91/EC.[69]

Pursuant to the new EPBD, member states shall particularly establish minimum energy performance requirements for new buildings and generally also for existing buildings undergoing major renovation in order to achieve cost-optimal levels (articles 4, 6 and 7). As regards new buildings, the feasibility of high-efficiency alternative systems, such as decentralised renewables, district heating, cogeneration and head pumps, if applicable, is to be taken into consideration. According to article 3, member states must base the calculation of the energy performance of buildings on a methodology that complies with the common framework laid down in annex I of Directive 2010/31. Member states may exempt certain categories of buildings from the application of minimum energy performance requirements, such as, under certain conditions, historic buildings and industrial sites (article 4 para 2).

Furthermore, member states shall make sure that by 31 December 2020 all new buildings are nearly zero-energy buildings. New public buildings already have to be nearly zero-energy buildings after 31 December 2018. The concept of nearly zero-energy buildings refers to buildings having a very high energy performance as defined in accordance with annex I, whereas the very low energy requirement should be covered mainly by energy from renewable sources.[70]

---

68 Commission website http://ec.europa.eu/energy/efficiency/buildings/buildings_en.htm, accessed 5 May 2016.

69 Directive 2010/31/EU of 19 May 2010 on the energy performance of buildings (recast) [2010] OJ L 153/13.

70 Cf art 2 no 2 Directive 2010/31/EU.

Directive 2010/31 provides for a range of further requirements. For instance, member states are to arrange the issuance of energy performance certificates for buildings or building units which are constructed, sold or rented out to new tenants.[71] Such certificates are to help prospective new buyers or tenants to decide whether to buy or to rent a new building or even to decide against buying or renting. Certifications must also be issued for public buildings used by authorities and frequently visited by the public, where certificates must be clearly visible displayed (see articles 11, 12 and 13 for detailed requirements). Member states are also to consider setting up financial support programmes and other instruments with a view to stepping up the energy performance of buildings (article 10). Furthermore, member states shall set requirements for technical building systems (article 8) and ensure regular inspection of heating and air-conditioning systems in buildings (articles 14 and 15).

5.2.3   Energy labelling

a)   *Household appliances*

In order to reduce the energy consumption of appliances typically used in households, the European Union has introduced the EU energy label. The label aims at increasing consumers' awareness of the real energy consumption of products. It reveals cost-saving opportunities and, thus, helps disseminate energy-efficient appliances. To date, the EU energy label has been governed by Directive 2010/30/EU (Energy Labelling Directive) which replaced the original Labelling Directive 92/75/EC[72] and which was partially amended by the Energy Efficiency Directive 2012/27/EU. According to the Energy Labelling Directive, household lamps and most white goods, such as refrigerators, washing machines, dryers, dishwashers, ovens, water heaters, and air-conditioning appliances must be accompanied by an EU energy label and a product fiche when offered for sale or rent. The label and product fiche provide information relating to the consumption of energy or of other essential resources.

The energy label, however, should not be confused with the EU Ecolabel (with a flower logo) which is a voluntary labelling system intended to encourage businesses to offer products and services that meet certain environmental criteria. By contrast, energy labels include coloured arrows combined with

---

71 See art 12 Directive 2010/31/EU.
72 Directive 2010/30/EU of the European Parliament and of the Council of 19 May 2010 on the indication by labelling and standard product information of the consumption of energy and other resources by energy-related products (recast) [2010] OJ L 153/1.

letters (generally from A to G) to differentiate the energy consumption of products, and they display further key information and characteristics of the relevant product, such as its annual energy consumption. The present design of the energy label is, however, criticised for its limited scale which suggests that there is no further need to improve energy efficiency once a product falls under categories A (or A+++).

The Energy Labelling Directive constitutes a framework directive which is implemented by a number of specific Commission regulations and directives with a focus on individual household appliances, such as electric refrigerators, household lamps, washing machines and so on.[73] All these acts determine details relating to the label and fiche required for a certain product.

b)   *Office equipment*

Promoting energy efficiency of office equipment, such as computers and displays, is the objective of the EU Energy Star programme set out in Regulation (EC) No 106/2008 (EU Energy Star Regulation).[74] In contrast to the rules applicable to typical household appliances, the EU Energy Star Regulation provides for manufacturers and retailers participating in the EU Energy Star programme on a voluntary basis. After registering their company and a product that meets the Energy Star energy efficiency criteria, they may use the Energy Star logo when marketing their products to attract new customers. The Energy Star label originated in the USA and is used worldwide today. The European and the US-American Energy Star programmes are co-ordinated with the result that products registered in the European Union are also recognised in the United States, and vice versa.

Back in 2001 the Commission concluded that the Energy Star programme had been successful and was particularly well suited for ICT products due to its dynamism and voluntary nature.[75] However, the Energy Star programme has also met with some scepticism concerning the effectiveness of self-certification of appliances by manufacturers[76] and the lack of an energy

---

73 For applicable acts see Commission's website http://ec.europa.eu/energy/en/topics/energy-efficiency/ energy-efficient-products, accessed 5 May 2016.

74 Regulation (EC) No 106/2008 of the European Parliament and of the Council of 15 January 2008 on a Community energy-efficiency labelling programme for office equipment (recast version) [2008] OJ L 39/1. Regulation (EC) No 106/2008 was amended meanwhile by Regulation (EU) No 174/2013.

75 European Commission, *Communication from the Commission on the implementation of the Energy Star programme in the European Union in the period 2006–2010* (COM(2011) 337 final) sec 4.4.

76 See *New York Times*, 'Why Obama's energy savings estimate may be skewed' (6 February 2009).

consumption rating comparable to that applicable to household appliances.[77] Indeed, it remains hard to understand how a certification label is supposed to effectively incentivise technical improvements when consumers are not enabled to easily differentiate between the energy consumption of products on a certain scale (for example, a scale from A to G). Once a product carries the Energy Star logo it implies that there is no great difference in energy consumption compared to similar products also furnished with an Energy star.

With a view to helping spread the use of Energy Star products, the EU Energy Star regulation requires that EU institutions and the central government authorities of the respective member states must define energy-efficiency requirements no less demanding than the Energy Star specifications for the public procurement of office equipment.[78] According to the Commission, manufacturers consider this provision as the main argument for Energy Star product registrations in the European Union.[79]

5.2.4   Eco-design of energy-related products

Making consumers aware of the energy expenditure of certain products through energy labels is only one way to scale down energy consumption. Apart from that, governments may also directly oblige manufacturers to develop energy efficient products. Defining such product-related requirements is the aim of the EU Eco-design policy and corresponding legislation. The general framework for setting Eco-design requirements, including efficiency requirements, follows from Directive 2009/125/EC (Eco-design Directive).[80] This directive applies to energy-related products (ErPs) including energy-using products (such as computers, televisions, transformers) and other energy-related products having an impact on energy consumption (such as windows, insulation material). The directive does not, however, apply to vehicles for transport, which come under a different set of rules (see below).[81]

The Eco-design Directive establishes a framework of setting and improving specific requirements for certain products, whereas such specific

---

77 See http://applianceadvisor.com/content/open-letter-steven-chu-obamas-choice-head-doe0099, acces sed 5 May 2016.

78 See art 6 Regulation (EC) No 106/2008 as amended by Regulation (EU) No 174/2013.

79 European Commission, *Communication from the Commission on the implementation of the Energy Star programme in the European Union in the period 2006–2010* (COM(2011) 337 final) sections 2.1 and 5.

80 Directive 2009/125/EC of the European Parliament and of the Council of 21 October 2009 establishing a framework for the setting of ecodesign requirements for energy-related product [2009] OJ L 285/10.

81 See section 5.3.3 below.

product-related requirements themselves are established only by various implementing measures or by self-regulation measures such as voluntary agreements. In cases where a given product is covered by an implementing measure, the manufacturer or its representative must assure the conformity of the product with all the requirements of that implementing measure by affixing a CE marking and issuing a declaration of conformity. Ultimately, the Eco-design Directive ensures the free movement of products that comply with implementing measures and bear the respective CE marking.

The preparation and adoption of implementing measures falls within the Commission's remit. The Commission is nonetheless obliged to ensure that member states and stakeholders are able to participate in the drafting process. For that reason, it has to involve the Ecodesign Consultation Forum, which consists of member states' representatives and interested parties, such as industry and consumer organisations, in defining and reviewing implementing measures. Furthermore, in drafting an implementing measure the Commission must take into account the opinion of the Ecodesign Regulatory Committee which again gathers representatives of the member states. Based on the Eco-design Directive, the Commission has adopted, in particular, implementing measures with regard to ecodesign requirements for household dishwashers,[82] household washing machines,[83] electric motors,[84] refrigerators and freezers,[85] televisions,[86] external power supplies,[87] and lighting products in the domestic and tertiary sectors.[88] The lighting products regulations are

---

82 Commission Regulation (EU) No 1016/2010 of 10 November 2010 implementing Directive 2009/125/EC of the European Parliament and of the Council with regard to ecodesign requirements for household dishwashers.

83 Commission Regulation (EU) No 1015/2010 of 10 November 2010 implementing Directive 2009/125/EC of the European Parliament and of the Council with regard to ecodesign requirements for household washing machines.

84 Commission Regulation (EU) No 4/2014 of 6 January 2014 amending Regulation (EC) No 640/2009 implementing Directive 2005/32/EC of the European Parliament and of the Council with regard to ecodesign requirements for electric motors; Commission Regulation (EC) No 640/2009 of 22 July 2009 implementing Directive 2005/32/EC of the European Parliament and of the Council with regard to ecodesign requirements for electric motors.

85 Commission Regulation (EC) No 643/2009 of 22 July 2009 implementing Directive 2005/32/EC of the European Parliament and of the Council with regard to ecodesign requirements for household refrigerating appliances.

86 Commission Regulation (EC) No 642/2009 of 22 July 2009 implementing Directive 2005/32/EC of the European Parliament and of the Council with regard to ecodesign requirements for televisions.

87 Commission Regulation (EC) No 278/2009 of 6 April 2009 implementing Directive 2005/32/EC of the European Parliament and of the Council with regard to ecodesign requirements for no-load condition electric power consumption and average active efficiency of external power supplies.

88 Commission Regulation (EC) No 1194/2012 of 12 December 2012 implementing Directive 2005/32/EC of the European Parliament and of the Council with regard to ecodesign requirements for directional lamps,

generally known as being responsible for withdrawing inefficient light bulbs from the market.[89]

5.3 Legislation and instruments related to environmental protection

EU environmental policy has assumed an ever greater importance in past decades. It deals with a range of issues, such as climate change, air pollution, the protection of nature, water and soil, and waste management, and thus constitutes a main instrument of shaping society in a sustainable way. EU environmental policy has a bearing on almost every other policy area and correlates with EU energy policy in particular.

Energy policy, on the one hand, constrains ambitious environmental targeting that might put an adequate energy supply at risk. On the other hand, environmental targets, on their part, have increasingly impinged on policies related to the generation, supply and consumption of energy. The promotion of climate-friendly energy sources and technologies, such as renewables and cogeneration, for instance, are reshaping energy generation. Environmental objectives constitute, furthermore, one driving force behind the EU policy on energy efficiency, as illustrated above, with its impact on the energy consumption side. Moreover, environmental policy encompasses a number of other instruments which may affect the establishment and running of certain facilities in the energy sector. Such measures relate in particular to the protection of habitats, environmental assessment, environmental liability, waste and air, soil and water quality.[90] The Commission's recommendation

---

for light emitting diode lamps and related equipment; Commission Regulation (EU) No 347/2010 of 21 April 2010 amending Commission Regulation (EC) No 245/2009 as regards the ecodesign requirements for fluorescent lamps without integrated ballast, for high intensity discharge lamps, and for ballasts and luminaires able to operate such lamps; Commission Regulation (EC) No 245/2009 of 18 March 2009 implementing Directive 2005/32/EC of the European Parliament and of the Council with regard to ecodesign requirements for fluorescent lamps without integrated ballast, for high intensity discharge lamps, and for ballasts and luminaires able to operate such lamps, and repealing Directive 2000/55/EC of the European Parliament and of the Council; Commission Regulation (EC) No 859/2009 of 18 September 2009 amending Regulation (EC) No 244/2009 as regards the ecodesign requirements on ultraviolet radiation of non-directional household lamps; Commission Regulation (EC) No 244/2009 of 18 March 2009 implementing Directive 2005/32/EC of the European Parliament and of the Council with regard to ecodesign requirements for non-directional household lamps.

89 European Commission, *Commission adopts two regulations to progressively remove from the market non-efficient light bulbs* (press release 18 March 2009, IP/09/411).

90 See also M Roggenkamp, C Redgwell, I del Guayo and A Rønne, *Energy Law in Europe* (2nd edn, OUP 2007) 315 et seq.

on minimum principles for using hydraulic fracturing ('fracking') represents one of the latest initiatives in this context.[91]

The following sections will illustrate legislation and instruments of environmental policy with a particular effect on various energy sub-sectors. Further information on current initiatives going beyond these may be gleaned in particular from the areas of energy, environmental and climate policy on the Commission's website. As regards the promotion of renewable energies and the measures of EU efficiency policy which also serve EU environmental policy, see the respective sections above.[92]

5.3.1 EU Greenhouse Gas Emission Allowance Trading Scheme (EU ETS)

The European Union Emissions Trading Scheme (EU ETS) is considered among the measures with a particular bearing on the energy branch. As one of the pillars of EU climate policy, the scheme aims at reducing emissions of greenhouse gases, such as carbon dioxide (CO_2) and methane (CH_4), with a view also to meeting European commitments on climate protection which were given in the framework of the Kyoto Protocol. The EU ETS particularly concerns energy production through the combustion of fossil fuels, but also pertains to numerous other activities emitting greenhouse gases, such as iron and steel production or aviation.[93] The legal framework of the EU ETS follows from Directive 2003/87/EC (ETS Directive),[94] Directive 2009/29/EC altering the ETS Directive[95] and various other amending and implementing measures.[96]

EU ETS is classed among the market-based instruments. It provides economic incentives for the reduction of emissions. The scheme operates on a

---

91 Commission Recommendation 2014/70/EU of 22 January 2014 on minimum principles for the exploration and production of hydrocarbons (such as shale gas) using high-volume hydraulic fracturing.

92 In terms of renewable energy see section 4.5 and in terms of energy efficiency see section 5.2. As regards relevant support programmes see also section 5.6 below.

93 For details and applicable temporary exemptions in terms of the inclusion of aviation into the scheme see Commission website http://ec.europa.eu/clima/policies/transport/aviation/index_en.htm, accessed 5 May 2016.

94 Directive 2003/87/EC of the European Parliament and of the Council of 13 October 2003 establishing a scheme for greenhouse gas emission allowance trading within the Community and amending Council Directive 96/61/EC [2003] OJ L 275/32.

95 Directive 2009/29/EC of the European Parliament and of the Council of 23 April 2009 amending Directive 2003/87/EC so as to improve and extend the greenhouse gas emission allowance trading scheme of the Community [2009] OJ L 140/63.

96 For details see Commission website http://ec.europa.eu/clima/policies/ets/index_en.htm, accessed 5 May 2016.

cap-and-trade approach. It limits overall emissions of greenhouse gases by all emitters and permits individual emissions on the basis of tradable allowances. Accordingly, installations emitting greenhouse gases covered by the scheme, such as power plants, must not only have a general permit to emit affected pollutants. They also require a certain number of allowances (known as European Union Allowances or EUAs) corresponding to the amount of their emissions. An emission allowance is the tradable unit under the EU ETS and represents one tonne of carbon dioxide equivalent. If a given undertaking reduces its emissions and subsequently does not reach the amount of emissions covered by allowances it has obtained by governmental allocation or auctioning, it may sell unused allowances. If the allowances it has at hand do not cover the actual amount of emissions, the undertaking must buy additional allowances. Eventually the installation of climate-friendly technologies should pay off given that the total amount of allowances available on the market remains limited and their price continues to be high.

The EU has progressively extended its emission trading scheme in the course of consecutive trading periods. The first period (2005–07) was considered as a 'learning by doing' phase and did not lead to major environmental benefits. Member states issued allowances overgenerously[97] and emissions were still slightly rising during that phase.[98] In the second period (2008–12), the European Union significantly tightened and enlarged the scheme. National emissions were capped at an average of 6.5% below 2005 levels in order to meet the Kyoto targets.[99] The EU decided to include emissions from aviation from 2012[100] and Norway, Iceland, and Liechtenstein joined the scheme. Moreover, the joint implementation (JI) and clean development mechanism (CDM) as Kyoto project-based mechanisms were explicitly linked with the EU ETS by the so-called Linking Directive.[101] Accordingly, credits generated under the JI and CDM (so-called ERUs and CERs) may be recognised as being equivalent to EU emission allowances.[102]

---

97 T Gilbertson and O Reyes, 'Carbon trading – How it works and why it fails' (November 2009) No 7 Critical Currents 51.

98 European Commission, *Emissions trading: 2007 verified emissions from EU ETS businesses* (press release of 23 May 2008, IP/08/787).

99 European Commission, *Questions and Answers on the Commission's proposal to revise the EU Emissions Trading System* (23 January 2008, MEMO/08/35).

100 For details and applicable temporary exemptions see Commission website http://ec.europa.eu/clima/policies/transport/aviation/index_en.htm, accessed 5 May 2016.

101 Directive 2004/101/EC of the European Parliament and of the Council of 27 October 2004 amending Directive 2003/87/EC establishing a scheme for greenhouse gas emission allowance trading within the Community, in respect of the Kyoto Protocol's project mechanisms.

102 Whereas CERs might already been allowed from 2005 onwards, recognition of ERUs was only provided for from 2008. See also L Massai, *The Kyoto Protocol in the EU: European Community and Member States under*

With the third phase (2013–20) further significant changes to the EU ETS have become effective.[103] Whereas in the first and second phases member states allocated the major part of allowances for free, in the third period free allocation is to be gradually substituted by auctioning. For instance, in 2020 member states may only grant 30% of emission allowances for free and in 2027 free allocation is set to cease, at least according to the currently applicable legislation.[104] As regards electricity generators and installations for carbon capture, the new scheme already bars free allocation from 2013 onwards.[105] However, electricity generators may obtain free allowances for district heating and cooling and high-efficiency cogeneration.[106] Moreover, for a transitional period until 2020, the new scheme also exempts under certain conditions electricity generators in areas with a particular need of modernisation by allowing the free allocation of allowances.[107] As it is particularly old coal-fired power stations in Eastern Europe that may benefit from this exemption, the transitional rules have met with sharp criticism.[108]

As regards the transitional free allocation of allowances, except for those granted to the aforementioned electricity generators in areas requiring modernisation[109], the Commission has adopted EU-wide harmonised rules in its so-called 'Benchmarking Decision'.[110] In conformity with the new ETS scheme, these rules move away from the originally applicable grandfathering principle under which allowances were granted to a certain facility on the basis of its emissions in a previous period.[111] Instead, the new harmonised rules provide for free allocation being led by benchmarks taking into account

---

International and European Law (Springer 2011) 125; M Roggenkamp, C Redgwell, I del Guayo and A Rønne, *Energy Law in Europe*, 321.

103 See Directive 2009/29/EC of the European Parliament and of the Council of 23 April 2009 amending Directive 2003/87/EC so as to improve and extend the greenhouse gas emission allowance trading scheme of the Community [2009] OJ L 140/63.

104 Cf art 1 para 12 of Directive 2009/29/EC (regarding inserted art 10a para 11 of Directive 2003/87/EC).

105 Cf art 1 para 12 of Directive 2009/29/EC (regarding inserted art 10a para 3 of Directive 2003/87/EC) and recital 19 of Directive 2009/29/EC.

106 Cf art 1 para 12 of Directive 2009/29/EC (regarding inserted art 10a para 4 of Directive 2003/87/EC) and recital 19 of Directive 2009/29/EC.

107 Art 1 para 12 of Directive 2009/29/EC (regarding inserted art 10c of Directive 2003/87/EC).

108 Cf Spiegel-Online, 'Klimabeschluss des EU-Gipfels Europas – Energie-Fresser kommen glimpflich davon' (report of 12 December 2008) http://www.spiegel.de/politik/ausland/0,1518,596108,00.html accessed 5 May 2016.

109 See art 2 Commission Decision 2011/278/EU.

110 Commission Decision 2011/278/EU of 27 April 2011 determining transitional Union-wide rules for harmonised free allocation of emission allowances pursuant to article 10a of Directive 2003/87/EC of the European Parliament and of the Council [2011] OJ L 130/1.

111 See also B Schmitt-Rady, 'A level playing field? Initial allocation of allowances in Member States' in M Peeters and K Deketelaere (eds), *EU Climate Change Policy: The Challenge of New Regulatory Initiatives* (Edward Elgar Publishing 2006) 87 et seq.

the best available technology, such as the most efficient techniques, high efficiency cogeneration and other specified methods.[112] Under the new approach installations meeting the set benchmarks will principally obtain all emission allowances for free. Other installations may attain just a part of required allowances and must, therefore, either buy additional allowances on the market or reduce their emissions.

The EU ETS with its ancillary costs for emission allowances may place European industries competing on a global market directly (through allowance procurement costs) or indirectly (through increased electricity costs) at a disadvantage (so-called 'carbon leakage'). In order to forestall such market distortion, sectors or sub-sectors which might be confronted with carbon leakage may attain more emission allowances for free than other European industries. The Commission has set up a list of sectors which may benefit from this preferential treatment.[113] Furthermore, subject to guidelines of the Commission, member states may grant energy-intensive industries potentially facing carbon leakage state aid designed to compensate for increases in electricity prices caused by EU ETS allowance costs being passed on to electricity customers.[114]

The EU ETS has ignited controversial debate throughout the years. The reason for this is not only the continued free allocation of allowances to old East-European energy generators and energy-intensive industries.[115] Additionally, a considerable surplus of allowances has piled up especially in the years of economic crises and led to a substantial drop in allowance prices, placing the attainment of the goals of the ETS in danger.[116] In order to react to this undesired development on a short-term basis, member states agreed in 2014 to the Commission's 'back-loading proposal', contemplating postponing the sale of 900 million allowances in the third ETS phase in order

---

112 Article 1 para 12 of Directive 2009/29/EC (regarding inserted art 10a para 1 of Directive 2003/87/EC); recital 8 of Commission Decision 2011/278/EU.

113 For the current list and the status of its revision see Commission websites http://ec.europa.eu/clima/policies/ets/cap/leakage/documentation_en.htm and http://ec.europa.eu/clima/policies/ets/cap/leakage/index_en.htm, both accessed 5 May 2016. See also European Commission, *Emissions trading: Member States approve list of sectors deemed to be exposed to carbon leakage* (press release of 18 September 2009, IP/09/1338.

114 See art 1 para 12 of Directive 2009/29/EC (regarding inserted art 10a para 6 of Directive 2003/87/EC) and European Commission, *Guidelines on certain State aid measures in the context of the greenhouse gas emission allowance trading scheme post-2012* (SWD(2012) 130 final) (SWD(2012) 131 final).

115 See also J Geiss, 'From agreement via legislation to implementation – will the climate and energy package delver until 2020?' in R Hinrichs-Rahlwes, *Sustainable Energy Policies for Europe* (CRC Press 2013) 59 et seq.

116 For details see K Neuhoff and A Schopp, 'Europäischer Emissionshandel: Durch Backloading Zeit für Strukturreform gewinnen' (2013) Nr 11 DIW Wochenbericht.

to temporarily reduce the number of allowances available in the market.[117] However, in order to solve the given problems in the long term, structural adjustments to the EU ETS need to be made and the Commission is envisaging these in the establishment of a market stability reserve in the fourth ETS phase.[118] As regards the period after 2020, in particular, EU institutions may consider further adjustments of the scheme outlined above. In this context the conclusions of the meetings of the European Council, like those of the one in October 2014, also have to be taken into account.

5.3.2 Greenhouse gas emission reduction outside EU ETS

The EU ETS does not cover emissions from all sectors. In order to be able to meet the overall emission reduction commitments, the European Union must nonetheless also limit emissions outside the EU ETS, for instance, in the areas of agriculture, buildings, transport and waste. The so-called 'Effort Sharing Decision'[119] of the Parliament and Council is aimed at serving that purpose and has been designed to contribute to about 10% reduction of emissions from non-ETS sectors. The decision determines minimum greenhouse gas emission targets for member states for the period from 2013 to 2020 and defines rules as to how to attain these goals. National emission targets were established according to a member state's relative wealth and span from a 20% reduction target for richer member states to a 20% emission increase opportunity for less wealthy member states.

Member states are responsible for adopting and implementing appropriate measures that contribute to their national emission targets. Measures may, for instance, include the improvement of the energy performance of buildings, the promotion of public transport or the use of renewable energy for heating. EU-wide policies, such as the provisions on the energy performance of buildings, on energy labelling and on Eco-design, as described above, help member states to attain their goals.

---

117 European Commission, *Europe strengthens its carbon market for a competitive low-carbon economy* (8 January 2014, MEMO/14/4). Upon member states approval the back-loading approach was eventually implemented by Commission Regulation (EU) No 176/2014 of 25 February 2014 amending Regulation (EU) No 1031/2010 in particular to determine the volumes of greenhouse gas emission allowances to be auctioned in 2013–20.

118 For details see Commission website http://ec.europa.eu/clima/policies/ets/reform/index_en.htm, accessed 5 May 2016.

119 Decision No 406/2009/EC of the European Parliament and of the Council of 23 April 2009 on the effort of Member States to reduce their greenhouse gas emissions to meet the Community's greenhouse gas emission reduction commitments up to 2020 [2009] OJ L 140/136.

5.3.3   Transport related policies

Aside from the energy sector, the transport sector is the field responsible for most greenhouse gas emissions, amounting to around 25% of total greenhouse gas emissions in the European Union.[120] Emissions in the sector still continue to rise and originate mainly from road transport. However aviation and maritime transport also contribute a considerable share. While aviation comes under the EU ETS and measures covering maritime transport are still in the planning phase, the European Union has already adopted several specific pieces of legislation designed to curb and eventually scale down emissions from road transport. Measures aim at decarbonising transport by stimulating the development and market penetration of clean and energy-efficient vehicles and by fostering the use of so-called 'alternative fuels'. Instruments include in particular the promotion of clean vehicles,[121] the setting of emission performance standards for vehicles,[122] the establishment of rules on fuel quality,[123] the introduction of labelling requirements in terms of tyres,[124] making transparent the fuel economy of cars and their CO_2 emissions (CO_2 labelling of cars)[125] as well as defining a common framework for the deployment of alternative fuels infrastructure.[126]

Under Directive 2009/33/EC on the promotion of clean and energy-efficient road transport vehicles, for instance, member states must ensure that in the framework of public procurement, contracting authorities, contracting entities and certain public service operators factor in lifetime energy and

---

120 See Commission website http://ec.europa.eu/clima/policies/transport/index_en.htm, accessed 5 May 2016.

121 Directive 2009/33/EC of the European Parliament and of the Council of 23 April 2009 on the promotion of clean and energy-efficient road transport vehicles.

122 Regulation (EC) No 443/2009 of the European Parliament and of the Council of 23 April 2009 setting emission performance standards for new passenger cars as part of the Community's integrated approach to reduce CO_2 emissions from light-duty vehicles; Regulation (EU) No 510/2011 of the European Parliament and of the Council of 11 May 2011 setting emission performance standards for new light commercial vehicles as part of the Union's integrated approach to reduce CO_2 emissions from light-duty vehicles.

123 Directive 2009/30/EC of the European Parliament and of the Council amending Directive 98/70/EC as regards the specification of petrol, diesel and gas-oil and introducing a mechanism to monitor and reduce greenhouse gas emissions and amending Council Directive 1999/32/EC as regards the specification of fuel used by inland waterway vessels and repealing Directive 93/12/EEC.

124 Regulation (EC) No 1222/2009 of the European Parliament and of the Council of 25 November 2009 on the labelling of tyres with respect to fuel efficiency and other essential parameters. See also Amending Regulations 228/2011 and 1235/2011.

125 Directive 1999/94/EC of the European Parliament and of the Council of 13 December 1999 relating to the availability of consumer information on fuel economy and CO_2 emissions in respect of the marketing of new passenger cars.

126 See, in particular Directive 2014/94/EU on the deployment of alternative fuels infrastructure.

environmental impacts when purchasing road transport vehicles.[127] That way, the public sector is to contribute substantially to bringing environmentally-friendly vehicles onto the market. Energy and environmental impacts to be considered in purchasing decisions must include at least energy consumption; emissions of CO_2; and emissions of oxides of nitrogen (NOx), non-methane hydrocarbons (NMHC) and particulate matter. Further acts establish emission performance standards for means of road transport with a view to directly improving the environmental compatibility of vehicles and enhancing their fuel economy. Acts currently in place include regulations on new passenger cars[128] and on new light commercial vehicles.[129] The Commission is also working on plans to cover emissions from heavy-duty vehicles.

5.3.4　EU Ecolabel

The EU Ecolabel enables customers to identify eco-sensitive products or services. That way it is intended to give environment-friendly goods a competitive advantage on the market and help them gain a footing. In contrast to the EU energy label, producers and service providers may use the EU Ecolabel on a voluntary basis. The legal framework of the underlying scheme is laid down in the so-called Ecolabel Regulation.[130] Accordingly, operators interested in using the Ecolabel, such as producers, importers or retailers, may apply to the national body responsible. The competent body awards the label on the basis of a contract with the applicant after having verified that a given product complies with defined environmental requirements.[131] The Commission has adopted such requirements for various product groups, whereas respective draft criteria had been elaborated before by Ad-Hoc Working Groups (AHWGs) formed from stakeholders and the European Union Ecolabelling

---

127　Directive 2009/33/EC of the European Parliament and of the Council of 23 April 2009 on the promotion of clean and energy-efficient road transport vehicles.

128　Regulation (EC) No 443/2009 of the European Parliament and of the Council of 23 April 2009 setting emission performance standards for new passenger cars as part of the Community's integrated approach to reduce CO_2 emissions from light-duty vehicles. Regulation (EU) No 333/2014 of the European Parliament and of the Council of 11 March 2014 amending Regulation (EC) No 443/2009 to define the modalities for reaching the 2020 target to reduce CO_2 emissions from new passenger cars.

129　Regulation (EU) No 510/2011 of the European Parliament and of the Council of 11 May 2011 setting emission performance standards for new light commercial vehicles as part of the Union's integrated approach to reduce CO_2 emissions from light-duty vehicles. Regulation (EU) NO 253/2014 of the European Parliament and of the Council amending Regulation (EU) No 510/2011 to define the modalities for reaching the 2020 target to reduce CO_2 emissions from new light commercial vehicles.

130　Regulation (EC) No 66/2010 of the European Parliament and of the Council of 25 November 2009 on the EU Ecolabel [2010] OJ L 27/1.

131　For details see Commission website http://ec.europa.eu/environment/ecolabel/index_en.htm, accessed 5 May 2016.

Board (EUEB). Ecolabel criteria shall take into account the most significant impacts of a product on the environment throughout its life cycle, from the extraction of raw materials, through to manufacturing, distribution and disposal.[132]

5.3.5 Low-carbon and clean coal technologies

Considering the huge environmental impacts of burning fossil fuels, especially coal, the development and dissemination of new technologies remains of paramount importance. In recent years technological transition has featured highly on the European Union's agenda and is intended to be achieved in particular through the promotion of low-carbon technologies (for example, renewable energy technologies) and clean coal technologies (for example, capture and storage of CO_2 and techniques that more efficiently convert coal into energy). Even though the term 'clean coal' has become established in politics, it remains misleading considering that combustion products still accumulate and are either released into the air or injected into the ground.

The European Union promotes the development and safe deployment of new technologies by a number of actions which fall within the scope of climate or energy policy. The mix of instruments to induce industry to use low-carbon or clean coal facilities and methods include the EU ETS, the Effort Sharing Decision, renewable energy policies and transport-related policies. Moreover, the European Union has adopted several financial programmes to fund the development and demonstration of new technologies and to help prepare these for the market (see section 5.6 below).

Carbon capture and geological storage (CCS) constitutes one of the relevant technologies to which the European Union attaches particular importance. CCS is a method for sequestering and compressing CO_2 and injecting it into the ground instead of releasing it into the atmosphere. The European Union considers CCS one of the key technologies for curbing CO_2 emissions from large point sources, such as coal power stations or industries combusting fossil fuels on a big scale. Apart from the funding of demonstration projects, EU legislation, namely Directive 2009/31/EC (CCS Directive), deals especially with the environmentally safe geological storage of CO_2, one of the

---

132 Recital 5 of Regulation (EC) No 66/2010.

main points of criticism in relation to CCS.[133] Other legislative acts cover the capture and transport of CO_2.[134]

Pursuant to the CCS Directive, it remains up to member states to decide whether to allow any storage sites in their territory. Member states are also free to determine the general area where storage sites may be located, whereas the selection of a single site within such an area comes under the conditions of the CCS Directive. Both the exploration and operation of storage sites require a permit granted by member states with respect to the provisions laid down in the CCS Directive. Once a storage site and an associated transport network have been opened, member states must generally ensure that third parties may in a transparent and non-discriminatory manner obtain access to these facilities for the purposes of CO_2 storage.

The CCS Directive also sets out provisions on the monitoring of sites, measures to be taken in the event of a leakage, conditions for the closure and post-closure obligations. When CO_2 injection comes to an end, a site has to be sealed and injection facilities must be removed. In general, initially the site operator remains responsible for the closed site, for instance in relation to monitoring, corrective measures and remedial actions pursuant to the Environmental Liability Directive 2004/35/EC.[135] After an interim period of principally no shorter than 20 years, when all available evidence indicates that the injected CO_2 is safely and permanently contained, responsibilities are transferred to the competent authority.[136]

Despite the role the European Union is earmarking for CCS, carbon sequestration has also been sharply criticised. The German *Sachverständigenrat für Umweltfragen* (Advisory Council on the Environment), for instance, has cited that uncertainty still remains as to the technical feasibility of CO_2 storage and its risks.[137] It has also been pointed out that CCS technology may serve as an excuse to stall the shift away from fossil fuels.[138] While more coal-fired power

---

133 Directive 2009/31/EC of the European Parliament and of the Council of 23 April 2009 on the geological storage of carbon dioxide and amending Council Directive 85/337/EEC, European Parliament and Council Directives 2000/60/EC, 2001/80/EC, 2004/35/EC, 2006/12/EC, 2008/1/EC and Regulation (EC) No 1013/2006.

134 E.g. Directive 2008/1/EC of the European Parliament and of the Council of 15 January 2008 concerning integrated pollution prevention and control (IPPC Directive).

135 For further details see art 17 CCS Directive.

136 For further details see arts 17 and 18 CCS Directive.

137 Sachverständigenrat für Umweltfragen, *Abscheidung, Transport und Speicherung von Kohlendioxid, Stellungnahme* (April 2009) p 10.

138 A Little, 'Bush admin isn't putting money where its mouth is on "clean coal"' (December 2004) http://grist.org/politics/little-coal/ accessed 5 May 2016.

plants could be established and operated, with the environmental impacts of coal extraction and remaining risks of CCS technology, the expansion of renewable energies will possibly be hampered, for instance through the diverting of investment.[139]

5.4 Legislation and instruments related to consumer protection

As is the case with environmental issues, the European Union's policy on consumer protection is of a cross-cutting nature. Questions of consumer protection, such as health, safety and economic interests of consumers and their right to information, are primarily realised through the defining of other policies (see articles 12 and 169 para 2 a TFEU). Accordingly, the European Union has also taken the interests of consumers in the energy sector into account when elaborating various sector-specific and non-sector specific strategies and legislative acts.[140] The elevated position of energy consumers has particularly been highlighted in the 2020 Energy Strategy.[141] This fundamental energy initiative has ascertained that consumers' interests are considered among the EU energy policy priorities in the years to come. EU action is to consequently make sure that secure and safe energy will also remain available at affordable prices in the future.

However, the setting of this objective does not mean that EU law has not addressed consumers' needs so far. Quite the contrary is the case. In actual fact, the corpus of provisions establishing and maintaining the internal energy market as laid down in the treaties and legislation already serve consumer interests by ensuring fair competition for prices and services. The Electricity and Gas Directives feature prominently in this context.[142] Apart from their general purpose of improving and integrating competitive electricity energy markets, both directives set forth a number of requirements which more directly strengthen the position of consumers.[143] For details, see above sections 4.1.1 d) and 4.2.1 d). Besides, the Energy Performance

---

139 Sachverständigenrat für Umweltfragen, *Abscheidung, Transport und Speicherung von Kohlendioxid, Stellungnahme* (April 2009) p 32; Amanda Little, ibid.

140 See also European Commission, *Commission Staff Working Paper, An Energy Policy for Consumers* (SEC(2010) 1407 final).

141 See European Commission, *Energy 2020 A strategy for competitive, sustainable and secure energy* (COM/2010/0639 final).

142 Directive 2009/72/EC of the European Parliament and of the Council of 13 July 2009 concerning common rules for the internal market in electricity and repealing Directive 2003/54/EC [2009] OJ L 211/55; Directive 2009/73/EC concerning common rules for the internal market in natural gas and repealing Directive 2003/55/EC [2009] OJ L 211/94.

143 See especially art 3 of both, Directive 2009/72/EC and 2009/73/EC.

of Buildings Directive and the Energy Labelling Directive seek to raise consumers' awareness of energy-saving potential with a view to promoting climate-friendly purchase decisions and to lowering final customers' energy bills.[144] Moreover, the Energy Efficiency Directive (Directive 2012/27/EU) requires member states to make sure under certain conditions that final customers for electricity, natural gas, district heating and cooling and domestic hot water obtain reliable individual meters.[145] Further requirements set out in the Energy Efficiency Directive concern intelligent metering systems, smart meters and billing information, which as a whole offer assurance that customers are provided with accurate consumption and billing information.

Apart from these acts which all feature an explicit relationship with the supply and consumption of energy, energy consumers' interests also fall within the scope of the general measures of EU consumer policy. These include in particular the Product Liability Directive,[146] the Unfair Contract Terms Directive,[147] the Unfair Commercial Practices Directive[148] and the Directive on Consumer Rights.[149] Whereas the latter three directives also seek to save energy consumers, for instance, from unfair standard contract terms, misleading advertising (such as misleading environmental claims),[150] aggressive sales practices, unsolicited doorstep selling and ill-judged distance contracts, the Product Liability Directive aims at protecting customers against damage caused by defective products. Electricity is explicitly considered as a 'product' within the interpretation of this directive.[151]

---

144 See also European Commission, *Commission Staff Working Paper, An Energy Policy for Consumers* (SEC(2010) 1407 final) p 5.

145 Cf art. 9 of Directive 2012/27/EU of the European Parliament and of the Council of 25 October 2012 on energy efficiency, amending Directives 2009/125/EC and 2010/30/EU and repealing Directives 2004/8/EC and 2006/32/EC [2012] OJ L 315/1.

146 Council Directive 85/374/EEC of 25 July 1985 on the approximation of the laws, regulations and administrative provisions of the Member States concerning liability for defective products, as amended by Directive 1999/34/EC.

147 Council Directive 93/13/EEC of 5 April 1993 on unfair terms in consumer contracts.

148 Directive 2005/29/EC of the European Parliament and of the Council concerning unfair business-to-consumer commercial practices in the internal market and amending Council Directive 84/450/EEC, Directives 97/7/EC, 98/27/EC and 2002/65/EC of the European Parliament and of the Council and Regulation (EC) No 2006/2004 of the European Parliament and of the Council.

149 Directive 2011/83/EU on consumer rights, amending Council Directive 93/13/EEC and Directive 1999/44/EC of the European Parliament and of the Council and repealing Council Directive 85/577/EEC and Directive 97/7/EC of the European Parliament and of the Council. As regards the application of the directive to contracts for the supply of water, gas, electricity or district heating, including by public providers, see art 3.

150 See also European Commission, *Commission Staff Working Document, Guidance on the implementation/application of directive 2005/29/EC on unfair commercial practices*, 37 et seq.

151 See in this context M Roggenkamp, C Redgwell, I del Guayo and A Rønne, *Energy Law in Europe*, 389.

5.5 Legislation and instruments related to energy security

A steady supply of energy represents the backbone of modern economy and is therefore the pivotal element of a highly industrialised and technology-based civilisation. Major interruptions of energy supply inevitably lead to severe economic damage and restrictions in daily life. Power outages in 2006 and the Russian cut in gas deliveries in 2009 exposed the susceptibility of the European energy supply. The issue of energy security has featured prominently in EU policy for years. Even though the history of legislation on energy security goes back to 1968,[152] it was formally given priority only with the Lisbon Treaty in 2007. This treaty made the security of energy supply a fundamental pillar of EU energy policy. With its 2008 Energy Security and Solidarity Action Plan (the '2nd Strategic Energy Review'),[153] its European Energy Security Strategy from 2014[154] and the strategy for an Energy Union from 2015,[155] the Commission introduced detailed ideas and priorities for the near future. Furthermore, the Commission has acknowledged the security of energy supply to be one of the central goals of energy policy in its landmark initiatives, the 2020 Energy Strategy,[156] the 2030 Framework for Climate and Energy Policy[157] and the Energy Roadmap 2050.[158] The core significance of the security of energy supply and the continuing need for action has after all been reaffirmed by the European Council on several occasions.[159] Present and envisaged measures are designed to address the various facets of energy security. According to the 2030 Framework for Climate and Energy Policy as published by the Commission, for instance, energy security is to be improved 'through common action, integrated markets, import diversification, sustainable development of indigenous energy sources, investment in the necessary infrastructure, end-use energy savings and supporting research and innovation'.

152 See M Roggenkamp, C Redgwell, I del Guayo and A Rønne, *Energy Law in Europe*, 313.

153 See European Commission, *Communication from the Commission to the European Parliament, the Council, the European Economic and Social Committee and the Committee of the Regions – Second Strategic Energy Review: an EU energy security and solidarity action plan* (COM/2008/0781 final).

154 European Commission, *Communication from the Commission to the European Parliament and the Council, European Energy Security Strategy* (COM/2014/0330 final).

155 European Commission, *Energy Union Package, A Framework Strategy for a Resilient Energy Union with a Forward-Looking Climate Change Policy* (COM(2015) 80 final), see annex one for related roadmap.

156 European Commission, *Energy 2020 – A strategy for competitive, sustainable and secure energy* (COM (2010) 0639 final); see also European Council 4 February 2011, *Conclusions* (EUCO 2/11).

157 Cf European Commission, *A policy framework for climate and energy in the period from 2020 to 2030* (COM (2014) 015 final).

158 European Commission, *Energy Roadmap 2050* (COM (2011) 0885 final).

159 See European Council 26/27 June 2014, *Conclusions* (EUCO 79/14) annex I: 'Strategic agenda of the Union in times of change'; European Council 23/24 October 2014, *Conclusions* (EUCO 169/14); European Council 19/20 March 2015, *Conclusions* (EUCO 11/15).

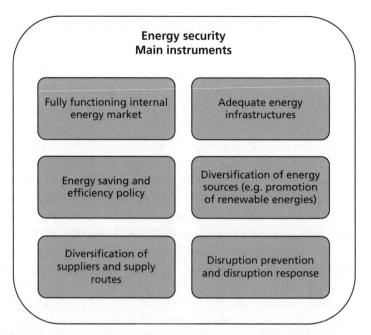

Figure 5.1 Main instruments to establish and maintain energy security

Against this background a range of the sector-specific and cross-sector instruments mentioned in this book address the issue of energy security (see also Figure 5.1). This holds especially true for the legislation safeguarding the functioning of the internal electricity and gas markets, the measures fostering the usage of renewable energy sources, the numerous instruments promoting energy efficiency and various initiatives coming under external energy policy (for the latter see also Chapter 6). Consequently, this section will merely highlight some of the issues concerned.[160]

Well functioning internal energy market: A fully functioning and integrated energy market constitutes a key element in obviating supply shortages and in making energy supply safer.[161] Due to the original partition of national energy markets, the necessary integration presents the European Union with a huge challenge. For the purpose of establishing and maintaining integrated markets in the various energy sub-sectors the European Union may resort to a range of instruments arising out of treaty law and specifically-

---

160 For further details on the EU's energy security policy see, for instance, J Vinois (ed.), *EU Energy Law: Volume VI, The Security of Energy Supply in the European Union* (Claeys & Casteels Publishing 2012); K Talus, *EU Energy Law and Policy – A Critical Account* (Oxford University Press 2013) 98 et seq.

161 See also M van Stiphout, 'The internal electricity and gas market, the best guarantee of security of supply' in J Vinois (ed.), *EU Energy Law: Volume VI, The Security of Energy Supply in the European Union.*

tailored legislation. As regards the electricity and gas markets, for instance, legislation tied up in the 3rd Energy Package plays a central role. The package is particularly intended to strengthen cross-border trade in energy, facilitate transnational collaboration and investment, and promote an increased solidarity among EU member states. For details on sector-specific legislation see Chapter 4 above.

Adequate pan-European energy infrastructure: A fully integrated and secure energy market presupposes adequate trans-European energy infrastructures. Energy infrastructures generally refer to technical facilities and organisational mechanisms necessary for the production, transmission, and storage of energy within its various forms (that is, electricity, natural gas, crude oil, or district heating).[162] Present infrastructures may still be described as partially outdated, insufficient to attain major goals of current energy and climate policies, and lacking essential interconnections between national partial markets.[163] Huge efforts remain necessary in order to adapt current infrastructure to future needs. With a view to mastering the challenges presented, the European Union has revised its energy infrastructure policy in recent years.[164] As a pivot for the new orientation, the European legislator adopted Regulation (EU) No 347/2013 (Energy Infrastructure Regulation) in 2013, repealing the previously applicable guidelines for trans-European energy networks (TEN-E) set out in Decision No 1364/2006/EC.[165]

The Energy Infrastructure Regulation establishes 12 priority corridors and areas in which the development of electricity, gas, oil or CO_2 infrastructures is to be primarily expedited and ultimately implemented by 2020.[166]

---

162 Cf G Reichert and J Voßwinkel, 'Europe's energy infrastructure – The European Commission's plan for an integrated European energy network' (2011) 4 IP Journal, Global Edition 29 et seq.

163 See European Commission, *Communication from the Commission to the European Parliament, the Council, the European Economic and Social Committee and the Committee of the Regions – Energy infrastructure priorities for 2020 and beyond – A Blueprint for an integrated European energy network* (COM(2010) 677 final).

164 See European Commission, *Communication from the Commission, Second Strategic Energy Review – An EU Energy Security and Solidarity Action Plan* (COM(2008) 781 final); *Communication from the Commission, Energy infrastructure priorities for 2020 and beyond – A Blueprint for an integrated European energy network* (COM(2010) 677 final); recital 3 of Regulation (EU) No 347/2013 on guidelines for trans-European energy infrastructure and repealing Decision No 1364/2006/EC and amending Regulations (EC) No 713/2009, (EC) No 714/2009 and (EC) No 715/2009.

165 Regulation (EU) No 347/2013 on guidelines for trans-European energy infrastructure and repealing Decision No 1364/2006/EC and amending Regulations (EC) No 713/2009, (EC) No 714/2009 and (EC) No 715/2009 [2013] OJ L 115/39.

166 For further details on the Energy Infrastructure Regulation see, for instance, C Sikow-Magny, K Nyitrai and N Siefken, 'The Regulation 347/2013 on guidelines for trans-European energy infrastructure' in J Vinois (ed.), *EU Energy Law: Volume VIII, The Energy Infrastructure Policy of the European Union* (Claeys & Casteels Publishing 2014) 153 et seq.

Contemplated measures include, for example, interconnections in the Baltic Sea region (cf the Baltic Energy Market Interconnection Plan (BEMIP)), infrastructure development in the northern seas in order to plug-in offshore wind parks, North-South electricity and gas interconnections in Central Eastern and South Eastern Europe, and smart grids deployment. First and foremost, the Energy Infrastructure Regulation lays down a framework for the identification of projects essential to realise the priority corridors and areas (projects of common interest), for the cross-border allocation of costs and risk-related incentives connected with these projects and for their promotion, for example, through speeding up permit granting procedures or the provision of European Union financial assistance.

Diversification of energy sources, suppliers and supply routes/energy saving and efficiency: In decades to come energy demand will keep growing while primary energy sources such as oil and gas become scarcer. These trends will tend to reinforce already existing dependencies on certain foreign suppliers and supply routes and may therefore lead to aggravated risks for the European Union's energy security. In order to counteract this likely scenario, the European Union has campaigned for various strategies in recent years. Actions have aimed either to curb still rising energy consumption (cf policies on energy efficiency) or to more strongly diversify the European Union's energy sources, suppliers and supply routes.

The envisaged diversification of energy sources is supposed to be brought about by making better use of indigenous fossil energy resources, by augmenting the share of renewable energy in the European energy mix and, in order to reduce the enormous dependence on oil in particular, by increasingly drawing on so-called 'alternative fuels' for transport.[167] In terms of renewable energy sources, the European Union already set a major milestone in 2007 with the adoption of the 20-20-20 targets, including the objective to boost the share of renewables so as to ensure that 20% of EU energy consumption will come from renewable resources by 2020.[168] For subsequent decades the Commission is even envisaging renewable energy sources taking centre stage in regard to the European energy mix,[169] which appears to be a demanding, but inevitable step to take for a Europe that is presently so dependent on fossil fuels.

---

167 As regards the latter aspect, particularly see Directive 2014/94/EU on the deployment of alternative fuels infrastructure.
168 See Brussels European Council 8/9 March 2007, *Presidency Conclusions* (doc 7224/1/07 REV1).
169 European Commission, *Energy Roadmap 2050* (COM(2011) 885/2) p 10.

Apart from that, the European Union has stepped up its efforts to diversify its gas and oil imports and supply routes. This is particularly to lessen dependence on Russian supplies, which might even continue to rise due to the enormous gas and oil needs of EU countries. On account of this, the European Union is seeking to promote in particular projects that link Europe to other regions rich in gas resources, such as the Caspian region, Central Asia and the Middle East (the so-called Southern Gas Corridor or 'SGC').[170] Although the Southern Gas Corridor bypassing Russia has taken top priority in recent years, its realisation is currently teetering on the brink. Reasons for this are the remaining uncertainties in some of the potential supply regions, such as Northern Iraq and Iran, and the abandonment of the Nabucco gas pipeline intended to haul Caspian gas directly to Central Europe. The frustrated Nabucco project exemplified the enormous obstacles the EU diversification plans may face when it comes down to economic and political realities. Not merely due to the fact that Russia put up fierce resistance, Nabucco also ultimately failed because not all member states and companies originally involved rallied behind the project.[171]

Disruption prevention and disruption response: Securing Europe's energy supply does not only require the European Union and member states to provide sufficient infrastructures and to diversify energy sources and suppliers. Moreover, it must also be ensured that energy infrastructures work in a reliable way, meaning adequate facilities and mechanisms must be available to prevent supply disruptions caused internally or externally and to mitigate eventual supply crises. Given the increasing integration of national energy networks and the growing dependencies on foreign energy imports, the risks of supply disruptions effecting more than one member state are rising, and this requires appropriate action at EU level.

In recent years the European Union has already established a number of measures supposed to avert trans-national risks and to promote the proper management of eventual cross-border crises in various energy sectors. These measures concern in particular:

---

170 See Regulation (EU) No 347/2013 on guidelines for trans-European energy infrastructure and repealing Decision No 1364/2006/EC and amending Regulations (EC) No 713/2009, (EC) No 714/2009 and (EC) No 715/2009 [2013] OJ L 115/39, annex I.

171 See Stefan Meister, 'Energy Security in the Southern Caucasus, The Southern Gas Corridor in its geopolitical environment', DGAPkompact, January 2014, No. 2. See in this context also V Feklyunina, 'The 'Great Diversification Game': Russia's Vision of the European Union's Energy Projects in the Shared Neighbourhood' (2008) 4(2) JCER 130–148; M Ratner, P Belkin, J Nichol and S Woehrel, 'Europe's Energy Security: Options and Challenges to Natural Gas Supply Diversification' (20 August 2013) published by Congressional Research Service.

- safeguarding security of electricity supply (Directive 2005/89/EC concerning measures to safeguard security of electricity supply),[172] see above section 4.1.2;
- strengthening the prevention and crisis response mechanisms in the gas sector (Regulation 994/2010 concerning measures to safeguard security of gas supply),[173] see above section 4.2.2;
- making available strategic oil stocks (Council Directive 2009/119/EC concerning the maintenance of minimum stocks of crude oil and/or petroleum products),[174] see above section 4.3.2;
- protecting critical infrastructure (Council Directive 2008/114/EC on the identification and designation of European critical infrastructures[175] and the European Programme for Critical Infrastructure Protection[176]).

Moreover, the Commission has adopted rules on the basis of which it may approve national state aid granted in the context of so-called capacity mechanisms meant to ensure the availability of a sufficient electricity supply at all times.[177] Such schemes have been used by a range of member states with a view to either secure the maintenance of existing capacity or to encourage investments in new capacity. For further information see Chapter 2.[178]

5.6   Support programmes

Support programmes form an integral part of the European Union's instruments to reinforce its internal policy agenda, but also to leverage its external action. Support programmes comprising, for instance, grants, loans and public procurement are drawn up to induce market participants, institutions and states to contribute to the implementation of European Union goals. Funding and other types of public support have also become central to the

---

172 Directive 2005/89/EC of the European Parliament and of the Council of 18 January 2006 concerning measures to safeguard security of electricity supply and infrastructure investment [2006] OJ L 33/22.

173 Regulation (EU) No 994/2010 of the European Parliament and of the Council of 20 October 2010 concerning measures to safeguard security of gas supply and repealing Council Directive 2004/67/EC [2010] OJ L 295/1.

174 Council Directive 2009/119/EC of 14 September 2009 imposing an obligation on Member States to maintain minimum stocks of crude oil and/or petroleum products [2009] OJ L 265/9.

175 Council Directive 2008/114/EC of 8 December 2008 on the identification and designation of European critical infrastructures and the assessment of the need to improve their protection [2008] OJ L 345/75.

176 European Commission, *Communication from the Commission on a European Programme for Critical Infrastructure Protection* (COM/2006/0786 final).

177 See section 3.9 of the Guidelines on State Aid for Environmental Protection and Energy 2014–2020 (EEAG) [2014] OJ C 200/1.

178 See section 2.2.5 b) ii).

carrying out of the EU's energy policy and ultimately affect all segments of the energy value chain. The present Multi-annual Financial Framework (MFF) applicable from 2014 to 2020 ensures that energy-related projects remain within the circle of potential beneficiaries of public aid over the coming years. Accordingly, assistance will be particularly directed at projects in the areas of energy infrastructures (for example, through the Connecting Europe Facility), energy technology (for example, through Horizon 2020), energy efficiency and renewable energies (for example, through Horizon 2020, EIB-ELENA Facility and the European Energy Efficiency Fund), as well as nuclear safety and decommissioning.

EU support programmes with relevance to energy-related projects particularly comprise the following:

- European Energy Programme for Recovery (EEPR)
  The programme aims at strengthening economic recovery through the granting of financial assistance to the energy sector. The EEPR's budget totals €3.98 billion and is allocated to projects in key areas, more specifically to gas and electricity infrastructure projects, offshore wind projects, carbon capture and storage as well as projects related to energy efficiency. Assistance to the latter projects is allocated through the European Energy Efficiency Fund (EEE-F).
- European Energy Efficiency Fund (EEE–F)
  The EEE-F supports the European Union and its member states in attaining the 20-20-20 climate and energy targets. Eligible projects mainly have a connection with energy efficiency, renewable energy or public transport. The fund provides both direct investments in such projects and investment in financial institutions such as local commercial banks which finance eligible projects. Final beneficiaries include municipal, local and regional authorities, but also public and private entities acting on their behalf.
- Connecting Europe Facility (CEF)
  The CEF provides financial assistance to improve trans-European networks in the fields of transport, telecommunications and energy. Supporting energy infrastructures features high on the European Union's agenda. Present electricity and gas networks are not considered appropriate for serving future energy needs, ensuring security of supply and allowing the large-scale use of renewable energy. Through the CEF, €4.7 billion is made available for upgrading and developing energy infrastructures until the year 2020.
- European Fund for Strategic Investments (EFSI)
  The EFSI supports private strategic investments in infrastructure and

innovation, and it provides risk finance for small businesses. The energy sector is one sector the fund is targeted at. Projects that the EFSI has particularly set its sights on include projects in energy infrastructure as well as those related to renewable energy and energy efficiency. The EFSI is managed by the European Investment Bank (EIB) and the European Investment Fund (EIF).

- Horizon 2020 – Framework Programme for Research and Innovation (2014–2020)
  Horizon 2020 represents the European Union's major funding programme to promote research and innovation. Its final goal is to secure the European Union's global competitiveness in future. The total budget of €77 billion is available from 2014 to 2020 with €5.9 billion being earmarked for non-nuclear energy research. More specific funding areas are laid down by the Commission in two-year work programmes. On the basis of these programmes the Commission publishes individual calls for concrete project proposals.

Apart from these programmes and facilities, the European Union and Euratom have set up or contributed to a range of further supportive resources which either specifically focus on energy-related activities or can at least potentially be made available for such activities. Without claiming to be exhaustive, the following list is merely intended to give an overview of these resources:

- Programme for the Competitiveness of Enterprises and small and medium-sized enterprises (COSME) (2014–20);
- Programme for the Environment and Climate Action (LIFE Programme) (2014–20);
- NER 300 Programme;
- Support for the European Joint Undertaking for ITER and the Development of Fusion Energy;
- Nuclear decommissioning assistance programmes;
- Euratom Research and Training Programme (2014–18);
- European Regional Development Fund (ERDF);
- Cohesion Fund;
- Instruments of the European Investment Bank (EIB), for example, ELENA Facility, and of the European Investment Fund (EIF);
- European Neighbourhood Instrument;
- Global Energy Efficiency and Renewable Energy Fund (co-financed by the European Union);
- Partnership Instrument (PI);
- Instrument for Nuclear Safety Cooperation.

The sheer number of programmes, which furthermore add to national support schemes, illustrates the complexity of promotional policy. It is apparent that the variety of programmes alone bears the risk of wasting development potential owing to deficient coordination and lacking cross-fertilisation. In order to effectively leverage public support, the European Union has stepped up its efforts in recent years to synchronise support programmes and generate synergies among them. Regulation 1303/2013 coordinating, among others, the European Regional Development Fund and the Cohesion Fund with a range of other funding sources, is indicative in this respect.[179]

The Commission's European Strategic Energy Technology Plan (SET Plan) represents another chief instrument in amplifying the European Union's promotional efforts in the field of energy.[180] The SET Plan is supposed to expedite the development and deployment of low-carbon energy technologies and it functions as a strategic reference point for public (EU and national) and private technology-related investments.[181] The plan builds on various funding sources, such as Horizon 2020, the Connecting Europe Facility and EIB lending,[182] and comprises various industrial initiatives (for example, in relation to wind energy, solar energy, electricity grids, carbon capture and storage, nuclear fission, bio-energy, smart cities) designed to pool and align innovation efforts.

? REVIEW QUESTIONS

1. By which general approaches may the European Union prevent national tax regimes from tarnishing the internal energy market? *See section 5.1.3.*
2. Which legislative acts in particular form the legal basis for augmenting energy efficiency at consumption level? *See sections 5.2.1–5.2.4.*
3. In which way does the approach of the EU eco-design policy fundamentally differ from that of the EU energy labelling policy? *See section 5.2.4.*
4. How does the EU ETS concern the energy sector? *See section 5.3.1.*

---

179 See Regulation (EU) No 1303/2013 of 17 December 2013 laying down common provisions on the European Regional Development Fund, the European Social Fund, the Cohesion Fund, the European Agricultural Fund for Rural Development and the European Maritime and Fisheries Fund and laying down general provisions on the European Regional Development Fund, the European Social Fund, the Cohesion Fund and the European Maritime and Fisheries Fund and repealing Council Regulation (EC) No 1083/2006, annex I.

180 European Commission, *Communication from the Commission, A European strategic energy technology plan (SET-plan) – 'Towards a low carbon future'* (COM/2007/0723 final). See also European Commission, *Investing in the Development of Low Carbon Technologies* (COM/2009/0519 final).

181 A E Malva, 'SET-Plan – Current status, future developments and Horizon 2020' ESTELA Summer Workshop, Brussels, 26 June 2013.

182 European Commission, *Investing in the Development of Low Carbon Technologies* (COM/2009/0519 final) sections 4 and 5; European Commission, *Energy Technologies and Innovation* (COM/2013/253 final).

5. Why has the EU ETS sparked controversial debate? *See section 5.3.1.*
6. By what features do the Electricity and Gas Directives, for instance, seek to strengthen the position of consumers? *See sections 5.4, 4.1.1 d) und 4.2.1 d).*
7. What are main instruments to establish and maintain energy security? See section 5.5.
8. What is the main subject matter of the Energy Infrastructure Regulation? *See section 5.5 under the heading 'Adequate pan-European energy infrastructure'.*
9. Give examples of support programmes that provide assistance for the development of energy infrastructures. *See section 5.6.*

 FURTHER READING

Joseph Curtin (ed.), *EU Energy Law: Volume VII, Energy Efficiency in the European Union* (Claeys & Casteels Publishing 2014)

Rainer Hinrichs-Rahlwes, *Sustainable Energy Policies for Europe* (CRC Press 2013)

Paul Hodson, Christopher Jones and Hans van Stehen (eds), *EU Energy Law: Volume III, Book 1, Renewable Energy Law and Policy in the European Union* (Claeys & Casteels Publishing 2010)

Jean-Arnold Vinois (ed.), *EU Energy Law: Volume VI, The Security of Energy Supply in the European Union* (Claeys & Casteels Publishing 2012)

Jean-Arnold Vinois, (ed.), *EU Energy Law: Volume VIII, The Energy Infrastructure Policy of the European Union* (Claeys & Casteels Publishing 2014)

6

External action

6.1 Preliminary remarks: legal basis and strategic framework

The European Union is highly dependent on external energy resources. Member states obtain roughly 88% of their required crude oil and 66% of their natural gas needs from outside sources.[1] Thus, the internal EU market may only function properly if member states develop effective strategies in their external relations with which they are able to safeguard continuous supply from third countries. Resource acquisition presents single member states with huge challenges due to the further intensifying global competition for resources, the location of many deposits in undemocratic or unstable regions and the additional need to reduce dependencies on single suppliers by diversifying supply sources and facilities. Therefore, there is an objective need to pool and pursue external energy strategies at EU level.

External energy policy as part of foreign policy is traditionally considered an inherent domain of sovereign nation states. Member states have therefore always been reluctant to transfer considerable powers, a reluctance which applies to foreign affairs in general and to external energy policy in particular. However, over the years the pruning of national external powers has proved to be unavoidable. Even though foreign policy still remains a core competence of member states, external EU responsibilities have successively been extended. Today, common external action is provided for in both the Treaty on European Union (TEU) and the Treaty on the Functioning of the European Union (TFEU). Besides, the Euratom Treaty also contains limited powers to maintain external relations.[2]

---

1 Cf European Commission, *Commission Staff Working Document, In-depth study of European Energy Security* (SWD (2014) 330 final/3), accompanying Communication, European energy security strategy (COM (2014) 330 final).
2 Cf arts 52, 64, 101–106 Euratom Treaty.

6.1.1 Legal basis

a)   *TEU*

The TEU empowers the European Union to establish a common foreign and security policy (CFSP), which is of inter-governmental character.[3] The CFSP may be described as coordinated foreign policy based on joint actions and common positions. In general, member states are required to take unanimous decisions in the European Council or the Council of the European Union. The adoption of legal acts is excluded, but the Union is authorised to conclude international agreements in the areas of the CFSP.

b)   *TFEU*

Apart from this inter-governmental sphere, the TFEU sets out external powers coming under the European Union's supranational domain (see articles 205 to 222 TFEU). Above all, these competences allow the European Union to conclude international agreements, to determine a common commercial policy as well as to take action in the fields of development cooperation, economic, financial and technical cooperation, and humanitarian aid.

The concluding of international agreements, meaning agreements with third countries and/or with international organisations, is particularly provided for where such agreements are necessary in order to achieve objectives referred to in the TFEU (see article 216 TFEU). This may, of course, also be the case in terms of meeting objectives falling under energy policy.

The common commercial policy (CCP) is understood as being the European Union's external trade policy concerning all measures to govern commercial relations with third countries.[4] It is set forth as an exclusive competence, meaning the European Union is in general solely responsible for decision-making in this area. The CCP enables the European Union to decide on unilateral action relevant to trade and to conclude bilateral and multilateral trade agreements (for example, WTO agreements). Unilateral actions concern imports and exports and encompass, for instance, common customs tariff duties. The European Union may also establish quantitative restrictions on imports, antidumping duties and export subsidies. However, when adopting unilateral measures, the European Union must observe the rules of the WTO and its own commitment to contribute to the

---

3 Cf arts 23 et seq TEU.
4 Cf articles 206 et seq TFEU.

development of world trade. As regards international agreements, in practice agreements are often composed of trade issues and other items which do not fall within the remit of the European Union, the consequence being that the European Union shares with the member states the competence to conclude such agreements.[5]

c)   *Euratom Treaty*

Ultimately, the European Union, or legally speaking Euratom, may under certain circumstances also fall back on the Euratom Treaty when there is a need for foreign action in the nuclear field. The Euratom Treaty provides, in Article 101, for the capacity of Euratom to conclude international agreements covering nuclear issues with third states, international organisations or third-country nationals. Euratom has signed such agreements with most of the main suppliers of nuclear fuels. The Commission requires that such agreements are not only deployed to secure supply, but also to promote nuclear safety and security by complying with the highest international safety and security standards.[6] Moreover, article 203 Euratom Treaty may be used as a legal basis to introduce measures other than international agreements, for instance financial instruments that promote nuclear safety in third-countries.[7]

6.1.2 Strategic framework

Based on all these powers laid down in the TEU, TFEU and Euratom Treaty, the European Union has subsequently developed its external energy policy. This area of foreign affairs draws on a number of different instruments and measures which primarily serve the security of energy supply, but also the protection of domestic industries, the fight against climate change and nuclear safety (for measures concerning nuclear safety see also section 4.6 above). In order to augment external energy efforts, the European Commission has set out relevant priorities and actions in a series of communications which include the following in particular: 'External energy relations – from principles to action' (2006),[8] 'Energy Policy for Europe' (2007),[9] 'Energy 2020 strategy' (2010),[10] 'EU Energy Policy: Engaging with Partners beyond

---

5 M J Hahn, in C Calliess and M Ruffert, *EUV/AEUV* (4th edn, C.H. Beck 2011) art 207 note 61.

6 European Commission, COM (2011) 539 final.

7 See Regulation (Euratom) No 237/2014 of 13 December 2013 establishing an Instrument for Nuclear Safety Cooperation.

8 European Commission, COM (2006) 590 final.

9 European Commission, COM (2007) 1 final.

10 European Commission, COM (2010) 639 final.

Our Borders' (2011),[11] 'European Energy Security Strategy' (2014)[12] and 'Framework strategy for an Energy Union' (2015).[13]

In referring to the European Commission proposal entitled 'EU Energy Policy: Engaging with Partners beyond Our Borders' the Council stressed in 2011 that current priorities are to comprise the strengthening of internal coordination; an intensified coordination with third countries and the deepening of bilateral energy partnerships, both especially with a view to diversify suppliers, supply routes and energy sources; and, ultimately, the facilitation of a sustainable and climate-friendly energy policy in developing countries.[14]

Seen from a technical perspective, the instruments available for executing the European Union's external energy policy may be classified as follows:

- international legal regimes and international cooperation (see section 6.2);
- regional legal regimes and regional cooperation (see section 6.3);
- unilateral actions in accordance with the EU common commercial policy (see section 6.4); and
- coordination of the European Union's and its member states' external energy activities (see section 6.4).

The present chapter is only intended to offer a glimpse into how the European Union deploys and prioritises in practice individual instruments coming under these categories. A more comprehensive picture is given in the Commission proposals mentioned, successive documents and corresponding conclusions of the European Council and the Council of Ministers.[15]

6.2 International legal regimes and international cooperation

At international level, there are a number of multilateral legal regimes and bilateral agreements which, to a greater or lesser extent, affect energy markets.

---

11 European Commission, COM (2011) 539 final.

12 European Commission, COM (2014) 330 final.

13 European Communication, COM (2015) 80 final.

14 Conclusions of the Council of the European Union of November 24, 2011 on Communication on Security of Energy Supply and International Cooperation – 'The EU Energy Policy: Engaging with partners beyond our borders', doc 17615/11.

15 For further details see also D Buschle, *EU Energy Law: Volume IX, European External Energy Law & Policy* (Claeys & Casteels Publishing 2015); K Talus, *EU Energy Law and Policy – A Critical Account* (Oxford University Press 2013) 212 et seq.

International regimes comprise, for instance, the WTO rules, the Energy Charter Treaty and the Kyoto Protocol. Bilateral arrangements include energy dialogues, programmes and agreements with individual players, such as energy suppliers and other energy consuming countries. The European Union is actively engaged in using all these instruments for the purpose of safeguarding EU energy supply, ensuring the competitiveness of domestic energy-intensive industries and fighting climate change.

6.2.1 WTO regime

The WTO regime represents the central legal framework pertaining to international trade. It also covers energy and energy-related services, such as investments and the obtaining of licenses for activities regarding energy.[16] The European Union has advocated a strict application and broad interpretation of WTO rules in the field of energy in recent years.[17] WTO rules are especially invoked to protect domestic energy-intensive industries against competitive disadvantages on the global market. The issue of dual pricing is an example of this approach. Dual pricing means that in countries rich in natural resources, such resources are sold at lower prices to domestic industries than to consuming countries and their industries. Dual pricing may therefore lead to lower production costs for energy-intensive industries (for example, steel manufacturers, petrochemical industry) in resource-rich countries and, as a consequence, to their advantageous position on the global market. As a community of net importing countries, the European Union has accordingly assumed a rather negative attitude towards dual pricing and considers this practice to be prohibited by the WTO Agreement on Subsidies and Countervailing Measures.[18] Producing countries oppose the EU stance, arguing that dual pricing is not explicitly addressed by the WTO agreement. In any case, so far the WTO has not officially condemned dual pricing and by virtue of the quite abstract wording contained in the WTO Agreement, it is questionable whether the WTO will do so in future.[19]

---

16 J Selivanova, 'The WTO and energy: WTO Rules and agreements of relevance to the energy sector' (2007) ICTSD Trade and Sustainable Energy Series Issue Paper No 1; M Roggenkamp, C Redgwell, I del Guayo and A Rønne, *Energy Law in Europe* (2nd edn, Oxford University Press 2007) 206.

17 See M Roggenkamp, C Redgwell, I del Guayo and A Rønne *Energy Law in Europe*, 204 et seq.

18 See for details: M Roggenkamp, C Redgwell, I del Guayo and A Rønne *Energy Law in Europe*, 204 et seq.

19 Cf also D Behn, 'The effect of dual pricing practices on trade, the environment, and economic development: Identifying the winners and the losers under the current WTO disciplines' (17 December 2007) http:// papers.ssrn.com/sol3/papers.cfm?abstract_id=1151553 accessed 8 May 2016.

6.2.2 Energy Charter Treaty

The Energy Charter Treaty (ECT) constitutes a binding multilateral agreement establishing a legal framework for international cooperation between net exporters of energy, net importers and transit countries.[20] The treaty and related documents deal with five general issues: the protection of foreign energy investments based on the principle of non-discrimination; the safeguarding of free trade in energy materials, products and energy-related equipment; the freedom of energy transit through pipelines and grids; the improvement of energy efficiency and the reduction of the negative environmental impact of the energy cycle; and the establishment of dispute settlement procedures.[21] As regards energy transit in particular, the ECT rules are to be enhanced by an additional Transit Protocol. To date, however, the protocol has not been adopted due to divergent positions of the European Union and Russia.[22]

The idea of the ECT dates back to the early 1990s when, at the end of the Cold War, an integration of the Eastern and Western energy sectors became realistic for the first time. At present, the treaty has been signed or acceded to by 51 countries, the European Community (now European Union) and Euratom. The European Union seeks to use the ECT as one of its central instruments to pursue its external energy goals. For that reason, the European Commission assigns the role of a key driver in implementing and extending the ECT to the European Union.[23] Whereas the ECT was originally meant to cover energy-related activities between European countries and successor states of the Soviet Union, the European Union intends to extend the charter's scope, for instance, also to North Africa and the Far East.[24] Particular emphasis is given to the role of Russia in the ECT process. Even though Russia as a leading energy exporter has signed the charter, it has omitted to ratify the agreement to date. Despite Russia's declaration to apply ECT rules nevertheless, particular European Union engagement is targeted at bringing the country to formally approve the charter and thereby institutionalising EU-Russia energy relations. The fact that these efforts have failed so far, provides ample proof of the general disparity of European and Russian strategic interests.[25]

---

20 For further details see also K Talus, *EU Energy Law and Policy – A Critical Account*, 233 et seq.

21 See Energy Charter Secretariat, *The Energy Charter Treaty and Related Documents – A Legal Framework for International Energy Cooperation* (Brussels 2004) p 14.

22 See A Johnston and G Block, *EU Energy Law* (Oxford University Press 2013) 290 et seq.

23 See, for instance, European Commission, COM (2006) 590 final.

24 European Commission, COM (2011) 0539 final.

25 See also Henry Helén, 'The EU's energy security dilemma with Russia' (2010) 4 POLIS Journal.

6.2.3 Kyoto Protocol and post-Kyoto regime

The Kyoto Protocol is an international instrument to fight climate change. The document was adopted within the framework of the United Nations Framework Convention on Climate Change (UNFCCC) and lays down legally binding commitments to reduce the emission of certain greenhouse gases (GHG). In doing so it indirectly impacts on power generators discharging GHGs and on energy consumption in general. The first commitment period under the protocol expired at the end of 2012. The second commitment period will run from 2013 until 2020, whereas further countries decided not to take part in that period.

The European Union has attempted to play a leading role in the process of the adoption and implementation of the Kyoto process for years. The European Union itself ratified the original protocol in 2002 and has been particularly engaged in urging ratification by other major GHG-emitting countries. While the United States has nonetheless rejected official approval, initial efforts have been successful in the case of Russia. Russian approval as part of a strategic compromise with Brussels, that also includes support for Russian accession to the WTO, has been crucial for the protocol to enter into legal effect.[26] Notwithstanding this, Russia ultimately declined to engage in the second commitment period, just as Canada and Japan did.[27] Ultimately, in December 2015 a new agreement was adopted with the aim of limiting global warming (the so-called Paris Agreement). This agreement is due to enter into force in 2020 and still requires a sufficient number of states to ratify it.

6.2.4 Other instruments

Apart from these international agreements, the European Union generally seeks to strengthen partnerships with key suppliers, transit countries and other large energy consumers.[28] For that reason, the European Union tries

---

26 M Roggenkamp, C Redgwell, I del Guayo and A Rønne, *Energy Law in Europe*, 210 et seq; BBC News, 'Russian MPs ratify Kyoto treaty' (22 October 2004) http://news.bbc.co.uk/2/hi/europe/3943727.stm accessed 8 January 2016; S Ferriter, 'Russian ratification of Kyoto could spark large-scale renewable energy development' http://www.climate.org/topics/international-action/russian-ratification-kyoto.html accessed 8 May 2016.

27 See Reuters.com, 'Russia will not cut emissions under extended Kyoto climate pact' (13 September 2012) http://www.reuters.com/article/2012/09/13/us-russia-kyoto-idUSBRE88C0QZ20120913 accessed 5 May 2016.

28 See European Commission, *Energy Policy for Europe* (COM (2007) 1 final) annex 1 EU 'International Energy Policy Priorities'; European Commission, *EU Energy Policy Engaging with Partners beyond Our Borders'* (COM (2011) 0539 final).

to use a variety of institutions and measures. The G7/8, the G20, the International Energy Forum (IEF) and the International Energy Agency (IEA), for instance, also serve as platforms to generally foster mutual understanding in terms of energy-related interests at international level. The OPEC and the Gulf Cooperation Council (GCC) in particular are considered as forums to consolidate the relationship with important oil-producing countries. A number of other resource-rich countries and regions have also been and will continue to be affiliated by individual arrangements, such as memoranda of understanding, partnership and cooperation agreements.[29] For instance, this is the case for a number of Central Asian countries.

Moreover, the European Union gives considerable weight to enhanced relations with other major energy consumers, such as the United States, China and India.[30] The European Union has established individual platforms of energy cooperation with these three countries, in order to promote open, competitive and transparent global energy markets, energy efficiency, renewable forms of energy and research cooperation.[31]

6.3 Regional legal regimes and regional cooperation

Naturally, regional energy relations with European neighbours play the predominant role for safeguarding the European Union's energy supply. Hence, the European Union has always sought to establish special ties with neighbouring energy producers and transit countries as well. The end of the Cold War has thereby provided particular opportunities enabling the European Union to orientate itself eastwards. Efforts have led to a complex framework of multilateral and bilateral dialogues, cooperation platforms and agreements supplementing the aforementioned instruments which are deployed on a global scale.

6.3.1 EU-Russia energy relations

Good energy relations with Russia are considered the key factor for attaining the European Union's external energy targets. For the time being, Russia

---

29 European Commission, *Energy Policy for Europe* (COM (2007) 1 final) annex 1 'EU International Energy Policy Priorities'.

30 European Commission, *Energy Policy for Europe* (COM (2007) 1 final) annex 1 'EU International Energy Policy Priorities'; European Commission, *EU Energy Policy Engaging with Partners beyond Our Borders* (COM (2011) 0539 final).

31 Cf the EU-US Energy Council, the European Commission (EC)-China Energy Dialogue and the EU-India Energy Panel.

remains the European Union's largest supplier of fossil fuels and uranium and might even strengthen its position in view of the still growing energy need in Europe. However, the dependency is mutual as the European Union in turn constitutes Russia's largest trade partner and for the time being it can hardly be replaced as such. Therefore, EU-Russia energy relations are based on a vital necessity for mutual trade.

Nonetheless cooperation has proved intricate and demanding for both sides as relations are strained by dissenting opinions on a range of issues with strategic and economic relevance. Challenging topics encompass, in particular, Moscow's attempts to maintain EU dependence on Russian fuels and the European Union's search for alternative energy sources and transport routes bypassing Russia, as exemplified by the aborted Nabucco pipeline project;[32] Brussels' Eastern partnership strategy prompting general geostrategic suspicion in Moscow; the EU energy market liberalisation process spoiling Gazprom's attempts at taking control over the whole gas supply chain; and repeated cuts in Russian gas supplies affecting not only transit countries Belarus and Ukraine but also a number of EU members.[33] Both sides' scramble for strategic influence in energy transit regions turned out to be a major cause of the Ukraine crisis that erupted in 2014 even though the crisis has to be understood in an even wider geopolitical context.

Given the Russian refusal to ratify the Energy Charter Treaty, EU-Russia energy relations have been primarily based on the 1994 Partnership and Cooperation Agreement (PCA), which the parties have been looking to replace since 2008. Within the PCA framework, cooperation has been strengthened through the EU-Russia Energy Dialogue established in 2000 and the agreed 'Common Space' initiative from 2003. The Energy Dialogue serves as a platform for continuous convergence and cooperation in the field of energy. Officially, the dialogue is broad in scope and is supposed to ensure reliability, security and predictability of energy relations. Nevertheless, in the past most contentious issues have remained outside the meetings.[34] In 2011 the parties decided to enhance the Energy Dialogue on particular issues that included an upgraded EU-Russia Early Warning Mechanism in the field of energy, a Joint Gas Advisory Council and a Roadmap of the EU-Russia Energy Cooperation until 2050.

---

32 See section 5.5 above.

33 A Cohen, 'Europe's strategic dependence on Russian energy' (5 November 2007) Backgrounder, No 2083, pp 3 et seq; D Averre, 'EU-Russia relations and the shared neighbourhood: an overview' (2011) Study, Directorate-General for External Policies of the Union, p 12.

34 M Roggenkamp, C Redgwell, I del Guayo and A Rønne, *Energy Law in Europe*, 218.

6.3.2 Relations with other eastern neighbours

External relations with individual Eastern neighbours are generally carried out within the framework of the European Neighbourhood Policy (ENP) and the EU enlargement process. Bilateral relations are based on Partnership and Cooperation Agreements (PCA) or Association Agreements (AA) which frequently define energy as one of the fields of collaboration. Agreements cover, for instance, cooperation in terms of security of supply, regulation of the energy sector in line with a market economy, and promotion of energy effectiveness. As regards Eastern neighbours, a variety of multilateral instruments have been created complementing bilateral relations, such as the Energy Community (formerly known as the European Energy Community or the Energy Community of South East Europe), the Eastern Partnership, the Black Sea Synergy and the INOGATE Programme.

a)   *Energy Community*

The Energy Community was founded by the European Union and a number of south-east European states in 2005. At present, the community includes the European Union, the Balkan States, Moldova and Ukraine. The Energy Community aims at establishing open and transparent energy markets within the contracting states by harmonising the applicable regulatory frameworks. Technically, harmonisation is effected by the implementation of the relevant *acquis communautaire* on energy, environment, competition and the renewable energy sources of the European Union. At its core, the legal package requiring implementation comprises the EU rules on the internal markets in electricity and gas. However, the relevant legal corpus also contains, for instance, EU efficiency legislation (for example, the Directive on the Energy Performance of Buildings and the one on Energy Labelling) and the competition rules of the TFEU. In fact, the Energy Community serves to extend EU energy policy to a number of non-EU countries. It paves the way to a single regulatory space for trade in energy, thereby attracting more investments in energy infrastructure whilst also enhancing the security of supply in the European Union and the contracting states.

The Energy Community is equipped with its own set of institutions, including the Ministerial Council as the primary decision-making body, the Permanent High Level Group (PHLG) preparing the work of the Ministerial Council, the Energy Community Regulatory Board (ECRB) and different thematic forums as advisory bodies, and the Secretariat administering the Energy Community and monitoring its progress.

b)   *Eastern Partnership (EaP)*

The Eastern Partnership represents an institutionalised forum to accelerate political association and economic integration between the European
Union and Armenia, Azerbaijan, Belarus, Georgia, Moldova and Ukraine.[35]
Founded in 2009 in Prague, the Eastern Partnership forms a special dimension of the European Neighbourhood Policy. It has been developed in parallel to other bilateral and multilateral initiatives and complements such
initiatives as the EU-Russia Partnership, the Union for the Mediterranean,
the Black Sea Synergy and the Energy Community in the cases of Moldova
and Ukraine. Four thematic platforms are organised in order to implement
the goals of the EaP. Platform 3 is dedicated to convergence and integration
in the field of energy security policy. Work is especially concentrated on the
following topics: enhancement of framework conditions, support for infrastructure development and promotion of increased energy efficiency.

c)   *Black Sea Synergy*

The Black Sea Synergy serves as a complementary forum to the above-
mentioned initiatives. It was initiated by the European Commission and
officially launched in 2008 in order to focus more attention on the vitally
important region of the Black Sea.[36] The synergy offers the countries in the
wider neighbourhood of the Black Sea a platform to invigorate ties within the
region, but also to deepen cooperation with the European Union alongside
existing cooperation initiatives. The Black Sea Synergy was launched to stim-
ulate democratic and economic reforms and development. Energy forms one
priority area on which cooperation is supposed to focus. In this respect, the
synergy is designed to strengthen the dialogue between energy producers,
consumers and transit countries in view of fair access to energy resources and
markets, enhanced energy security and environmental sustainability.[37]

d)   *INOGATE (Interstate Oil and Gas Transport to Europe) Programme*

The INOGATE Programme represents another component of the
European Union's strategy to improve energy security through the building of enhanced energy partnerships in strategically significant regions.

---

35 Council of the European Union, 'Joint Declaration of the Prague Eastern Partnership Summit Prague',
(press release of 7 May 2009, 8435/09 (Presse 78)).

36 See European Commission, *Communication Black Sea Synergy – A New Regional Cooperation Initiative*
(COM(2007) 160 final).

37 Joint Statement of the Ministers of Foreign Affairs of the countries of the European Union and of the wider
Black Sea area (Kiev, 14 February 2008).

INOGATE concentrates on a strip ranging from Eastern Europe to Central Asia, including the Black Sea and the Caspian region. The programme constitutes a cornerstone for the development of alternative energy sources and supply routes which may bypass Russia's Southern borders, and as such, it is one of the key initiatives to turn the Southern Gas Corridor into a reality.[38]

INOGATE is organised by a technical secretariat, located in Kiev, and currently financed through the European Neighbourhood and Partnership Instrument (ENPI). The programme covers 12 countries; with Kazakhstan, Kyrgyzstan, Tajikistan, Turkmenistan and Uzbekistan, INOGATE also embraces countries not addressed by the European Neighbourhood Policy. In principle, INOGATE is geared to objectives comparable to those of other programmes: converging local energy markets along the lines of the EU internal market, enhancing energy security (for example, by energy supply diversification), developing energy efficiency and renewable energies, and advancing conditions for investment in energy projects.

With a view to putting INOGATE into practice, partners adopted the Baku Initiative in 2004 and the Astana Declaration in 2006 which determined a more detailed work plan – the Energy Road Map. The plan specifically provides for the harmonisation of legal and technical standards, and the extension and modernisation of existing energy transit infrastructures with a view to diversifying the supply routes towards Europe. However, the effectiveness of INOGATE remains to be seen.[39] Implementation is particularly dependent on the progress of reforms within the countries concerned, on their external orientation, especially towards Russia, and finally on the EU member states' unity and determination to realise certain key infrastructure projects.

6.3.3 Relations with the Mediterranean region

Enhanced cooperation with littoral states of the Mediterranean reaches back to the mid-1990s. In 1995 the EU and 14 Mediterranean states launched the Euro-Mediterranean Partnership (EUROMED), also known as the Barcelona Process. EUROMED made available a platform for dialogue and cooperation in a variety of fields regarding political and security matters, economic and financial issues, as well as social, cultural and human questions.

---

38 Cf Czech Presidency of the European Union, *Declaration – Prague Summit, Southern Corridor* (8 May 2009), with particular reference to the Baku initiative; N Sartori, 'The European Commission's policy towards the Southern Gas Corridor: Between national interests and economic fundamentals' (January 2012) IAI Working Papers issue 1201, pp 5 et seq. See also section 5.5 above.

39 S Nies, 'Oil and gas delivery to Europe – An overview of existing and planned infrastructures' (2008) French Institute for International Relations (Ifri) 22 et seq.

In economic terms, for instance, partners provided for the creation of Free Trade Areas and accordingly the elimination of customs duties. Energy was also incorporated as one of the areas of collaboration. Partner countries especially emphasised their will to create appropriate framework conditions necessary for the extension of energy networks and link-ups. Later, in 2007, Euromed Energy Ministers adopted a Five-Year Action plan devoted to the harmonisation of energy markets, sustainable development in the energy sector and the elaboration of projects of common interest in key areas.

In 2008 EUROMED was re-launched as the Union for the Mediterranean (UfM). Today, the UfM encompasses, in addition to the EU member states, 15 states of the Mediterranean region. A secretariat, headquartered in Barcelona, enhances coordination of regional and trans-regional projects. UfM persists with the goals of the Barcelona Process and upgrades cooperation in the aforementioned fields, ranging from political reforms, peace and stability in the Middle East and North Africa (MENA) region to economic integration. It remains to be seen whether all the set goals can be achieved. UfM activities are generally burdened with a number of political difficulties, which may jeopardise success in particular fields. General suspicion in relation to the predominant position of the European Union within the partnership, as well as tensions originating from the unresolved Arab-Israeli conflict, constitute only two out of a number of obstacles officials have to cope with when driving the UfM agenda ahead.

With the UfM founding declaration, the 2008 Paris Declaration, member states re-affirmed energy as one of the areas that cooperation is supposed to focus on. The fostering of alternative energy, and the use of solar energy generated in the MENA region in particular, was assigned a pivotal role. For that reason, the partner countries elevated the creation of a Mediterranean Solar Plan (MSP) to an UfM top priority. In this regard, UfM cooperates especially with Desertec/Dii GmbH and Medgrid. Both industrial initiatives aim at the development of alternative energy generation capacities and electricity networks in the MENA region.

From the viewpoint of the European Union, the Union for the Mediterranean also ranks among the tools of the European Neighbourhood Policy (ENP), just like the Eastern Partnership. In addition to this multilateral level, the European Union maintains bilateral relations with all the MENA countries, which are primarily based on association agreements concluded under the EUROMED framework. Agreements lay down conditions for individual dialogue and cooperation covering, among other things, the field of energy (for example, promotion of renewable energy and development of energy networks as well as links to European networks). Furthermore, association agreements serve as a basis for the establishment of a Mediterranean free trade area. Considering the fact that energy sources remain among the main products exported from MENA countries to the EU members, the EU energy sector would be a main profiteer from facilitations granted under a free trade scheme.

Finally, in addition to the aforementioned intergovernmental actions, the European Union also promotes transnational energy-related projects which coincide with UfM goals and the European Union's southern-neighbourhood agenda. MED-ENEC I and II, and MED-EMIP were prime examples in this respect. Whereas MED-ENEC aimed at increasing energy efficiency and the use of renewable energy sources in the building and the construction sectors within the Mediterranean region, MED-EMIP was meant to accelerate the development of an integrated energy market and to boost the share of clean energy in the energy mix through reinforced dialogue and the sharing of information.

6.4   Other instruments of external energy policy

Further to the multilateral and bilateral tools described above, the European Union may also use unilateral and introversive measures to supplement and strengthen its external energy action. Unilateral instruments include in particular defensive measures based on the European Union's common commercial policy. Such tools may be necessary to protect the European energy market and to ensure rights under international trade rules (in particular WTO rules). Defensive actions may concern imports and exports and especially comprise the imposition of anti-dumping and anti-subsidy duties,[40] and measures provided for in the Trade Barriers Regulation,[41] such as the raising of existing customs duties, the introduction of any other charge on imports, and the introduction of quantitative restrictions.[42]

Introversive measures aim at improving the coordination of EU and member states' external energy activities with a view to facilitating the attainment of

---

40 See Council Regulation (EC) No 1225/2009 of 30 November 2009 on protection against dumped imports from countries not members of the European Community, and Council Regulation (EC) No 597/2009 of 11 June 2009 on protection against subsidised imports from countries not members of the European Community.
41 Council Regulation (EC) No 3286/94 of 22 December 1994 laying down Community procedures in the field of the common commercial policy in order to ensure the exercise of the Community's rights under international trade rules, in particular those established under the auspices of the World Trade Organization.
42 See art 12 para 3 of the Trade Barriers Regulation.

EU objectives.[43] In 2011 the European Commission outlined feasible options for pertinent action in its communication 'EU Energy Policy Engaging with Partners beyond Our Borders'.[44] First, transparency on energy agreements concluded between member states and third countries was to be increased. Based on a corresponding initiative by the European Commission, the European Union adopted an information exchange mechanism for intergovernmental agreements in 2012.[45] The scheme supplements the notification requirements applicable to gas contracts[46] and agreements in the field of nuclear energy.[47] It enables the European Commission to monitor bilateral agreements and recommend changes reflecting EU energy goals.[48]

Second, with a view to fostering the European Union's external energy policy, the European Commission also encouraged member states to use its legal support when negotiating agreements that touch on the area of internal market legislation[49]. The European Commission volunteers to assess the conformity of prospective agreements with EU law. The pertinent legal basis was also established with the adoption of the aforementioned information exchange mechanism.[50] Third, the Commission even considered going one step further by assuming negotiating mandates in cases where international agreements have an effect on EU energy policy. This may be true for agreements on large infrastructure projects. A good example of authorising the European Commission to act in this way is a mandate from 2011 granted for negotiating an agreement on the legal framework for a Trans-Caspian gas pipeline system.

However, the introversive measures applied so far have not appeared to be sufficient. For instance, it turned out that the South Stream pipeline agreements concluded between Russia and the member states through which the pipeline was meant to pass, run contrary to the EU law establishing the internal energy market and backing up the European Union's security of supply

---

43 See also European Council 4 February 2011, *Conclusions* (EUCO 2/1/11) para 11.

44 See COM (2011) 0539 final.

45 Decision No 994/2012/EU of the European Parliament and of the Council of 25 October 2012 establishing an information exchange mechanism with regard to intergovernmental agreements between Member States and third countries in the field of energy [2012] OJ L 299/13.

46 See Regulation (EU) No 994/2010 of the European Parliament and of the Council of 20 October 2010 concerning measures to safeguard security of gas supply and repealing Council Directive 2004/67/EC [2010] OJ L 295/1.

47 See art 103 Euratom Treaty also for further requirements concerning third party agreements concluded by member states in the field of nuclear energy.

48 See European Commission, press release IP/12/1070 of 04 October 2012.

49 See European Commission, COM (2011) 0539 final.

50 See European Commission, press release IP/12/1070 of 04 October 2012.

agenda.[51] This incident seems to be one reason why the Commission has proposed measures going beyond the previously applied scheme in its strategy for an Energy Union.[52] According to the new plans, the Commission is envisaging an obviously obligatory ex-ante assessment of the compatibility of intergovernmental agreements with EU law conducted by itself, giving it the chance to object to any contradictory provisions before these are agreed. Furthermore, the Commission is also planning to bring commercial gas supply contracts that may have an impact on EU energy security under transparency requirements.

The fathers of the original idea of an Energy Union would still call into question whether these measures, are sufficient in themselves from a security of supply point of view. The original vision for an Energy Union has notably provided for a joint purchasing of gas considering, in particular, the weak position of several member states vis-à-vis Russia when negotiating gas supply contracts.[53] The Commission's strategy for an Energy Union makes for somewhat sobering reading in this context by solely expressing the Commission's intention to assess certain options for collective purchasing. Moreover, whether such options, if proposed by the Commission, would finally meet with member states' approval remains unclear, given the fact that member states have already been split over establishing more transparency in terms of gas deals.[54] However, so far the door does not seem to be totally shut yet for smaller EU member states in terms of having mechanisms at their disposal in future that might offer real negotiating power, especially in crisis situations or in cases where they are dependent on a single supplier.

 REVIEW QUESTIONS

1. On the basis of which provision of the TFEU may the European Union conclude international agreements in the field of energy policy? *See section 6.1.1 b).*
2. What is the subject matter of the Energy Charter Treaty? *See section 6.2.2.*

---

51 Cf O Geden and J Grätz, 'Die EU-Politik zur Sicherung der Gasversorgung' (September 2014) CSS Analysen zur Sicherheitspolitik Nr. 159, p 3; euractiv report of 18 Februar 2015 'EU-Kommission will nationale Energieabkommen vorab prüfen' http://www.euractiv.de/sections/energie-und-umwelt/eu-kommission-will-nationale-energieabkommen-vorab-pruefen-312226 accessed 8 May 2016.

52 European Commission, *Energy Union Package, A Framework Strategy for a Resilient Energy Union with a Forward-Looking Climate Change Policy* (COM(2015) 80 final), see annex one for related roadmap.

53 See J Buzek and J Delors, 'Towards a new European Energy Community' (5 May 2010) http://www.notre-europe.eu/media/en_buzek-delors_declaration.pdf?pdf=ok accessed 8 May 2016; D Buchan and M Keay, 'Europe's 'Energy Union' plan: a reasonable start to a long journey' (March 2015) Oxford Energy Comment, p 5.

54 See Reuters report of 18 March 2015 'Debate on gas contract secrecy overshadows EU quest for energy union' http://uk.reuters.com/article/2015/03/18/us-eu-energy-idUKKBN0ME0W520150318 accessed 8 May 2015.

3. In what way does the Energy Community seek to harmonise relevant law in contracting states? *See section 6.3.2 a).*
4. What does INOGATE stand for? *See section 6.3.2 d).*
5. In what way does the current concept of an Energy Union differ from the original idea? *See section 6.4.*

 FURTHER READING

Dirk Buschle, *EU Energy Law: Volume IX, European External Energy Law & Policy* (Claeys & Casteels Publishing 2015)

Alan Dashwood and Marc Maresceau (eds), *Law and Practice of EU External Relations, Salient Features of a Changing Landscape* (Cambridge University Press 2011)

Christopher Hill and Michael Smith, *International Relations and the European Union* (2nd edn, Oxford University Press 2011)

Kim Talus, *EU Energy Law and Policy – A Critical Account* (Oxford University Press 2013)

Bart van Vooren and Ramses A Wessel, *EU External Relations Law: Text, Cases and Materials* (Cambridge University Press 2014)

Bibliography

Andoura, S, L Hancher and M van der Woude, 'Towards a European Energy Community: A Policy Proposal' (March 2010) http://www.delorsinstitute.eu/011-2155-Towards-a-European-Energy-Community-A-Policy-Proposal.html accessed 10 May 2016

Ashe-Taylor, J and V Moussis, 'EU competition law and third party access to gas transmission networks' (2005) 14(3) Utilities Law Review 105

Averre, D, 'EU-Russia Relations and the shared neighbourhood: an overview' (2011) Study, Directorate-General for External Policies of the Union

Bacon, K (ed.), *European Union Law of State Aid* (2nd edn, Oxford University Press 2013)

Behn, D, 'The effect of dual pricing practices on trade, the environment, and economic development: Identifying the winners and the losers under the current WTO disciplines' (17 December 2007) http://papers.ssrn.com/sol3/papers.cfm?abstract_id=1151553 accessed 10 May 2016

Bomberg, E, J Peterson and R Corbett, *The European Union: How Does It Work?* (3rd edn, Oxford University Press 2012)

Bovis, C H, *EU Public Procurement Law* (2nd edn, Edward Elgar Publishing 2012)

Bradbrook, A, 'Energy law as an academic discipline' (1996) 14 JERL 193, 194

Buchan, D, 'Energy policy – sharp challenges and rising ambitions' in H Wallace, M A Pollack and A R Young (eds), *Policy-making in the European Union* (6th edn, Oxford University Press 2010)

Buchan, D and M Keay, 'Europe's "Energy Union" plan: a reasonable start to a long journey' (March 2015) Oxford Energy Comment

Bungenberg, M and C Nowak, 'Europäische Umweltverfassung und EG-Vergaberecht – zur Berücksichtigung von Umweltschutzbelangen bei der Zuschlagserteilung' (2003) Zeitschrift für Umweltrecht (ZUR)

Buschle, D, *EU Energy Law: Volume IX, European External Energy Law & Policy* (Claeys & Casteels Publishing 2015)

Buzek, J and Delors, J, 'Towards a new European Energy Community' (5 May 2010) http://www.notre-europe.eu/media/en_buzek-delors_declaration.pdf?pdf=ok accessed 10 May 2016

Calliess, C and M Ruffert, *EUV/AEUV* (4th edn, C.H. Beck 2011)

Cameron, P, *Competition in Energy Markets: Law and Regulation in the European Union* (2nd edn, Oxford University Press 2007)

Chalmers, D, G Davies and G Monti, *European Union Law* (3rd edn, Cambridge University Press 2014)

Cohen, A, 'Europe's strategic dependence on Russian energy' (5 November 2007) Backgrounder, No 2083, pp 3 et seq

Craig, P and G de Burca, *EU Law: Text, Cases, and Materials* (5th edn, Oxford University Press 2011)

Curtin, J (ed.), *EU Energy Law: Volume VII, Energy Efficiency in the European Union* (Claeys & Casteels Publishing 2014)

Dashwood, A and M Maresceau (eds), *Law and Practice of EU External Relations, Salient Features of a Changing Landscape* (Cambridge University Press 2011)

de Hauteclocque, A, *Market Building Through Antitrust: Long-Term Contract Regulation in EU Electricity Markets* (Edward Elgar Publishing 2013)

de Rijke, M, 'Third-party access: Implementing EU legislation' (08 November 2004) http://www.internationallawoffice.com/Newsletters/detail.aspx?g=dbc384ba-54af-4770-9083-6a1ed81e8fa1 accessed 10 May 2016

Delvaux, B, *EU Law and the Development of a Sustainable, Competitive and Secure Energy Policy: Opportunities and Shortcomings* (Intersentia 2013)

Delvaux, B, M Hunt and K Talus (eds), *EU Energy Law and Policy Issues, vol 4* (Intersentia 2014)

Durand, É and M Keay, 'National support for renewable electricity and the single market in Europe: the Ålands Vindfraft case' (August 2014) Oxford Energy Comment, https://www.oxfordenergy.org/wpcms/wp-content/uploads/2014/08/National-support-for-renewable-electricity-and-the-single-market-in-Europe-the-%C3%85lands-Vindkraft-case.pdf accessed 10 May 2016

Feklyunina, V, 'The "great diversification game": Russia's vision of the European Union's energy projects in the shared neighbourhood' (2008) 4(2) JCER 130–148

Feltkamp, R, 'Insider trading and market manipulation in wholesale energy markets: the impact of REMIT' in B Delvaux, M Hunt and K Talus (eds), *EU Energy Law and Policy Issues, vol 4* (Intersentia 2014) 307 et seq

Ferriter, S, 'Russian ratification of Kyoto could spark large-scale renewable energy development' http://www.climate.org/topics/international-action/russian-ratification-kyoto.html accessed 10 May 2016

Fischer, S and O Geden, 'Die Energieziele sind nicht besonders ehrgeizig' (Handelsblatt 26 January 2014) http://www.handelsblatt.com/meinung/gastbeitraege/klima-und-eu-die-energieziele-sind-nicht-besonders-ehrgeizig/9369846.html accessed 10 May 2016

Foster, N, *EU Law – Directions* (Oxford University Press 2008)

Foster, N, *Foster on EU Law* (4th edn, Oxford University Press 2013)

Fouquet, D, 'Erarbeitung eines Antwortkataloges im Hauptprüfverfahren der Europäischen Kommission, Staatliche Beihilfe SA.34947 (2013/C) (ex 2013/N) – Investitionsvertrag' (legal opinion submitted to the Austrian Ministry of Agriculture, Forestry, Environment and Water Management on 5 March 2014)

Fouquet, D and C Jones (eds), *EU Energy Law: Volume III – Book Two, Renewable Energy in the Member States of the EU* (2nd edn, Claeys & Casteels Publishing 2015)

Geden, O and S Fischer, 'Moving targets, Die Verhandlungen über die Energie- und Klimapolitik-Ziele der EU nach 2020' (January 2014) SWP-Studie

Geden, O and J Grätz, 'Die EU-Politik zur Sicherung der Gasversorgung' (September 2014) CSS Analysen zur Sicherheitspolitik Nr. 159

Geiss, J, 'From agreement via legislation to implementation – will the climate and energy package delver until 2020?' in R Hinrichs-Rahlwes, *Sustainable Energy Policies for Europe* (CRC Press 2013) 59 et seq

Gilbertson, T and O Reyes, 'Carbon trading – How it works and why it fails' (November 2009) No 7 Critical Currents

Grabitz, E and M Hilf (eds), *Das Recht der Europäischen Union: EUV/AEUV* (C. H. Beck 2013)

Grabmayr, N, M Kahles and F Pause, 'Warenverkehrsfreiheit in der Europäischen Union und nationale Förderung erneuerbarer Energien' Würzburger Berichte zum Umweltenergierecht Nr. 4, dated 18 June 2014 http://www.stiftung-umweltenergierecht.de/forschung/forschungsergebnisse/wuerzburger-berichte-zum-umweltenergierecht.html accessed 10 May 2016

Grunwald, J, *Das Energierecht der Europäischen Gemeinschaften* (de Gruyter 2003)

Hackländer, D, *Die allgemeine Energiekompetenz im Primärrecht der Europäischen Union* (Peter Lang Verlag 2010)

Hancher, L, T Ottervanger and P J Slot, *EU State Aids* (4th edn, Sweet & Maxwell 2012)

Haucap, J, 'The costs and benefits of ownership unbundling' (November/December 2007) Intereconomics

Helén, H, 'The EU's energy security dilemma with Russia' (2010) 4 POLIS Journal

Hill, C and M Smith, *International Relations and the European Union* (2nd edn, Oxford University Press 2011)

Hinrichs-Rahlwes, R, *Sustainable Energy Policies for Europe* (CRC Press 2013)

Hodson, P, C Jones and H van Stehen (eds), *EU Energy Law: Volume III, Book 1, Renewable Energy Law and Policy in the European Union* (Claeys & Casteels Publishing 2010)

Howes, T, 'The EU's new Renewable Energy Directive (2009/28/EC)' in S Oberthür and M Pallemaerts (eds), *The New Climate Policies of the European Union* (VUB Press 2010) 138 et seq

Johnston, A and G Block, *EU Energy Law* (Oxford University Press 2013)

Jones, A and B Sufrin, *EC Competition Law: Text, Cases, and Materials* (3rd edn, Oxford University Press 2008)

Jones, C (ed.), *EU Energy Law: Volume I, The Internal Energy Market: The Third Liberalisation Package* (3rd edn, Claeys & Casteels Publishing 2010)

Jones, C, (ed.), *EU Energy Law: Volume II, EU Competition Law and Energy Markets* (3rd edn, Claeys & Casteels Publishing 2011)

Jones, C and V Landes, V, 'Part 4 – Merger Control' in C Jones (ed.), *EU Energy Law: Volume II, EU Competition Law and Energy Markets* (3rd edn, Claeys & Casteels Publishing 2011)

Kahles, M and T Müller, 'Powerful national support systems versus Europe-wide harmonisation – assessment of competing and converging support instruments' in R Hinrichs-Rahlwes, *Sustainable Energy Policies for Europe* (CRC Press 2013) 69 et seq

Kahles, M and T Müller, 'Legal assessment of "discriminating market barriers" in national support schemes' in R Hinrichs-Rahlwes, *Sustainable Energy Policies for Europe* (CRC Press 2013) 65 et seq

Lenz, C and K Borchardt, *EU-Verträge* (5th edn, Bundesanzeiger Verlag 2010)

Little, A, 'Bush admin isn't putting money where its mouth is on "clean coal"' (December 2004) http://grist.org/politics/little-coal/ accessed 10 May 2016

Malva, A E, 'SET-Plan – Current status, future developments and Horizon 2020' ESTELA Summer Workshop, Brussels, 26 June 2013

Massai, L, *The Kyoto Protocol in the EU: European Community and Member States Under International and European Law* (Springer 2011)

Meister, S, *Energy Security in the Southern Caucasus, The Southern Gas Corridor in its geopolitical environment* (January 2014) 2 DGAPkompact

Monti, G, *EC Competition Law* (Cambridge University Press 2007)

Neuhoff, K and A Schopp, 'Europäischer Emissionshandel: Durch Backloading Zeit für Strukturreform gewinnen' (2013) Nr 11 DIW Wochenbericht

Nies, S, 'Oil and gas delivery to Europe – An overview of existing and planned infrastructures' (2008) French Institute for International Relations (Ifri) 22 et seq

Peeters, M and T Schomerus (eds), *Renewable Energy Law in the EU: Legal Perspectives on Bottom-Up Approaches* (Edward Elgar Publishing 2014)

Peterson, J and M Shackleton (eds), *The Institutions of the European Union (The New European Union Series)* (3rd edn, Oxford University Press 2012)

Piebalgs, A, 'Towards a Single European Gas and Electricity Market' (speech delivered at the VDEW Congress Berlin on 24 May 2007, European Commission Speech/07/335, 24/05/2007)

Pielow, J, G Brunekreeft and E Ehlers, 'Legal and economic aspects of ownership unbundling in the EU' (2009) 2(2) Journal of World Energy Law & Business 96–116

Pisal, R, *Entflechtungsoptionen nach dem Dritten Energiebinnenmarktpaket* (Nomos 2011)

Ptasekaite, R, 'Competition law and nuclear regulation: A European perspective' in B Delvaux, M Hunt and K Talus (eds), *EU Energy Law and Policy Issues* (vol 4, Intersentia 2014)

Ratliff, J and R Grasso, *EU Energy Law: Volume X, Insider Trading and Market Manipulation in the European Wholesale Energy Markets – REMIT* (Claeys & Casteels Publishing 2015)

Ratner, M, P Belkin, J Nichol and S Woehrel, 'Europe's energy security: Options and challenges to natural gas supply diversification' (20 August 2013) published by Congressional Research Service

Reichert, G and J Voßwinkel, 'Europe's energy infrastructure – The European Commission's plan for an integrated European energy network' (2011) 4 IP Journal, Global Edition 29 et seq

Ritter, L and D Braun, *European Competition Law: A Practitioner's Guide* (3rd edn, Kluwer Law International 2004)

Roggenkamp, M, C Redgwell, I del Guayo and A Rønne, *Energy Law in Europe* (2nd edn, Oxford University Press 2007)

Salas, M F, R Klotz, S Moonen and D Schnichels, 'Access to gas pipelines: lessons learnt from the Marathon case', in European Commission, Competition Policy Newsletter (no 2, summer 2004) 41 et seq

Sartori, N, 'The European Commission's policy towards the Southern Gas Corridor: Between national interests and economic fundamentals' (January 2012) IAI Working Papers issue 1201, pp 5 et seq

Schill, S W, 'The interface between national and international energy law', in K Talus (ed.), *Research Handbook on International Energy Law* (Edward Elgar Publishing 2014)

Schmidt-Preuß, M, 'OU – ISO – ITO: Die Unbundling-Optionen des 3. EU-Liberalisierungspakets' ("et" Energiewirtschaftliche Tagesfragen, September 2009) http://www.et-energie-online.de/ AktuellesHeft/Topthema/tabid/70/Year/2009/Month/9/NewsModule/423/20099.aspx accessed 10 May 2016

Schmitt-Rady, B, 'A level playing field? Initial allocation of allowances in Member States' in M Peeters and K Deketelaere (eds), *EU Climate Change Policy: The Challenge of New Regulatory Initiatives* (Edward Elgar Publishing 2006) 87 et seq

Schneider, A M, *EU-Kompetenzen einer Europäischen Energiepolitik* (Nomos 2010)

Scholz, U and S Purps, 'The application of EU competition law in the energy sector' (2013) 4(1) Journal of European Competition Law & Practice 63–82

Schwarze, J (ed.), *EU-Kommentar* (3rd edn, Nomos 2012)

Schwarze, J and P D Cameron, 'European energy policy in Community law' in E Mestmäcker (ed.), *Natural Gas in the Internal Market, A Review of Energy Policy* (Nomos 1993)

Selivanova, J, 'The WTO and Energy: WTO Rules and Agreements of Relevance to the Energy Sector' (2007) ICTSD Trade and Sustainable Energy Series Issue Paper No 1

Sikow-Magny, C, K Nyitrai and N Siefken, 'The Regulation 347/2013 on guidelines for trans-European energy infrastructure' in J Vinois (ed.), *EU Energy Law: Volume VIII, The Energy Infrastructure Policy of the European Union* (Claeys & Casteels Publishing 2014) 153 et seq

Simm, M, 'The interface between energy, environment and competition rules of the European Union' (Institutional Report to the FIDE Congress 2012) http://www.fide2012.eu/ General+and+EU+Reports/id/217/ accessed 10 May 2016

Staab, A, *The European Union Explained: Institutions, Actors, Global Impact* (Indiana University Press 2008)

Streinz, R (ed.), *EUV/AEUV* (2nd edn, C.H. Beck 2012)

Szyszczak, E (ed.), *Research Handbook on European State Aid Law* (Edward Elgar Publishing 2011)

Talus, K, 'Wind of change: long-term gas contracts and changing energy paradigms in the European Union' in C Kuzemko, A Belyi, A Goldthau and M F Keating (eds), *Dynamics of Energy Governance in Europe and Russia* (Palgrave Macmillan 2012), 237 et seq

Talus, K, *EU Energy Law and Policy – A Critical Account* (Oxford University Press 2013)

Tudway, R H (ed.), *Energy Law and Regulation in the European Union* (Sweet & Maxwell 2016)

van Stiphout, M, 'The internal electricity and gas market, the best guarantee of security of supply' in J Vinois (ed.), *EU Energy Law: Volume VI, The Security of Energy Supply in the European Union* (Claeys & Casteels Publishing 2012)

van Vooren, B and R A Wessel, *EU External Relations Law: Text, Cases and Materials* (Cambridge University Press 2014)

Vinois, J (ed.), *EU Energy Law: Volume VI, The Security of Energy Supply in the European Union* (Claeys & Casteels Publishing 2012)

Vinois, J, (ed.), *EU Energy Law: Volume VIII, The Energy Infrastructure Policy of the European Union* (Claeys & Casteels Publishing 2014)

von Bogdandy, A and J Bast (eds), *Principles of European Constitutional Law* (2nd edn, Hart Publishing and C.H. Beck 2010)

von Danwitz, T, 'Regulation and liberalization of the European electricity market – A German view' (2006) 27 Energy Law Journal 423 et seq

Wallace, H, M A Pollack and A R Young (eds), *Policy-making in the European Union* (6th edn, Oxford University Press 2010)

Willems, B and E Ehlers, 'Cross-subsidies in the electricity sector' (2008) 9(3) Competition and Regulation in Network Industries 216

Index